T0344275

Theory and Practice of
Computation

Theory and Practice of
Computation

Proceedings of Workshop on Computation: Theory and Practice WCTP2015

The University of the Philippines Cebu, Cebu City, The Philippines
22 – 23 September 2015

Editors

Shin-ya Nishizaki
Tokyo Institute of Technology, Japan

Masayuki Numao
Osaka University, Japan

Jaime D L Caro
University of the Philippines Diliman, Philippines

Merlin Teodosia C Suarez
De La Salle University, Philippines

World Scientific

NEW JERSEY · LONDON · SINGAPORE · BEIJING · SHANGHAI · HONG KONG · TAIPEI · CHENNAI · TOKYO

Published by

World Scientific Publishing Co. Pte. Ltd.
5 Toh Tuck Link, Singapore 596224
USA office: 27 Warren Street, Suite 401-402, Hackensack, NJ 07601
UK office: 57 Shelton Street, Covent Garden, London WC2H 9HE

British Library Cataloguing-in-Publication Data
A catalogue record for this book is available from the British Library.

THEORY AND PRACTICE OF COMPUTATION
Proceedings of Workshop on Computation: Theory and Practice WCTP2015

ISBN 978-981-3202-80-1

Printed in Singapore

Preface

Computation should be a good blend of theory and practice. Researchers in the field should create algorithms to address real world problems putting equal weight to analysis and implementation. Experimentation and simulation can be viewed as yielding to refined theories or improved applications. WCTP 2015 is the fifth workshop organized by the Tokyo Institute of Technology, The Institute of Scientific and Industrial Research-Osaka University, University of the Philippines-Diliman and De La Salle University-Manila that is devoted to theoretical and practical approaches to computation. It aims to present the latest developments by theoreticians and practitioners in academe and industry working to address computational problems that can directly impact the way we live in society. Following the success of the Workshop on Computation: Theory and Practice 2011 (WCTP 2011) , held in the University of the Philippines Diliman, Quezon City, on September 2011, and of WCTP 2012, held in De La Salle University–Manila, on September 2012, WCTP 2013, held both in the University of the Philippines Diliman, on September 30 and October 1, 2013 and in the University of San Jose-Recoletos, Cebu, on September 28 and 29, 2013, and WCTP 2014, held both in Century Park Hotel – Manila on October 3, 2014 and in the University of the Philippines Cebu, on October 6 and 7, 2014, WCTP 2015 was held in the University of the Philippines Cebu, on Septmber 22 and 23, 2015. This post-proceedings is the collection of the selected papers that were presented at WCTP 2015.

The program of WCTP 2015 consisted of selected research contributions. It included the most recent visions and researches of 9 talks in work-in-progress session, 18 contributions. We collected the original contributions after their presentation at the workshop and began a review procedure that resulted in the selection of the papers in this volume. They appear here in the final form.

WCTP 2015 required a lot of work that was heavily dependent on members of the program committee, and lastly, we owe a great debt of gratitude to the University of the Philippines Cebu, specifically, Ryan Ciriaco Dulaca,

Kurt Junshean Espinosa, Julie Nieva, Yuleta Orillo, and Robert Roxas, for organizing the workshop.

July, 2016

Shin-ya Nishizaki
Masayuki Numao
Jaime Caro
Merlin Teodosia Suarez

PROGRAM CO-CHAIRS

Shin-ya Nishizaki	Tokyo Insitute of Technology, Tokyo, Japan
Masayuki Numao	Osaka University, Osaka, Japan
Jaime Caro	Univeristy of the Philippines – Diliman, Philippines
Merlin Teodosia Suarez	De La Salle Univeristy – Manila, Philippines

PROGRAM COMMITTEES

Koichi Moriyama, Ken-ichi Fukui,
     – Osaka University, Japan

Satoshi Kurihara,   – The University of Electro-Communications, Japan

Ryutaro Ichise   – National Institute of Technology, Japan

Mitsuharu Yamamoto – Chiba University, Japan

Hiroyuki Tominaga – Kagawa University, Japan

Takuo Watanabe, Shigeki Hagihara
     – Tokyo Institute of Technology, Japan

Raymund Sison, Jocelynn Cu, Gregory Cu, Rhia Trogo, Judith Azcarraga, Ethel Ong, Charibeth Cheng, Nelson Marcos, Rafael Cabredo, Joel Ilao
     – De La Salle University, Philippines

Rommel Feria, Henry Adorna, Prospero C. Naval Jr.
     – University of the Philippines Diliman, Philippines

Robert Roxas, Kurt Junshean Espinosa
     – University of the Philippines Cebu, Philippines

John Paul Vergara, Mercedes Rodrigo
     – Ateneo De Manila University, Philippines

Allan A. Sioson   – Ateneo de Naga University, Philippines

Randy S. Gamboa – Univeristy of Southeastern Philippines, Philippines

GENERAL CO-CHAIRS

Hirofumi Hinode   Tokyo Tech Philippines Office, Tokyo Institute of Technology, Japan

Masayuki Numao   International Collaboration Center, The Institute of Scientific and Industrial Research, Osaka University, Japan

ORGANIZING COMMITTEES

Kurt Junshean Espinosa, Robert Roxas, Ryan Ciriaco Dulaca, Yuleta Orillo, Julie Nieva
- University of the Philippines Cebu, Philippines

Contents

Polynomial-time Algorithm for Translocation Syntenic Distance

Corina Belenzo, Carmelyne Salve Corpuz, Henry Adorna, Jhoirene Clemente,

Richelle Ann Juayong and Jan Michael Yap*

*Department of Computer Science, University of the Philippines Diliman,
Quezon City, Philippines*
* E-mail: jcyap@dcs.upd.edu.ph
www.aclab.dcs.upd.edu.ph

Syntenic distance, an evolutionary distance model, is the minimum number of fusions, fissions, and translocations required to transform one genome into another. The problem of computing for the syntenic distance between two genomes has been proven to be NP-hard. Translocation syntenic distance is a special case of syntenic distance wherein operations are restricted to translocations. This restriction leads to the limitation of input instances to square instances only. As of writing, there remains no available computational complexity results for the problem of finding the minimum translocation syntenic distance between two genomes. In this paper, we focus on the translocation syntenic distance of square input instances with square connected components. A BFS-based polynomial-time algorithm for translocation syntenic distance is devised and proven effective. The algorithm runs on $O(n^2)$ time and takes up $O(n^2)$ space. A conjecture on the NP-hardness of the minimum translocation synteny problem is also presented. The idea behind the conjecture comes from the relationship between the translocation syntenic distance problem and the unsigned translocation distance problem, which was already proven to be NP-hard.

Keywords: Syntenic Distance, Translocation Synteny, Computational Biology.

1. Introduction

In molecular biology and genetics, the genome is the genetic material of an organism. It is encoded either in the DNA or, for many types of viruses, in the RNA. It also includes both the genes and the non-coding sequences of the DNA or RNA[16]. Genomes evolve through events called rearrangements[1].

Genome rearrangements reorganize the genetic material along chromosomes. They cut out large parts of a chromosome and put it back into the sequence at another position or in reverse orientation. The cuts usually occur between genes, because cutting the gene itself may lead to the gene's destruction, and this may further lead to the decrease of the fitness of the organism or worse, its death[1]. This means that these mutations alter not the gene content, but only the gene order and the gene orientation.

The analysis of the genome arrangements was first studied by Dobzhansky and Sturtevant in 1938[8]. They published a paper on an evolutionary tree presenting a rearrangement scenario with 17 inversions for the species *Drosophila pseudoobscura* and *Drosophila miranda*[15]. The number of genome rearrangements needed to transform one genome into another is used as a measure of evolutionary distance. There are two types of transformations that can rearrange genes. The first one is intrachromosomal transformations, wherein the change in the order of the gene happens within one chromosome. Examples of these are reversal and transposition. The second one is interchromosomal transformations, wherein different chromosomes exchange part of their gene sequences. Three possible types of which are fusion, fission and translocation. It has been observed that intrachromosomal events occur more frequently than interchromosomal.

There have been numerous proposed models for the evolutionary distance. There is one using transposition or the relocation of a segment of a chromosome to another location within the same chromosome, and it is called transposition distance. Another one called reversal distance uses reversal or the replacement of a segment of a chromosome by the same segment in reversed order. Reversal distance uses the number of reversals needed to transform one genome into another as a measure of the distance between two genomes[2]. In the special case wherein each genome consists of exactly one chromosome, and it is assumed that there are no multiple occurrences of the same gene within a genome, the computation for reversal distance boils down to the sorting of a directed or an undirected permutation into the identity permutation.

Ferretti, Nadeau, and Sankoff introduced another evolutionary distance model in 1996, the syntenic distance[9]. The syntenic distance between two genomes is the minimum number of fusions, fissions, and translocations required to transform one into another. Contrary to reversal distance, in syntenic distance, the order of the genes within chromosomes is irrelevant. Instead, it focuses on the assignment of genes within chromosomes. Data of exact gene sequence in genomes are generally unavailable whereas the chromosomal assignment of genes is more studied. This makes syntenic distance more convenient to consider in computing for genomic distance [13].

The problem of finding the minimum syntenic distance is widely studied and several algorithms of different approaches have been formulated in attempt to solve it. Computing for the syntenic distance between genomes has already been proven to be an NP-Hard problem by DasGupta *et al.* Furthermore, they provided a simple polynomial-time 2-approximation algorithm for it [7].

The original algorithm presented by Ferreti *et al.* was characterized by a heuristic determining which operation is used at each step so that the next step is at the most advantageous situation. Liben-Nowell gave an analysis of this algorithm and presented further some structural properties of the minimum syntenic distance problem such as monotonicity and non-redundancy [12]. Years later, he was able to provide an improved approximation algorithm using the Gossip Problem [13].

Currently, all proposed approximation algorithms work on move sequences constrained within connected components, such instance of synteny problem is defined by Liben-Nowell as the *connected synteny problem*. It has been proven that this approach cannot be better than a 2-approximation [12].

In this paper, we focus on translocation syntenic distance, a special case of syntenic distance wherein there exists a restriction on the operations to translocations alone. In most cases, especially in mammals, translocations occur more frequently than fusions and fissions. We formulate an algorithm for computing translocation syntenic distance and determine its time and space complexities. We also provide a conjecture on the computational complexity of the translocation syntenic distance.

2. Preliminaries

The same representation of genomes as in related papers will be used [2,9,12,13]. A *gene* is usually represented by a signed letter. However, in this paper, the sign is omitted because the orientation of a gene does not matter in solving for the syntenic distance [2]. A *chromosome* is represented as an unordered non-empty set of genes, and a *genome* is an unordered collection of chromosomes. A genome can be transformed by any sequence of the following syntenic operations: *fusion, fission,* and *translocation.* These representations and operations are formally defined in Ref. 2 and the definition is as follows.

Definition 1. Let $G = \{g_1, ..., g_m\}$ be a set and let $G_1 = \{S_1, ..., S_k\}$ and $G_2 = \{T_1, ..., T_n\}$, where $S_i \subseteq G$, $S_i \neq \emptyset$, for all $1 \leq i \leq k$, and $\bigcup_{i=1}^{k} S_i = G$; and $T_j \subseteq G$, $T_j \neq \emptyset$, for all $1 \leq j \leq n$, and $\bigcup_{j=1}^{n} T_j = G$.

We call G_1 and G_2 *genomes* over G. We denote the set of all genomes over G by Γ_G. The following three operations are called syntenic operations:

- A *fusion* is a function $\phi : \Gamma_G \to \Gamma_G$ such that the following holds for $G_2 = \phi(G_1)$: There exist $i_1, i_2 \in \{1, ..., k\}$ and $j_1 \in \{1, ..., n\}$ such that $S_{i_1} \cup S_{i_2} = T_{j_1}$ and $\{S_i | i \notin \{i_1, i_2\}\} = \{T_j | j \neq j_1\}$ hold.
- A *fission* is a function $\psi : \Gamma_G \to \Gamma_G$ such that the following holds for $G_2 = \psi(G_1)$: There exist $i_1 \in \{1, ..., k\}$ and $j_1, j_2 \in \{1, ..., n\}$ such that $S_{i_1} = T_{j_1} \cup T_{j_2}$ and $\{S_i | i \neq i_1\} = \{T_j | j \notin \{j_1, j_2\}\}$ hold.
- A *translocation* is a function $\rho : \Gamma_G \to \Gamma_G$ such that the following holds for $G_2 = \rho(G_1)$: There exist $i_1, i_2 \in \{1, ..., k\}$ and $j_1, j_2 \subsetneq \{1, ..., n\}$ such that $S_{i_1} \cup S_{i_2} = T_{j_1} \cup T_{j_2}$ and $\{S_i | i \notin \{i_1, i_2\}\} = \{T_j | j \notin \{j_1, j_2\}\}$ hold.

In a fusion, two chromosomes merge into a single chromosome. In a fission, one chromosome splits into two chromosomes. Lastly, in a translocation, two chromosomes exchange arbitrary subsets of their genes resulting to two new chromosomes. Now, let us formally define *syntenic distance* and give an example to illustrate its definition.

Definition 2. The *syntenic distance* $syn(G_1, G_2)$ of G_1 and G_2 is the minimum number of syntenic operations required to transform G_1 into G_2.

Example 2.1. Let $G = \{a, ..., h\}$ be a set of genes and let $G_1 = \{\{a, c, d\}\{b, f\}\{e, g, h\}\}$ and $G_2 = \{\{a, b\}\{c, d, e\}\{f, g, h\}\}$ be two genomes over G.

Applying the following transformations to G_1 will transform it into G_2.

$$G_1 = \{\{a, c, d\}\{b, f\}\{e, g, h\}\}$$
$$\xrightarrow{fusion} \{\{a, c, d\}\{b, e, f, g, h\}\}$$
$$\xrightarrow{translocation} \{\{a, b\}\{c, d, e, f, g, h\}\}$$
$$\xrightarrow{fission} \{\{a, b\}\{c, d, e\}\{f, g, h\}\} = G_2$$

The first operation that was performed on the genome G_1 was a fusion of its second and third chromosome, decreasing the number of the chromosomes of G_1 by one. Next, a translocation was performed, exchanging gene b from the first chromosome with the genes c and d from the second chromosome. Finally, G_1 becomes equal to G_2 by applying a fission, splitting the genes of the second chromosome into two as shown above. Now, let us show that the syntenic distance is indeed a distance or a metric over Γ_G.

Lemma 2.1. *The syntenic distance is a metric, or a distance function, on Γ_G.*

The proof for Lemma 2.1 is found in Ref. 2. The proof only states that the syntenic distance satisfies all four properties of a distance function, namely, the non-negativity, identity, symmetry, and triangle inequality properties. Formally, they are stated as follows: $syn(G_1, G_2) \geq 0$, $syn(G_1, G_2) = 0$ if and only if $G_1 = G_2$, $syn(G_1, G_2) = syn(G_2, G_1)$, and $syn(G_1, G_2) \leq syn(G_1, G_3) + syn(G_3, G_2)$ for all $G_1, G_2, G_3 \in \Gamma_G$.

Now, let us formally define the optimization problem of computing for the syntenic distance between two genomes. In mathematics and computer science, an *optimization problem* is the problem of finding the best solution from all feasible solutions.

Definition 3. The MINIMUM SYNTENY problem, the problem of computing for the syntenic distance, is an optimization problem as follows:
Input: A finite set G and two genomes $G_1, G_2 \in \Gamma_G$
Feasible Solutions: Every sequence $\theta_1, \ldots, \theta_l$ of syntenic operations satisfying $G_1 \theta_1 \ldots \theta_l = G_2$
Costs: For a feasible solution $\theta_1, \ldots, \theta_l$, the costs are $cost(\theta_1, \ldots, \theta_l) = l$
Optimization goal: Minimization

The computational complexity of the MINIMUM SYNTENY problem is discussed in the Review of Related Literature section. For the meantime, we present a further definition of a method of converting any input instance to the MINIMUM SYNTENY problem into a normal form called *compact representation*.

Definition 4. Let G be a finite set and let $G_1 = \{S_1, \ldots, S_k\} \in \Gamma_G$ and $G_2 = \{T_1, \ldots, T_n\} \in \Gamma_G$ be two genomes over G, where $n \geq k$.
We define $G' = \{1, \ldots, n\}$, $G_2' = \{\{1\}, \ldots, \{n\}\}$, and $G_1' = \{S_1', \ldots, S_k'\}$, where

$$S_i' = \bigcup_{x \in S_i} \{j | x \in T_j\}$$

for all $1 \leq i \leq k$. The triple (G', G_1', G_2') is then called the *compact representation* of (G, G_1, G_2).

The formal definition for the compact representation in Definition 4 was borrowed from Ref. 2. To understand better how to transform an input instance to the MINIMUM SYNTENY problem into its compact representation, see the following example.

Example 2.2. Consider the $G = \{a, ..., h\}$, and the genomes $G_1 = \{\{a, c, d\} \{b, f\} \{e, g, h\}\}$ and $G_2 = \{\{a, b\} \{c, d, e\} \{f, g, h\}\}$. Then, $G' = \{1, 2, 3\}$ and $G_2' = \{\{1\} \{2\} \{3\}\}$. We check each gene in each chromosome of G_1 to form G_1'. For every gene we encounter in G_1, we determine in which chromosome of G_2 we can find the its copy. Then, we replace the gene with the number that represents the chromosome in G_2'. In our example, G_1' becomes $\{\{1, 2\} \{1, 3\} \{2, 3\}\}$.

The compact representation of an input instance to the MINIMUM SYNTENY problem is computable in polynomial time[6]. The compact representation of an input instance can now replace the input instance itself to the problem as supported by the following lemma.

Lemma 2.2. *Let G be a finite set and let $G_1 = \{S_1, \ldots, S_k\} \in \Gamma_G$ and $G_2 = \{T_1, \ldots, T_n\} \in \Gamma_G$ be two genomes over G, where $n \geq k$. Moreover, let (G', G_1', G_2') be the compact representation of (G, G_1, G_2). Then, $syn(G_1, G_2) = syn(G_1', G_2')$.*

The proof idea for Lemma 2.2 was also presented in Ref. 2. It only states that the compact representation groups together all the elements in each of the chromosomes in G_1' that needs to be transferred to be able to reach G_2'. Given the compact representation, we can build a graph representing the input instance to the MINIMUM SYNTENY problem. We call this graph a *synteny graph* and it is defined as follows.

Definition 5. Let $I = (G, G_1, G_2)$ be the compact representation of an input instance to the MINIMUM SYNTENY problem. The *synteny graph* for I is an undirected graph $Syngraph(I) = (V, E, \Sigma, S)$, where

- $|V| = |G_1|$
- $S : V \to G_1$
- $\Sigma = G$

- $\{v_i, v_j\} \in E$ if and only if $i \neq j$ and $S(v_i) \cap S(v_j) \neq \emptyset$, $1 \leq i, j \leq k$, $v_i, v_j \in V$

If p is the number of connected components of $Syngraph(I)$, we say that p is the number of components of I.

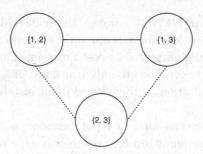

Fig. 1.   The synteny graph of the compact representation in Example 2.

The synteny graph is also described as the intersection graph of the chromosomes or sets from the genome G_1. Figure 1 shows the synteny graph of the compact representation we have computed in Example 2. Since there is exactly one connected component in the synteny graph, we say that $p = 1$ and that the number of components of the input instance is also 1. Moreover, given a value of p, we can derive a lower bound on the syntenic distance as stated in the following lemma.

Lemma 2.3. *Let $I = (G, G_1, G_2)$ be the compact representation of an input instance for the* MINIMUM SYNTENY *problem with p components.*
Then, $syn(G_1, G_2) \geq n - p$.

The proof for Lemma 2.3 is also found in Ref. 2. The proof states that an optimal sequence of syntenic operations for I must be able to produce at most one more component for every performed syntenic operation from the solution sequence.

Narrowing down from the MINIMUM SYNTENY problem, we are able to find another problem called the MINIMUM TRANSLOCATION SYNTENY problem.

Definition 6. The MINIMUM TRANSLOCATION SYNTENY problem, the problem of computing for the syntenic distance using only translocations, is the following optimization problem:

Input: A finite set G and two genomes $G_1, G_2 \in \Gamma_G$ such that $n = k$

Feasible Solutions: Every sequence $\theta_1, \ldots, \theta_l$ of translocations satisfying $G_1 \theta_1 \ldots \theta_l = G_2$

Costs: For a feasible solution $\theta_1, \ldots, \theta_l$, the costs are $cost(\theta_1, \ldots, \theta_l) = l$

Optimization goal: Minimization

Like the MINIMUM SYNTENY problem, the defined MINIMUM TRANSLO-CATION SYNTENY problem above is also an optimization problem with the goal of minimizing the output of its cost function. This problem restricts the allowed syntenic operations to only translocations. Moreover, this restriction led to a limitation on the allowed input instance to the problem.

We define this special kind of input instance as the a *square* input instance[13]. A square input instance is the only type of instance that the MINIMUM TRANSLOCATION SYNTENY problem can accept as input.

Definition 7. Let $I = (G, G_1, G_2)$ be the compact representation of an input instance. Furthermore, let $G_1 = \{S_1, ..., S_k\}$ and $G_2 = \{\{1\}, \ldots, \{n\}\}$. We say that our input instance is a *square* instance if and only if $n = k$.

The following example is an illustration of the definition.

Example 2.3. Let $I = (G, G_1, G_2)$ be the compact representation of an input instance. Suppose $G_1 = \{\{1, 3, 4\}, \{2, 3\}, \{1, 2, 4\}, \{1, 4\}\}$ and $G_2 = \{\{1\}, \{2\}, \{3\}, \{4\}\}$. We call this input instance a square instance since $n = 4$, and $k = 4$.

3. The Minimum Synteny Problem

In 1998, DasGupta *et al.* was able to prove that computing for the syntenic distance between two genomes is computationally hard[7].

Theorem 3.1. *The* MINIMUM SYNTENY *problem is NP-hard.*

The proof for Theorem 3.1 is found in Ref. 7. The reduction used two problems, the *largest balanced quasi-independent set* (LBQIS) problem and the *largest balanced independent set* (LBIS) problem.

Recall the definition of an NP-hard problem. We say that a problem H is NP-hard if every problem L in NP can be reduced to H in polynomial-time. We also say that a problem G is NP-complete when it is both in NP and NP-hard.

In the proof, it was first shown that if the LBQIS problem is 'NP-hard, then the MINIMUM SYNTENY problem is also NP-hard by the reduction of the LBQIS problem to the MINIMUM SYNTENY problem. Then, the LBQIS problem was shown to be NP-complete by the reduction of the LBIS problem to the LBQIS problem. The LBQIS problem, being NP-complete and being NP-hard at the same time, shows that the MINIMUM SYNTENY problem is also NP-hard, since it was first shown that if it is NP-hard then the MINIMUM SYNTENY problem is also NP-hard, and since any problem L in NP reduces in polynomial time to a problem G in NP-Complete.

Upon showing the NP-hardness of the MINIMUM SYNTENY problem, DasGupta *et al.* presented an approximation algorithm for the problem with an approximation ratio of 2^7. In computer science, approximation algorithms are algorithms used to find approximate solutions to optimization problems. Since it is unlikely that there can ever be an efficient polynomial-time exact algorithm solving the MINIMUM SYNTENY problem because it is NP-hard, we settle for polynomial-time sub-optimal solutions, such as the algorithm below.

Algorithm 3.1 MINSYNTENY(I)

1: Construct the synteny graph $Syngraph(I)$ and determine its connected components $C_1, ..., C_p$.
2: For each connected component, perform as many fusions as necessary to shrink it to a single vertex.
3: Separate the single elements within each vertex by a sequence of fissions.
4: **Output:** The sequence of performed fusions and fissions.

The first thing that the approximation algorithm does is build the synteny graph of the given input instance and keep a record of its connected components. For each connected component in its record, it performs a series of fusions until all the vertices in the connected component become one vertex. When each connected component in the record consists of a single vertex, the algorithm performs a series of fissions in each of these vertices to produce a vertex for each single element. In the end, we get a graph with a set of vertices, each vertex containing a single element, and no edges connecting these vertices. Thus, we were able to transform G_1 to G_2. Let us give an example to further illustrate the algorithm.

Example 3.1. Given the compact representation produced in Example 2.3, we have built a synteny graph which is shown in Figure 1. As we can see, the synteny graph contains one connected component. In this connected component, we perform a series of fusions that will shrink the vertices into one. The resulting synteny graph is shown in Figure 2.

$$\{1,2\}, \{1,3\}, \{2,3\}$$
$$\xrightarrow{fusion} \{1,2,3\}, \{2,3\}$$
$$\xrightarrow{fusion} \{1,2,3\}$$

Fig. 2. The synteny graph after the series of fusions by Algorithm 3.1.

Since we now have each connected component, in this case, our only component, consisting of a single vertex, we perform a series of fission over the vertex and separate each element. The resulting synteny graph is shown in Figure 3. Thus, we were able to transform G_1 to G_2.

$$\{1,2,3\}$$
$$\xrightarrow{fission} \{1\}, \{2,3\}$$
$$\xrightarrow{fission} \{1\}, \{2\}, \{3\}$$

Fig. 3. The synteny graph after the series of fissions by Algorithm 3.1.

DasGupta *et al.* were also able to determine the approximation ratio of the approximation algorithm they posed. In the study of approximation algorithms, approximation ratio is the ratio between the actual result of the approximation algorithm and the optimal result. In other words, it gives us an idea on how close an approximation is to the optimal solution.

Theorem 3.2. MINSYNTENY *is a polynomial-time 2-approximation algorithm for the* MINIMUM SYNTENY *problem.*

The proof for Theorem 3.2 can also be found in Ref. 7. For each connected component C_i, $1 \leq i \leq p$, MINSYNTENY performs exactly $k_i - 1$ fusions, given that k_i is the number of vertices in the component C_i, and exactly $n_i - 1$ fissions, given that n_i is the number of all unique elements in all sets of C_i. Summing these up for all connected components, we get $n + k - 2p$ syntenic operations. Since $n \geq k$, we can say that $n + k - 2p \leq 2(n - p)$. Recall that Lemma 2.3 states that $n - p$ serves as the lower bound for the MINIMUM SYNTENY problem. Thus, dividing $2(n - p)$ by $n - p$, gives us an approximation ratio of 2 for this approximation algorithm.

Furthermore, DasGupta *et al.* say that the approximation ratio of 2 is already tight, because in the case wherein the given compact representation of the input instance is $I = (G, G_1, G_2)$, where $G = \{1, ..., n\}$, $G_2 = \{\{1\}, ..., \{n\}\}$ and $G_1 = \{\{1\}, \{1, 2\}, \{1, 2, 3\}, ..., \{1, 2, ..., n\}\}$, the optimal solution would perform $n - 1$ translocations while MINSYNTENY would execute $2n - 2$ moves consisting of $n - 1$ fusions and $n - 1$ fissions.

The time complexity of MINSYNTENY was also determined in Ref. 7. The total time needed to construct the synteny graph and find its connected components is $O((4k + nk)A^{-1}(4k + nk, k)) = O(nkA^{-1}(nk, k))$, where the function $A^{-1}(x, y)$ is the inverse of the Ackermann function. The remaining time for the fusions and fissions is at most $O(nk)$.

4. The Minimum Translocation Synteny Problem

We already know that if we want to restrict our move sequences to consist of translocations only, or try to solve the MINIMUM TRANSLOCATION SYNTENY problem, then we can only work on square input instances[13]. This is because a translocation only transforms two non-empty sets into two other non-empty sets. There is no way that a sequence of translocations will alter the number of non-empty sets. Each i, $1 \leq i \leq n$, must be left alone in one vertex in the synteny graph. Therefore, after the initial construction of the synteny graph, there must exist exactly n vertices.

Moreover, currently, there are still no available computational complexity results for the MINIMUM TRANSLOCATION SYNTENY problem. Therefore, it is not yet known whether the problem is computationally hard like the MINIMUM SYNTENY problem or not.

On another note, in 2005, a closely-related distance problem called the UNSIGNED TRANSLOCATION DISTANCE problem was proved to be NP-Hard by Zhu *et al.*[18]. The problem was first studied by Kececioglu and Ravi[11], who gave a 2-approximation algorithm relying on a conjecture that the said problem was indeed NP-Hard. Similar to the MINIMUM TRANSLOCATION SYNTENY problem, the goal of the UNSIGNED TRANSLOCATION DISTANCE problem is to find the mininum number of translocations that will transform one genome into another. However, it differs with the MINIMUM TRANSLOCATION SYNTENY problem in the way the chromosomes are represented. In the UNSIGNED TRANSLOCATION DISTANCE problem, chromosomes are represented as a sequence of genes, not a set. The genes, therefore, within the chromosomes are ordered. But it is important to note that the UNSIGNED TRANSLOCATION DISTANCE problem deals with genes without orientation or sign, and in this aspect, it is also similar to the MINIMUM TRANSLOCATION SYNTENY problem.

5. An Algorithm for Translocation Syntenic Distance

In this section, we will discuss the details of the algorithm we have formulated and some of the properties that it holds. This section also contains a conjecture on the computational complexity of the UNSIGNED TRANSLOCATION DISTANCE problem. Before we begin, there is a need to define a square synteny graph and a square connected component.

Suppose $I = (G, G_1, G_2)$ is the compact representation of a square input instance, then $Syngraph(I) = (V, E, \Sigma, S)$ is a *square synteny graph* where $|V| = |\Sigma|$. Let $C_i, 1 \leq i \leq p$, be the connected components of $Syngraph(I)$. $C_i = (V_i, E_i, \Sigma_i, S_i)$ is an undirected connected graph, where:

- $V_i \subseteq V$, $\bigcup_{i=1}^{p} V_i = V$, and $V_i \cap V_j = \emptyset, 1 \leq i, j \leq p, i \neq j$
- $S_i \subseteq S$, S_i contains the original mapping of v for all $v \in V_i$, $\bigcup_{i=1}^{p} S_i = S$, and $S_i \cap S_j = \emptyset, 1 \leq i, j \leq p, i \neq j$
- $\Sigma_i \subseteq \Sigma$, $\Sigma_i = \bigcup S_i(v)$, for all $v \in V_i$, $\bigcup_{i=1}^{p} \Sigma_i = \Sigma$, and $\Sigma_i \cap \Sigma_j = \emptyset, 1 \leq i, j \leq p, i \neq j$

- $E_i \subseteq E$ which contains all adjacent edges of v for all $v \in V_i$, $\bigcup_{i=1}^{p} E_i = E$, and $E_i \cap E_j = \emptyset, 1 \leq i, j \leq p, i \neq j$.

Furthermore, we say that C_i, $1 \leq i \leq p$, is a *square connected component* if and only if $|V_i| = |\Sigma_i|$.

The Algorithm 5.1, SCTRANSLOCATIONSYNTENY, is designed to run once on each square connected component C_i, $1 \leq i \leq p$, of a square synteny graph $Syngraph(I)$. Upon entry to the algorithm, the necessary queues and lists are initialized and the starting vertex v, such that v contains the most number of elements among all of the vertices which have the highest degree, or the greatest number of edges connected to them, in V_i, is determined using the function STARTINGVERTEX.

The algorithm calls on two more functions, namely, ISVALIDTRANSLOCATION and TRANSLOCATION. The first function checks whether a translocation to be performed between two vertices will produce an empty vertex or not. If it will do so, the operation is not executed. The second function is the translocation operation itself. Upon termination of Algorithm 5.1, a list T containing all translocation operations performed on C_i is returned, and the list of singletons α is expected to contain all $v \in V_i$. Moreover, C_i boils down from one square connected component to n square connected components, $n = |\Sigma_i|$. Each of these square connected components consists of one vertex and each vertex takes on a unique element from Σ_i. Although not explicitly done or show in the algorithm, the translocation synteny distance as computed by SCTRANSLOCATIONSYNTENY is the length of the list T.

The SCTRANSLOCATIONSYNTENY algorithm consists of a nested loop that performs a *breadth first search*-based procedure on each square connected component C_i, $1 \leq i \leq p$. It visits each adjacent vertex b from the last dequeued vertex a from Q, $a, b \in V_i$, and checks if a and b will produce a valid translocation output. If it will do so, it executes a translocation operation between them. Note that the order of parameters in calling Algorithm 5.2 and Algorithm 5.3, the function ISVALIDTRANSLOCATION and TRANSLOCATION, respectively, should be as follows.

- The first parameter is the vertex $u \in V_i$ that we are currently trying to transform into a singleton. In TRANSLOCATION, we keep the first element of $S_i(u)$ to itself. An assumption made is that the elements of $S_i(v)$ for all $v \in V_i$ are presorted and that the set data structure used maintains an order (e.g. ArrayList in Java).

- The second parameter is the adjacent vertex $v \in V_i$. In TRANSLO-CATION, we transfer to $S_i(v)$ all the elements of $S_i(u)$, excluding the first element, that are also in $S_i(v)$, and if the first element of $S_i(u)$ is also in $S_i(v)$, then we transfer it from $S_i(v)$ to $S_i(u)$.

5.1. *Proof of Effectiveness*

After a translocation between vertex a and and its adjacent vertex b, the edge e connecting them is removed since $S_i(a) \cap S_i(b)$ becomes empty. When the dequeued vertex a from Q has finished visiting and performing translocations with none or more of its adjacent vertices, there are three possible cases in which a could fall into, depending on the value of the *repeat* boolean.

- **Case 1**: The *repeat* boolean is true. If this is the case, then vertex a failed one or more times in the valid translocation test and still has one or more adjacent vertices connected to it. The vertex a is re-enqueued in the queue Q.
- **Case 2**: The *repeat* boolean is false and $S_i(a)$ has exactly one element. If this is the case, then vertex a has successfully passed the valid translocation test with all of its adjacent vertices, and it no longer has any edge connected to it. The element that $S_i(a)$ contains is unique to itself, therefore, vertex a is added to the list of singletons α.
- **Case 3**: The *repeat* boolean is false and $S_i(a)$ has more than one element. If this is the case, then vertex a has successfully passed the valid translocation test with all of its adjacent vertices, and it no longer has any edge connected to it. The elements that $S_i(a)$ contains are also unique to itself. However, since $S_i(a)$ has more than one element, we cannot add vertex a to the list of singletons α yet. What we do is perform a translocation that will transfer the elements of a, excluding its first element, to the next vertex to be dequeued from Q. Since these elements that we are going to transfer are unique to vertex a, there is no need to update the edges of the square connected component. After this operation, vertex a is added to the list of singletons α.

The extra translocation that occurs in Case 3 provides the solution for the re-enqueued vertices in Case 1. Failing the valid translocation test actually means that the translocation between a vertex and its adjacent vertex will produce an empty vertex, which is, by definition, an empty chromosome and it is not allowed. However, the vertices that fall into Case 3 hold the extra elements that can be placed into the supposed-to-be empty vertices. Therefore, it is only necessary that these elements be transferred to the vertices that are still in the queue. Since the input connected component C_i is a square connected component, that is $|V_i| = |\Sigma_i|$, the algorithm will never enter an infinite loop.

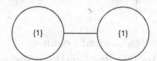

Fig. 4.   A non-square connected component.

Consider the simplest non-square connected component in Figure 4. Suppose this connected component becomes an input to the algorithm. The vertex u will fail the valid translocation test with v, and will be re-enqueued to the queue Q. When vertex v becomes the current vertex, it will also fail the valid translocation test with u, and will also be re-enqueued to the queue Q. The vertex u becomes the current vertex again, and the cycle goes on and on.

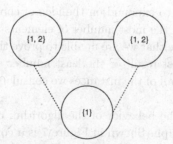

Fig. 5.   A non-square connected component with three vertices.

If we extend the non-square connected component to three vertices and two distinct elements as in Figure 5, and start at vertex u, vertex v will eventually take on the element 2. The vertices u and w will remain connected, both with exactly one and the same element 1. The algorithm will loop infinitely as the two vertices will continuously be enqueued in and dequeued from the queue Q, forever failing the valid translocation test, just like in Figure 4.

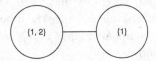

Fig. 6.   A square connected component.

To transform Figure 4 to a square connected component, we add one distinct element from 1 to any of its vertices, say adding 2 to vertex u, as shown in Figure 6. In this case, the vertex u will still fail the valid translocation test with v, and will be re-enqueued to the queue Q. However, when vertex v becomes the current vertex, it will pass the valid translocation test with u, and will contain the element 1. The vertex u becomes the current vertex again and we'll see that it is already a singleton containing the element 2. The queue Q, therefore, will be emptied and the algorithm will come to a halt. In a square connected component, there is enough amount of elements to place in each of the vertices because $|V_i| = |\Sigma_i|$.

5.2. *Choosing the Start Vertex*

In this section, we try to expound on the idea of choosing the vertex with the highest degree and the most number of elements as the starting vertex for our algorithm. Note that we are unable to prove that this kind of vertex indeed perform the best result or the least number of translocations. We relied on the fact that all of the instances we considered are consistent with the idea.

Here, we observe the behavior of the algorithm on a complete and an incomplete synteny graph. Shown in Figure 7 is a complete synteny graph with its vertices labeled a, b, c, and d arbitrarily. We find all permutations of these vertices and run the algorithm for each of those. We treat each permutation as a priority order in the algorithm, more specifically, in visiting all the adjacent vertices from a certain vertex. For example, taking the priority order, d, c, b, a, will make our starting vertex, the vertex d. From

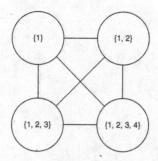

Fig. 7.   A vertex-labeled complete synteny graph.

Table 1.   The relationship between the priority order of vertices and the number of performed translocations for the synteny graph in Figure 7.

Priority Order	No. of Translocations	Priority Order	No. of Translocations
a, b, c, d	6	a, b, d, c	6
a, c, b, d	6	a, c, d, b	6
a, d, b, c	6	a, d, c, b	6
b, a, c, d	5	b, a, d, c	5
b, c, d, a	5	b, c, a, d	5
b, d, c, a	5	b, d, a, c	5
c, a, b, d	5	c, a, d, b	5
c, b, a, d	5	c, b, d, a	5
c, d, a, b	5	c, d, b, a	5
d, a, b, c	4	d, a, c, b	4
d, b, a, c	4	d, b, c, a	4
d, c, b, a	4	d, c, a, b	4

d, we visit all its adjacent vertices and perform, if valid, a translocation with each, starting from c, then b, and lastly, a. The same priority will be considered all through out the algorithm. The summary of the observation for the complete synteny graph in Figure 7 is shown in Table 1.

Starting from the vertex d, the vertex with the most number of elements, that is 4, decreased the number of performed translocations by 2 compared to when the starting vertex used was the vertex a. The vertex a contains the least number of elements, that is 1, while the vertices b and c contain 2 and 3 elements, respectively.

18

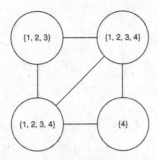

Fig. 8. A vertex-labeled incomplete synteny graph.

Table 2. The relationship between the priority order of vertices and the number of performed translocations for the synteny graph in Figure 8.

Priority Order	No. of Translocations	Priority Order	No. of Translocations
a, b, c, d	4	a, b, d, c	4
a, c, b, d	4	a, c, d, b	5
a, d, b, c	5	a, d, c, b	5
b, a, c, d	4	b, a, d, c	4
b, c, d, a	4	b, c, a, d	4
b, d, c, a	5	b, d, a, c	5
c, a, b, d	4	c, a, d, b	5
c, b, a, d	4	c, b, d, a	4
c, d, a, b	5	c, d, b, a	5
d, a, b, c	5	d, a, c, b	5
d, b, a, c	5	d, b, c, a	5
d, c, b, a	5	d, c, a, b	5

The same experiment is performed with the incomplete synteny graph shown in Figure 8. Like the complete synteny graph we considered above, the vertices of this synteny graph were also labeled a, b, c, and d, arbitrarily. We also run the algorithm on the synteny graph 24 times, each time using a priority order given by a certain permutation of all its vertices. The observation on the number of translocations performed for each priority order of this synteny graph is summarized in Table 2.

The results for the incomplete synteny graph seems to be varying. However, it becomes noticeable that starting with the vertex d, the vertex with the least number of elements and one of the vertices with the least number of edges connected to them, performed the most number of translocations in the table. On the other hand, starting with vertex b, the vertex with the most number of elements and one of the vertices with the most number of edges connected to them, performed the least number of translocations for 4 out of 6 times. Starting with vertices a and c both produced the least number of translocations for 3 out of 6 times. Vertex a is one of the vertices with the lowest degree, while vertex c is one of the vertices with the highest degree.

5.3. *Time and Space Complexities*

In this section, we determine the time and space complexities of our algorithm.

Theorem 5.1. *The time complexity of* SCTRANSLOCATIONSYNTENY *is* $O(n^2)$.

Proof. The algorithm consists mainly of a nested loop. The outer loop iterates over Q, while the inner loop iterates over all the adjacent vertices of a dequeued vertex v from Q, $\forall v \in V_i$ 2. Suppose $|V_i| = n$, since we are using a breadth first search approach in traversing the connected component C_i, the maximum number of vertices Q may contain is n. Thus, the outer loop iterates n times. Moreover, the maximum number of adjacent vertices that a vertex may have is $n - 1$. Thus, the inner loop may iterate for at most $n - 1$ times. This gives us an upperbound of $n(n - 1)$ or n^2 iterations.

Searching for the starting vertex takes a linear amount of time, since the function STARTINGVERTEX is composed of a sequence of loops, wherein each takes also a linear amount of time. The case of re-enqueuing a vertex which failed the valid translocation test does not affect the quadratic time of the algorithm. This is because even though vertices are being re-enqueued, the size of the list of singletons α increases. In other words, the number of adjacent vertices a vertex has is expected to decrease. Therefore, the running time of SCTRANSLOCATIONSYNTENY will still be dominated by the nested loop of the algorithm as the size of the synteny graph increases, giving the time complexity of the algorithm an asymptotic upper bound of $O(n^2)$. □

Theorem 5.2. *The space complexity of* SCTRANSLOCATIONSYNTENY *is* $O(n^2)$.

Proof. The auxilary space needed for each translocation is n, and there can be at most $n - 1$ translocations for each vertex. This means that the maximum capacity of the list T is $n(n-1)$ as well. Thus, the total space required for the computation of translocations is $O(n^2)$. □

5.4. *On the Minimum Translocation Synteny Problem*

In this section, we present a conjecture based on the relationship found between the unsigned translocation distance problem and MINIMUM TRANSLOCATION SYNTENY problem.

Conjecture 1. *The* MINIMUM TRANSLOCATION SYNTENY *problem is NP-Hard.*

As defined, genome is a set of chromosomes and a chromosome is a non-empty set of genes. In this part, we define a chromosome to be a sequence of genes such that chromosome $X = x_1, ..., x_p$. In a signed genome, each gene x_i is represented as a signed integer. For unsigned genomes, each gene of its chromosomes is represented as a positive integer. Here, the direction of the genes is disregarded just as the order of genes is disregarded in computing for syntenic distance. The problem of computing for translocation distance of unsigned genomes is called the *Unsigned Translocation Distance* problem or UT DISTANCE problem. Given two unsigned genomes A and B, UT DISTANCE is the minimum translocation sequence performed to transform A to B[18].

Daming Zhu and Lusheng Wang proved that the unsigned translocation distance problem is NP-Hard[18]. With its similarities to MINIMUM TRANSLOCATION SYNTENY problem, we conjectured that the MINIMUM TRANSLOCATION SYNTENY is also NP-Hard.

6. Summary and Recommendations

A conjecture was also posed regarding the computational complexity of the MINIMUM TRANSLOCATION SYNTENY problem, saying that the problem might possibly be an NP-hard problem because of its relationship to the UNSIGNED TRANSLOCATION DISTANCE problem which is already known to be NP-hard.

In this paper, we focused on the translocation syntenic distance problem. We devised a breadth first search-based algorithm that computes the translocation syntenic distance between two genomes. We were able to prove that the algorithm is effective by saying that the algorithm reaches its goal of the returned list T containing all translocation operations performed on C_i and the list of singletons α containing all $v \in V_i$, and by saying that the algorithm reaches a halt. We were also able to determine that the time complexity of the algorithm is $O(n^2)$, and by finding out the component of the algorithm which takes up the most amount of space at any given time, the space complexity of the algorithm was determined to be $O(n^2)$. The behavior of the algorithm on different priority order of vertices was observed and was used as basis for choosing the starting vertex of the algorithm to be the vertex with the most number of elements among the vertices with the highest degree.

For future works, we recommend devising an algorithm for the translocation syntenic distance that would work, not only on square instances with square connected components, but on square instances in general. Another recommendation would be proving that choosing a starting vertex for the algorithm such that the vertex has the most number of elements among the vertices with the highest degree indeed improves the algorithm. Researchers may also incorporate into the algorithm a priority order on all vertices of the input connected component instead of choosing only a starting vertex. The algorithm may be improved to reduce time and space complexity Lastly, it is recommended to prove the computational complexity of the MINIMUM TRANSLOCATION SYNTENY problem as we have only conjectured that it is NP-hard.

References

1. Bergeron, A., Chauve, C. and Gingras, Y. (2007). Formal Models of Gene Clusters. In: I. Mandoiu and A. Zelikovsky (Eds.) *Bioinformatics Algorithms Techniques and Applications* (pp. 177–202). New Jersey, USA: Wiley-Interscience.
2. Bockenhauer, H. and Bongartz, D. (2007). *Algorithmic Aspects of Bioinformatics*. New York, USA: Springer Berlin Heidelberg.
3. Caprara, A. (1999). Sorting Permutations by Reversals and Eulerian Cycle Decompositions. *SIAM Journal on Discrete Mathematics*, 12(1), 91–110.
4. Chauve, C. and Fertin, G. (2003). On maximal instances for the original syntenic distance. *Theoretical Computer Science, 326*, 29–43. doi:10.1016/j.tcs.2004.05.006.
5. Choffrut, C. (2004). Syntenic Distance: A survey. Retrieved from

http://www.liafa.jussieu.fr/~cc/MBI/synteny.pdf

6. Cormen, T., Leiserson, C. E., Rivest, R. and Stein, C. (2001). Chapter 21: Data Structures for Disjoint Sets. In: *Introduction to Algorithms* (3rd ed.). Cambridge, USA: MIT Press.

7. DasGupta, B., Jiang, T., Kannan, S., Li, M. and Sweedyk, E. (1998). On the complexity and approximation of syntenic distance. *Discrete Applied Mathematics, 88*, 59–82. doi:10.1016/S0166-218X(98)00066-3.

8. Dobzhansky, T. and Sturtevant, A. H. (1938). Inversions in the Chromosomes of Drosophila Pseudoobscura. *Genetics, 23(1)*, 28–64.

9. Ferretti, V., Nadeau, J. and Sankoff, D. (1996). Original synteny. In D. Hirschberg and G. Myers (Eds.) *7th CPM '96 Proceedings of the 7th Annual Symposium on Combinatorial Pattern Matching*, 159–167.

10. Hannenhalli, S. (1996). Polynomial-time algorithm for computing translocation distance between genomes. *71*, 137–151. doi:10.1016/S0166-218X(96)00061-3.

11. Kececioglu, J. and Ravi, R. (1995). Of mice and men: Algorithms for evolutionary distances between genomes with translocation. *In: Proceedings of the 6th Annual ACM-SIAM Symposium on Discrete Algorithms*, 604–613.

12. Liben-Nowell, D. (2001). On the structure of syntenic distance. *Journal of Computational Biology, 8(1)*, 53–67.

13. Liben-Nowell, D. (2002). Gossip in synteny: Incomplete gossip and syntenic distance between genomes. *Journal of Algorithms, 43(2)*, 264–283.

14. Mullighan, C. G., Hunger, S. P. and Meshinchi, S. (2012). Molecular Genetics in Children, adolescents and young adults with acute lymphoblastic leukemia and acute myeloid leukemia. In: M. S. Cairo and S. L. Perkins (Eds.) *Hematological Malignancies in Children, Adolescents and Young Adults* (pp. 122–124). World Scientific Publishing Co. Pte. Ltd.

15. Pevzner, P. and Tesler, G. (2003). Genome Rearrangements in Mammalian Evolution: Lessons From Human and Mouse Genomes. *Genome Research, 13(1)*, 37–45. doi:10.1101/gr.757503.

16. Ridley, M. (1999). *Genome: the Autobiography of a Species in 23 Chapters*. New York, USA: Harper Perennial.

17. Sankoff, D. and Nadeau, J. H. (1996). Conserved synteny as a measure of genomic distance. *Discrete Applied Mathematics, 71*, 247–257. doi:10.1016/S0166-218X(96)00067-4.

18. Zhu, D. and Wang, L. (2006). On the complexity of unsigned

translocation distance. *Theoretical Computer Science*, *352*, 322-328. doi:10.1016/j.tcs.2005.09.078.

Algorithm 5.1 SCTRANSLOCATIONSYNTENY(C)

1: create queue Q
2: create lists α, T
3: $v = \text{STARTINGVERTEX}(C)$
4: $Q.enqueue(v)$
5: **while** Q is not empty **do**
6:    $a \leftarrow Q.dequeue()$
7:    $repeat \leftarrow FALSE$
8:    **for** each $e \in C.adjacent\_edges(a)$ **do**
9:      $b \leftarrow C.adjacent\_vertex(a, e)$
10:      **if** b is not in Q **then**
11:        $Q.enqueue(b)$
12:      **end if**
13:      **if** ISVALIDTRANSLOCATION(a, b) **then**
14:        **if** $intersection(S(a), S(b))$ is not null **then**
15:          $T.add(\text{TRANSLOCATION}(a, b))$
16:        **end if**
17:        $C.delete\_edge(e)$
18:      **else**
19:        $repeat \leftarrow TRUE$
20:      **end if**
21:    **end for**
22:    **if** repeat is true **then**
23:      $Q.enqueue(a)$
24:    **else**
25:      **if** $S(a)$ is a singleton **then**
26:        $\alpha.add(a)$
27:      **else**
28:        $x \leftarrow set\_difference(S(a), S(a).first\_element)$
29:        $b \leftarrow Q.peek()$
30:        $S(b) \leftarrow union(S(b), x)$
31:        $T.add(\text{TRANSLOCATION}(a, b))$
32:        $\alpha.add(a)$
33:      **end if**
34:    **end if**
35: **end while**
36: **return** T

Algorithm 5.2 TRANSLOCATION(u, v)

1: $x \leftarrow intersection(set\_difference(S(u), S(u).first\_element), S(v))$
2: $y \leftarrow S(u).first\_element$
3: $S(u) \leftarrow union(set\_difference(S(u), x), y)$
4: $S(v) \leftarrow union(set\_difference(S(v), y), x)$
5: **return** $((u, x), (v, y))$

Algorithm 5.3 ISVALIDTRANSLOCATION(u, v)

1: **if** v is a singleton **and** $S(v).first\_element$ equals $S(u).first\_element$ **then**
2:    **return** FALSE
3: **end if**
4: **return** TRUE

Algorithm 5.4 STARTINGVERTEX(C)

1: $highest\_degree = 0$
2: **for** each v in C **do**
3:    **if** $degree(v) >= highest\_degree$ **then**
4:       $highest\_degree = degree(v)$
5:    **end if**
6: **end for**
7: create list β
8: **for** each v in C **do**
9:    **if** $degree(v) == highest\_degree$ **then**
10:      $\beta.add(v)$
11:    **end if**
12: **end for**
13: $greatest\_size = 0$
14: **for** each v in $beta$ **do**
15:    **if** $size(v) >= greatest\_size$ **then**
16:       $greatest\_size = size(v)$
17:    **end if**
18: **end for**
19: **for** each v in β **do**
20:    **if** $size(v) == highest\_degree$ **then**
21:       **return** v
22:    **end if**
23: **end for**

Towards Unbounded Realizability Checking

Masaya Shimakawa[1], Shigeki Hagihara[1] and Naoki Yonezaki[2]

[1] *Department of Computer Science,*
Graduate School of Information Science and Engineering,
Tokyo Institute of Technology, Tokyo, Japan

[2] *The Open University of Japan, Chiba, Japan*

Realizability verification of reactive system specifications can detect dangerous situations that may arise that were not expected while drawing up the specifications. However, such verification typically involves complex, intricate analyses. To avoid this difficulty, progress has been made in developing bounded or approximate approaches for realizability verification. By contrast, few unbounded approaches have been studied. We anticipate the potential of unbounded approaches. While the strongest advantage of bounded approaches is that they can apply symbolic technique, which is an implementation-level (low-level) technique, we expect that by using semi-symbolic techniques, unbounded approaches can perform competitively. Moreover, algorithm-level (high-level) techniques with unbounded approaches might be applied more flexibly than in bounded approaches. Therefore, we expect that unbounded approaches could verify numerous specifications efficiently. In this paper, we present several ideas about improvements for unbounded approaches, and discuss the potential of unbounded approaches.

Keywords: Realizability; Reactive System; Specification; ω-automata; Temporal Logic.

1. Introduction

Many critical safety systems, such as those that control nuclear power plants or air traffic control systems, are reactive systems. Reactive systems are systems that interact with their environments. Such systems must be designed to respond appropriately to any request from the environment at any time. When developing such a system, the requirements should be analyzed and then described as specifications for the system. If there exists a situation that is not considered when describing the specifications, the developed system may become endangered. Therefore, it is important to verify that a specification does not contain flaws of this kind. Verification during the specification phase reduces development reworking.

In designing a reactive system, it is effective to describe the specifications in a formal language, such as linear temporal logic (LTL) or check realizability.[1,2] Realizability is the property such that there exists a system model that satisfies given specifications in all situations. Realizability verification can detect dangerous situations, and a system model can be synthesized if the specification is realizable.[1]

However, such verification typically involves complex, intricate analyses. Therefore, realizability verification can be applied only to limited scale specifications. Realizability is checked as follows: we construct a deterministic ω-automaton D that accepts behaviors that satisfy the specifications, and then analyze the automaton D. The construction uses Safra's determinization,[3] which is intricate. It is considered difficult to get an efficient implementation with it.

To avoid this difficulty, many bounded approaches (approximation approaches) for realizability verification have been studied.[4-10] In bounded approaches, the size of the witness or the acceptance condition of ω-automaton is bounded, which simplifies checking procedures. For simplicity, we can apply symbolic techniques to bounded realizability verification, which is an efficient implementation-level (low-level) technique that uses a BDD (Binary Decision Diagram) or SAT (Satisfiability) solver. This is the greatest advantage of bounded approaches. Many tools for realizability checking adopt this approach (e.g., Acacia+[11] and Unbeast[12]).

In comparison, few unbounded approaches for realizability verification have been studied. To our knowledge, no tool based on an unbounded approach exists. We think that this is because it is difficult to apply symbolic techniques to unbounded realizability checking.

We have developed a semi-symbolic technique that uses BDD in part, and this technique has been successful in other fields of verification.[13,14] The technique is widely applicable, and can be used for unbounded realizability checking based on Safra's determinization. We expect that the efficiency of semi-symbolic unbounded realizability checking, which does not use approximation, will be competitive with that of symbolic bounded realizability checking.

Moreover, algorithm-level (high-level) techniques with unbounded approaches might be applied more flexibly than in bounded approaches. For example, compositional realizability verification based on a bounded approach can deal only with $\wedge$-specification (in which sub-specifications are connected by a conjunction operator),[15] because the approximation in a bounded approach negatively affects the verification. In comparison, we expect that with an unbounded approach, the compositional technique can also deal with other types of specification because, in this approach, we do not use approximation.

In this paper, we present several ideas about improvements for unbounded realizability checking, and discuss the potential of unbounded realizability checking. We describe an idea about a semi-symbolic technique for unbounded realizability checking, and report an experimental result. Moreover, we present ideas about techniques for automata reduction and compositional verification.

The remainder of this paper is organized as follows. In Sec. 2, we describe related works. In Sec. 3, we introduce the concept of realizability of reactive system specifications. Moreover, we outline a procedure for realizability checking using ω-automata. In Sec. 4, we present an idea about a semi-symbolic technique for unbounded realizability checking, and report an experimental result. In addition, we describe ideas about automaton reduction techniques and a compositional verification technique for unbounded realizability checking. We present our conclusion in Sec. 5.

2. Related Works

Bounded Realizability Checking

As described above, unbounded realizability checking uses Safra's determinization of ω-automaton,[3] which is intricate, and it is thought difficult to get an efficient implementation.

Therefore, Refs. 4, 5 and 7 have proposed procedures that avoid Safra's determinization. The procedures in Refs. 5 and 7 are refinements of the procedure in Ref. 4. In the procedures in Refs. 5 and 7, the acceptance condition of ω-automaton is bounded. The condition that the number of occurrences of accepting states is *at most* k, instead of *finite* is used as an acceptance condition. Moreover, the checking is done incrementally for $k = 0, 1, \ldots$. Several tools that are based on these procedures have been developed, including Acacia+[11] and Unbeast[12]. Acacia+ and Unbeast are based on symbolic techniques.[a]

In addition, a procedure that considers witnesses of size k is proposed in Refs. 5 and 6, and an improved version of this is given in Ref. 8. In these procedures, bounded realizability checking is reduced to a SAT problem or

---

[a]Acacia+ uses an antichain-based symbolic technique and Unbeast uses a BDD-based symbolic technique.

a satisfiability modulo theories (SMT) problem, and the problem is solved using an efficient SAT solver or SMT solver.

Realizability checking for Fragments

Fragments of linear temporal logic (LTL) as specification languages that can avoid Safra's determinization have also been studied.

Reference 16 shows the complexities of constructing deterministic ω-automata and checking realizability for $LTL(op_1, op_2, \ldots, op_n)$, where $LTL(op_1, op_2, \ldots, op_n)$ is a fragment that allows only $op_1, op_2, \ldots, op_n$ operators (e.g., $LTL(\mathbf{F}, \mathbf{X})$, $LTL(\mathbf{G}, \mathbf{F})$, and so on).

In Ref. 17, an LTL fragment called *generalized reactivity (1)* is proposed, together with a checking procedure based on a symbolic technique. Specifications written in the fragment can be translated into deterministic automata briefly. Therefore, a BDD-based symbolic technique can be applied. The tools Anzu[18] and Ratsy[19] based on the procedure have been developed.

Reference 20 proposes a procedure for the common fragment of LTL and computational tree logic (CTL). Since specifications written in the fragment can be translated into universal automata[b] that have a structural characteristic, we can determinize the automaton briefly, using the characteristic. Therefore, a symbolic technique can also be applied to the method.

3. Realizability Checking

In this section, we introduce the notion of realizability for reactive system specifications, and outline a procedure for (unbounded) realizability checking.

3.1. *Realizability for reactive system specifications*

A reactive system is a system that responds to requests from the environment in a timely fashion, and is considered a reaction function $f : (2^X)^+ \to 2^Y$, where X is a set of events caused by the environment and Y is a set of events caused by the system. We refer to events caused by the environment as *input events*, and those caused by the system as *output events*. The

---

[b]Universal automata are dual to non-deterministic automata. That is, in universal automata, if all of the runs of a σ satisfy the acceptance condition, the automaton accepts σ.

reaction function f relates sequences of sets of previously occurring input events to a set of current output events. The behavior of reactive system f for input sequence $a_0 a_1 \ldots \in (2^X)^\omega$ of sets of input events is as follows: $(a_0 \cup f(a_0))(a_1 \cup f(a_0 a_1)) \ldots \in (2^{X \cup Y})^\omega$.

A specification of a reactive system provides a set of correct behaviors. Linear temporal logic (LTL) is a suitable language for describing reactive system specifications. In LTL, in addition to the operators $\land, \lor, \rightarrow \neg, \top$, and $\perp$, we can use the temporal operators $\mathbf{X}, \mathbf{G}, \mathbf{F}$, and $\mathbf{U}$. The notation $\mathbf{X}\psi$ means that 'ψ holds the next time', $\mathbf{G}\psi$ means that 'ψ always holds', $\mathbf{F}\psi$ means that 'ψ eventually holds', and $\psi_1 \mathbf{U} \psi_2$ means that 'ψ_1 always holds until ψ_2 holds'. We treat input and output events as atomic propositions. $\sigma \models \varphi$ means that behavior σ satisfies formula φ, which is defined as usual (see e.g., Refs. 1 and 9).

Intuitively, realizability for a reactive system specification is the property such that there exists a reactive system such that all behaviors satisfy the specification. Formally, a reactive specification $Spec$ is realizable if there exists a reactive system f such that $\forall a_0 a_1 \ldots \in (2^X)^\omega ((a_0 \cup f(a_0))(a_1 \cup f(a_0 a_1)) \ldots \models Spec)$.

Example

Let us consider a simple specification for a door control system. The initial specification is as follows.

(a) If the open button is pushed, the door eventually opens.
(b) While the close button is pushed, the door remains shut.

The events 'the open button is pushed' and 'the close button is pushed' are both input events. We denote these events by x_1 and x_2, respectively. The event 'the door is open (closed)' is an output event. We denote this event by y (resp., $\neg y$). The initial specification is then represented by $Spec_1 : \mathbf{G}((x_1 \rightarrow \mathbf{F}y) \land (x_2 \rightarrow \neg y))$ in LTL. There seems to be no problem. However, the specification is not realizable, since no system can behave in ways such that the behavior satisfies the specification for the environmental behavior in which the close button is still being pushed after the open button has been pushed. Formally, there does not exist a system f such that $(a_0 \cup f(a_0))(a_1 \cup f(a_0 a_1)) \ldots \models Spec$ holds for $a_0 a_1 a_2 \ldots = \{x_1, x_2\}\{x_2\}\{x_2\} \ldots$.

Suppose that constraint (b) in the initial specification can be weakened to (b'):

(b') If the close button is pushed, the door eventually closes.

Then, the modified specification is represented by $\mathbf{G}((x_1 \to \mathbf{F}y) \wedge (x_2 \to \mathbf{F}\neg y))$, and this is realizable.

3.2. *A Procedure for checking Realizability*

Realizability can be checked using ω-automata[c] as follows:

(1) We obtain a non-deterministic (or universal) ω-automaton A such that A accepts the behavior that satisfies the specification.
(2) From A, we construct a deterministic ω-automaton D using Safra's determinization.[3]
(3) We analyze D, and check whether there exists a system such that all of the behaviors satisfy the specification.

As described above, Safra's determinization is intricate, and it has been considered difficult to get an efficient implementation. In the next section, we present an implementation-level technique and ideas about algorithm-level techniques.

4. Improvement of Unbounded Realizability Checking

4.1. *Semi-symbolic technique*

Since Safra's determinization is intricate, it is difficult to apply a symbolic technique that is efficient to unbounded realizability checking. In a symbolic technique, we represent an entire automaton by one BDD or one logical formula, and analyze it. Unbounded realizability checking uses Safra's determinization and a state of deterministic automaton is a tree in which a node of the tree is a set of states of a non-deterministic automaton. We cannot represent such an intricate automaton by one BDD or one logical formula effectively.

In this work, we apply a semi-symbolic technique to unbounded realizability checking in which MTBDD (Multi-Terminal BDD) is used partially. This technique has succeeded in other fields of verification,[13,14] and can be used widely. We are investigating a semi-symbolic technique for unbounded realizability checking. In this technique, transitions of each state are represented by one MTBDD, and each state that has an intricate struc-

---

[c]ω-automaton is an automaton that deals with infinite words.

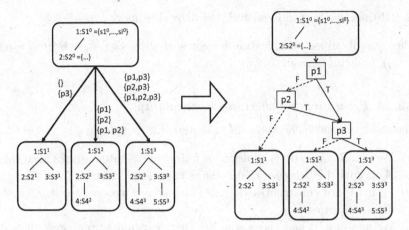

Fig. 1. The representation of transitions of each state in the semi-symbolic technique. Here, the alphabet of the automaton is $\Sigma = 2^{\{p1,p2,p3\}}$. The transition through the edge labeled by T (resp. F) from p_i corresponds to the transition with the letter that contains p_i (resp. does not contain p_i).

ture is dealt with explicitly, as illustrated in Fig. 1. The advantage of this technique is that transitions of each state can be represented compactly.

Preliminary Experiment

We implemented a prototype unbounded realizability checker using the semi-symbolic technique, and compare the execution time with the symbolic bounded realizability checkers Acacia+[11] and Unbeast,[12] to evaluate the semi-symbolic technique in unbounded realizability checking.[d]

Our prototype is implemented as follows: The construction of non-deterministic ω-automata in Step 1 of the procedure in Sec. 3.2 is based on LTL3BA.[21] The determinization of non-deterministic ω-automata in Step 2 and the analysis of deterministic ω-automata in Step 3 are implemented using the BDD package CUDD[22] and Python. In a preliminary experiment, we used the following three specifications: (a) Ele_n: n-floor elevator specifications,[23] (b) Arb_n: n-process arbiter specifications,[18] (c) LB_n: n-server load balancing specifications.[12]

Table 1 shows the total checking time for realizability for each specification. The notation "T/O" corresponds to a calculation that required more than 1000 s. Although we did not apply other improvement techniques,

---

[d]The environment was OS Ubuntu 12.04; CPU Core i7 2.6 GHz, 16 GB memory.

Table 1. The checking time (in seconds) of realizability.

	Our method	Acacia+	Unbeast
Ele_2	0.13	6.45	0.15
Ele_3	23.24	540.97	T/O
Arb_2	2.82	0.52	66.43
Arb_3	945.73	223.71	T/O
LB_8	111.67	T/O	88.91
LB_9	248.61	T/O	246.57

our method is faster than the other checkers in the verification of Ele_n. In the verification of Arb_n and LB_n, our method is competitive with the other checkers. The result shows that a semi-symbolic technique also works well in unbounded realizability checking. We expect that superior results will be obtained by using other improved techniques.

4.2. *Techniques for automata reduction*

In a symbolic technique, reductions of automata are not necessarily effective. This is because the reduction may increase the representation, which is described by BDD or logical formula, of the automata. In comparison, when a semi-symbolic technique is used, reductions of automata are effective.

Several reduction techniques for ω-automata have been studied, which use simulation relation, strong connected components, etc. Many of them are applied to automata after construction. In this work, we focus on *on-the-fly* reduction of ω-automata determinization. In on-the-fly reduction, we reduce the automaton in the middle of determinization. Since the reduction decreases the number of states and transitions that need to be dealt with, the reduction also decreases the cost of constructing the deterministic automaton. We have showed that in other fields of verification, such reductions with the semi-symbolic technique are effective. [14] We plan to investigate on-the-fly reductions for determinization of ω-automata or unbounded realizability checking, based on Ref. 14.

4.3. *Technique for compositional verification*

Here, we describe a technique for compositional verification. In compositional realizability checking, the sub-specification ψ_i is written for each module of the system, and is checked as follows:

(1) For each ψ_i, we translate sub-specifications ψ_i to a deterministic ω-automaton D_i.
(2) For each D_i, we construct D_i' where the local information for each module is removed.
(3) We combine each D_i' into one automaton D', and analyze it.

Since the local information is removed in step (2), the method can check more efficiently. The technique has been successful for satisfiability checking and bounded realizability checking.[15,23,24] Compositional realizability verification based on a bounded approach can deal only with $\wedge$-specification (in which sub-specifications are connected by a conjunction operator).[15] This is because the approximation in a bounded approach negatively affects the verification. In comparison, we expect that with an unbounded approach, the compositional technique can also deal with other types of specification because, in this approach, we do not use approximation. We plan to investigate a method based on the idea in Ref. 24, in which the local information on events is removed.

5. Conclusion

In this paper, we present several ideas on how to improve unbounded realizability verification, and discuss its prospects. While the greatest advantage of bounded approaches is that symbolic (implementation-level) techniques can be applied, unbounded approaches perform competitively using semi-symbolic techniques. We compared the prototype of our method, in which only a semi-symbolic technique is applied, with other checkers, and confirmed an example in which our method can check faster. We expect that by applying other techniques discussed in this paper, our method will deliver better performance. We believe that our method contributes to specification analysis for developing safety in critical systems.

References

1. A. Pnueli and R. Rosner, On the synthesis of a reactive module, in *Proc. 16th ACM SIGPLAN-SIGACT Symposium on Principles of Programming Languages*, (ACM, 1989).
2. M. Abadi, L. Lamport and P. Wolper, Realizable and unrealizable specifications of reactive systems., in *Proc. 16th International Colloquium on Automata, Languages, and Programming*, LNCS Vol. 372 (Springer, 1989).

3. S. Safra, On the complexity of omega-automata, in *Proc. 29th Annual Symposium on Foundations of Computer Science*, (IEEE Computer Society, 1988).

4. O. Kupferman and M. Y. Vardi, Safraless decision procedures, in *Proc. 46th Annual IEEE Symposium on Foundations of Computer Science*, (IEEE Computer Society, 2005).

5. S. Schewe and B. Finkbeiner, Bounded synthesis, in *Proc. 5th International Symposium on Automated Technology for Verification and Analysis*, LNCS Vol. 4762 (Springer, 2007).

6. B. Finkbeiner and S. Schewe, SMT-based synthesis of distributed systems, in *Proc. Second Workshop on Automated Formal Methods*, (ACM, 2007).

7. E. Filiot, N. Jin and J.-F. Raskin, An antichain algorithm for LTL realizability, in *Proc. 21st International Conference on Computer Aided Verification*, LNCS Vol. 5643 (Springer, 2009).

8. M. Shimakawa, S. Hagihara and N. Yonezaki, SAT-based bounded strong satisfiability checking of reactive system specifications, in *Proc. International Conference on Information and Communication Technology (ICT-EurAsia2013)*, LNCS Vol. 7804 (Springer, 2013).

9. M. Shimakawa, S. Hagihara and N. Yonezaki, Bounded strong satisfiability checking of reactive system specifications, *IEICE Trans. Inf. & Syst.* **E97-D**, 1746 (2014).

10. M. Shimakawa, S. Hagihara and N. Yonezaki, Reducing bounded realizability analysis to reachability checking, in *Proc. 9th International Workshop on Reachability Problems*, (Springer, 2015, to appear).

11. A. Bohy, V. Bruyère, E. Filiot, N. Jin and J.-F. Raskin, Acacia+, a tool for LTL synthesis, in *Proc. 24th International Conference on Computer Aided Verification*, LNCS Vol. 7358 (Springer, 2012).

12. R. Ehlers, Unbeast: Symbolic bounded synthesis, in *Proc. 17th International Conference on Tools and Algorithms for the Construction and Analysis of Systems*, LNCS Vol. 6605 (Springer, 2011).

13. T. Aoshima, K. Sakuma and N. Yonezaki, An efficient verification procedure supporting evolution of reactive system specifications, in *Proc. 4th International Workshop on Principles of Software Evolution*, (ACM, 2001).

14. S. Mochizuki, M. Shimakawa, S. Hagihara and N. Yonezaki, Fast translation from LTL to Büchi automata via non-transition-based automata, in *Proc. 16th International Conference on Formal Engineering Methods*, LNCS Vol. 8829 (Springer, 2014).

15. E. Filiot, N. Jin and J.-F. Raskin, Compositional algorithms for LTL synthesis, in *Proc. 8th International Conference on Automated Technology for Verification and Analysis*, LNCS Vol. 6252 (Springer, 2010).

16. R. Alur and S. La Torre, Deterministic generators and games for LTL fragments, *ACM Trans. Comput. Logic* **5**, 1 (ACM, 2004).

17. N. Piterman and A. Pnueli, Synthesis of reactive(1) designs, in *Proc. Verification, Model Checking, and Abstract Interpretation*, LNCS Vol. 3855 (Springer, 2006).

18. B. Jobstmann, S. Galler, M. Weiglhofer and R. Bloem, Anzu: A tool for property synthesis, in *Proc. 19th International Conference on Computer Aided Verification*, LNCS Vol. 4590 (Springer, 2007).

19. R. Bloem, A. Cimatti, K. Greimel, G. Hofferek, R. Könighofer, M. Roveri, V. Schuppan and R. Seeber, Ratsy – a new requirements analysis tool with synthesis, in *Proc. 22nd International Conference on Computer Aided Verification*, LNCS Vol. 6174 (Springer, 2010).

20. R. Ehlers, ACTL ∩ LTL synthesis, in *Proc. 24th International Conference on Computer Aided Verification*, LNCS Vol. 7358 (Springer, 2012).

21. T. Babiak, M. Křetínský, V. Řehák and J. Strejček, LTL to Büchi automata translation: Fast and more deterministic, in *Proc. 18th International Conference on Tools and Algorithms for the Construction and Analysis of Systems*, LNCS Vol. 7214 (Springer, 2012).

22. Fabio Somenzi, CUDD: CU Decision Diagram Package Release 2.5.0 http://vlsi.colorado.edu/ fabio/CUDD/.

23. T. Aoshima and N. Yonezaki, Verification of reactive system specification with outer event conditional formula, in *Proc. International Symposium on Principles of Software Evolution*, (IEEE Computer Society, 2000).

24. S. Ito, T. Ichinose, M. Shimakawa, N. Izumi, S. Hagihara and N. Yonezaki, Qualitative analysis of gene regulatory networks by temporal logic, *Theor. Comput. Sci.* **594**, 151 (Elsevier, 2015).

Quantum Approximate String Matching for Large Alphabets

Jeffrey A. Aborot

Computer Software Division,
Advanced Science and Technology Institute,
Department of Science and Technology,
Quezon City, 1101, Philippines
E-mail: jep@asti.dost.gov.ph
http://www.asti.dost.gov.ph

Algorithms and Complexity Laboratory,
Department of Computer Science,
University of the Philippines Diliman,
Quezon City, 1101, Philippines
E-mail: jaaborot@up.edu.ph
http://aclab.dcs.upd.edu.ph

In this article we present a quantum algorithm for finding approximate copies of a pattern within a much longer text. The algorithm is based mainly on amplitude amplification technique used in Grover's quantum search algorithm and is more suited for instances in which the size of the alphabet is at least twice as the number of distinct symbols of the pattern. The algorithm is composed of a filtering phase for trimming the search space and a verification phase for determining solution indices in the text. We present details of each subroutine used in the algorithm. The algorithm returns all solution indices within the text with number of iterations proportional to the ratio of the size of the text and the number of distinct symbols in the pattern with high probability. Overall, the time complexity of the algorithm is mainly influenced by the size of the text.

Keywords: Approximate String Matching; Amplitude Amplification; Quantum Computing; Quantum Algorithm; Filtering and Verification.

1. Introduction

In this paper we focus into a model of the generalized search problem defined on strings of symbols of a finite alphabet called *string matching problem*. A string is defined to be a sequence of symbols from a finite alphabet Σ. The string matching problem is the problem of finding matches of a sample string, called a *pattern*, within a much longer string, called *text*. The similarity, or *distance*, of the pattern and the substrings of the text are defined with respect to the exact problem being modeled. Some distance measures allow operations like insertion, deletion and substitution of symbols into either the pattern or the substring and the distance of the pattern from the substrings of the text under this distance measure is the number of performed operations on the substring to convert it into an exact copy of the pattern, or vice versa. A more basic distance measure allows only substitution of symbols in either the pattern or the substring. The distance under this measure is the total number of substitutions performed to convert the substring into an exact copy of the pattern. We use the latter distance measure in this paper.

Several classical algorithms [1–7] has already been proposed for the many variants of the string matching problem but the interest of authors in this paper lie on *quantum computation* [8–10]. This computing model abstracts the computation of a machine which makes use of quantum mechanical behavior of certain physical systems. The motivation of this paper is in finding out if there is a quantum algorithm which computes solutions to an *approximate* matching variant of the string matching problem. Using the circuit model of a quantum computer and one of the earliest quantum search algorithms [11] developed we could find a single solution within a space of possible solutions in $O\left(\sqrt{N}\right)$ quantum time where N is the size of the search space. Further analysis of this algorithm [12] showed that t number of solutions can be found in time complexity $O\left(\sqrt{\frac{N}{t}}\right)$.

2. Approximate string matching

In this paper we denote the length of input text T as N and that of the input pattern P as M. We denote the text as $T = t_0 \ldots t_{N-1}$ and the pattern as $P = p_0 \ldots p_{M-1}$. We denote an M-length substring of T starting at index i as $T[i, i + M - 1]$, $0 \leq i < N$. We also denote the distance between any substring of T and P as $Dist(T[i, i + M - 1], P)$. We limit the scope of this paper into a variant of string matching problem in which the number of mismatches is allowed up to some predefined threshold. We call this variant as *Approximate String Matching Problem*.

Definition 2.1 (Approximate String Matching Problem). *Let* Σ *be any alphabet.*
Input: *Text* $T \in \Sigma^N$, *pattern* $P \in \Sigma^M$, *threshold distance d, where d is defined with respect to some distance metric* $Dist(\cdot, \cdot)$.
Output: *All text indices i for which* $Dist(T[i, i + M - 1], P) \leq d$.

Also, in this paper we define the distance metric between substring $T[i, i + M - 1]$ and P for the Approximate String Matching problem to be the *Hamming* distance:

$$H(T[i, i + M - 1], P) = \sum_{j=0}^{M-1} g(T[i + j], P[j])$$

where $g(\cdot, \cdot)$ is defined as

$$g(a, b) = \begin{cases} 1, & a \neq b \\ 0, & otherwise. \end{cases}$$

This variant of the string matching problem models the search problems on data in which mutation is highly to occur due to internal or external influences. Example of this data are genomic data, communication data and viruses.

3. Preliminaries on quantum computing

Quantum computing models computation using physical systems which exhibit quantum mechanical effects[8-11,13,14]. Concepts in classical computing also have counterparts in quantum computing. Bits correspond to quantum bits or *qubits* which can be in state $|0\rangle$ or $|1\rangle$. Unlike bits, qubits can also be in an initial combination of states $|0\rangle$ and $|1\rangle$ called a superposition state. A qubit in a superposition state takes a definite classical state once it is subjected to a measurement operation. A quantum state is associated with a so called *complex amplitude* which describes its probability of its occurrence as classical state when the qubit is subjected to a measurement operation. A quantum state $|0\rangle$ with complex amplitude α_0 can be represented using the vector $\alpha_0[1, 0]^T = [\alpha_0, 0]^T$ and the state $|1\rangle$ with amplitude α_1 with the state $\alpha_1[0, 1]^T = [0, \alpha_1]^T$. One requirement on the amplitude of states of a quantum system is that the sum of modulo square of its amplitudes should equate to unity, $\sum_i |\alpha_i|^2 = 1$. Computation on a quantum system is then operation on a complex vector space and can be represented with matrix operations on vectors. Another requirement in quantum computation is that operations on a quantum system must be reversible, i.e. $UU^\dagger = I$ where U is some quantum operator, $U^\dagger$ is its conjugate transpose and I is the identity operator.

A *quantum register* is composed of one or more qubits and is denoted as $|q_1 q_2 \ldots q_n\rangle$, $q_i \in \{0, 1\}$. Quantum operation on a register is a matrix operation on the tensor product of the vectors corresponding to its individual qubits. An operator for an n-qubit register represented as a $2^n \times 1$ complex vector is a $2^n \times 2^n$ matrix operator with a normalizing factor.

One of the most well studied models of a quantum computer is the quantum circuit. A transformation of the state of a quantum register can be represented as a series of quantum gate operations in a quantum circuit corresponding to a sequence of unitary quantum operations on the individual qubits of the register. The last operation in a quantum circuit is usually a measurement operation which puts the qubits in a register into a definite classical state.

4. Quantum algorithm for approximate string matching

We present a quantum algorithm for the approximate string matching problem for the case of large alphabets. It is composed of a filtering phase and a verification phase. In the filtering phase elements of the solution space which do not meet a certain criteria are discarded. This leaves only probable candidate solutions for later verification. The details of these phases are discussed in the succeeding sections.

We initialize several registers for the computation in the filtering and verification phase. We allot a $(\log_2 N)$-qubit register, register A, for representing all indices in T and a $(\log_2 N + 1)$-qubit register, register B, for representing index of first occurrence of each distinct symbol in P and eventually all highly possible starting locations of P in T. We also allot a register of ancillary qubits for scratch throughout the computation which we will not include anymore in the composite superposition state of the registers. The initial state of these registers will be the quantum superposition state

$$|\psi_{\text{init}}\rangle = \sqrt{\frac{1}{N}} \sum_{i=0}^{N-1} |i\rangle |\mathbf{0}\rangle \tag{1}$$

4.1. *Filtering phase*

We would like to discard substrings in T which have more than d mismatches in comparison to P. All substrings $T[i,i+M\text{-}1]$ such that $H(T[i,i+M\text{-}1],P)>d$, $0 \leq i < N\text{-}M\text{+}1$ will be discarded. We use the classical filtering method by Amir *et al.*[7] This method assumes that the number of distinct symbols in P is greater than or equal to $2d$. We denote the set of distinct symbols in P as $P_{\text{Sym}} = \{\alpha_1, \alpha_2, \ldots, \alpha_q\}$. We denote the index of first occurrence of a symbol α_j in P as i_j. That is, for all

$j = 1, \ldots, q$, $P[i_j] = \alpha_j$ and $P[k] \neq \alpha_j, k = 0, \ldots, i_j - 1$. Given $T[i] = \alpha_j$, index $i - i_j$ is a possible starting index of an approximate occurrence of P in T since i_j is the index of first occurrence of symbol α_j in P and the first symbol in P is only $i_j - 1$ steps prior to this index. The first symbol of P must then be in index $i - i_j$. Repeating this analysis to the succeeding indices in T, $i + 1, i + 2, \ldots$, may result to the same possible starting index of P in T, i.e. $i - i_j$, if the succeeding symbols $T[i+1], T[i+2], \ldots$, matches their corresponding symbols in P. In Amir et al.[7] a *mark* is accounted to each index $i - i_j, 0 \leq i < N - 1$. Indices $i - i_j$ in T with marks $< d$ will be discarded and only the remaining indices will be considered for passing into the succeeding phase of the algorithm. We denote the set of indices $i - i_j$ with marks $\geq d$ as *Loc*. The filtering phase of the quantum algorithm will then first require identification of indices of first occurence i_j and then identification of possible starting indices of approximate occurrences of P in T, $i - i_j$.

4.1.1. *Operator U_{Loc}*

We encode the data given by P_{Sym} and the corresponding indices of first occurrence i_j in P into a unitary operator which we denote as U_{Loc}. Given a state $|i\rangle|\mathbf{0}\rangle$ in the superposition state in Equation 1 the effect of application of operator U_{Loc} is the identification of index of first occurrence i_j as follows

$$U_{\mathrm{Loc}}\left(|i\rangle|\mathbf{0}\rangle\right) = |i\rangle|i_j\rangle \tag{2}$$

The application of operator U_{Loc} into state $|\psi_{\mathrm{init}}\rangle$ will then result to

$$U_{\mathrm{Loc}}\left(|\psi_{\mathrm{init}}\rangle\right) = U_{\mathrm{Loc}}\left(\sqrt{\frac{1}{N}} \sum_{i=0}^{N-1} |i\rangle|\mathbf{0}\rangle\right)$$

$$|\psi_{\mathrm{loc}}\rangle = \sqrt{\frac{1}{N}} \sum_{i=0}^{N-1} |i\rangle|i_j\rangle \tag{3}$$

Let $\log_2(N) = n$. The encoding of P_{Sym} and i_j into operator U_{Loc} will require a unitary matrix of dimension $\left(2^n \times 2^{n+1}\right) \times \left(2^n \times 2^{n+1}\right)$. The factor 2^n is accounted to the indices $i = 0, \ldots, N - 1$ of T while the factor 2^{n+1} is accounted to the indices which may result from the succeeding operation $i - i_j$. The operation $i - i_j$ may result to a negative value and so we allot an extra qubit as sign indicator.

4.1.2. *Operator U_{Sub}*

The succeeding operation from identification of indices i_j will be the identification of possible starting indices of P in T, $i - i_j$. We facilitate this operation using an operator we denote as U_{Sub}. Given a state $|i\rangle|i_j\rangle$ from superposition state $|\psi_{\text{loc}}\rangle$ the effect of application of operator U_{Sub} will be

$$U_{\text{Sub}}\left(|i\rangle|i_j\rangle\right) = |i\rangle|i - i_j\rangle \tag{4}$$

and its overall effect into state $|\psi_{\text{loc}}\rangle$ will be as follows

$$U_{\text{Sub}}\left(|\psi_{\text{loc}}\rangle\right) = U_{\text{Sub}}\left(\sqrt{\frac{1}{N}}\sum_{i=0}^{N-1}|i\rangle|i_j\rangle\right)$$
$$|\psi_{\text{sub}}\rangle = \sqrt{\frac{1}{N}}\sum_{i=0}^{N-1}|i\rangle|i - i_j\rangle \tag{5}$$

A possible implementation of operator U_{Sub} is a quantum adder circuit. One design of such circuit is that of A. Barenco *et al.*[15] A complete addition operation on quantum states of registers of any size will utilize a cascade of a quantum full adder circuit. Since the operation $i - i_j$ will require a subtraction operation we will apply a complementation operation prior to execution of the adder circuit. This complementation operation will represent each value i_j in state $|\psi_{\text{loc}}\rangle$ in its 2's complement notation, i.e. $-i_j$.

The complementation operation for all the qubits of register B can be executed in parallel and so will require time complexity $O(1)$. The addition operation on each corresponding qubit between i and i_j will require only a fixed amount of steps and can be performed in parallel for each corresponding qubits of i and i_j using a cascade of the circuit for a quantum full adder. The addition operation then will require time complexity $O\left(\log_2(N)\right)$.

4.1.3. *Measurement of register state*

To identify the candidate solution indices in T we measure the state of the register B. In state

$$|\psi_{\text{sub}}\rangle = \sqrt{\frac{1}{N}}\sum_{i=0}^{N-1}|i\rangle|i - i_j\rangle$$

the states $|i-i_j\rangle$ of register B are in a superposition state and so we need to execute the quantum filtering algorithm several times to get all candidate solution indices $i - i_j$. We assume each measurement step requires only $O(1)$ time complexity.

4.1.4. *Iterations of the quantum filtering subroutine*

Equation 5 can be rewritten such that states $|i\rangle$ with same $|i - i_j\rangle$ are grouped together as follows

$$|\psi_{\text{sub}}\rangle = \sqrt{\frac{c_{l_1}}{N}} \sum_{i\ s.t.\ (i-i_j)=l_1} |i\rangle|l_1\rangle + \ldots + \sqrt{\frac{c_{l_m}}{N}} \sum_{i\ s.t.\ (i-i_j)=l_m} |i\rangle|l_m\rangle \quad (6)$$

where $c_{l_k}, 1 \leq k \leq m$, is the count of marks accounted to index l_k of T. Note that indices l_k with higher count of marks will have a higher probability of occurring as result of the measurement operation on register B. The probability of occurrence as result for an index l_k will be $\frac{c_{l_k}}{N}$.

Since we do not have knowledge of each value c_{l_k} we cannot directly apply the discarding step in Amir *et al.*[7] to disqualify those indices in T which have less than d marks. Instead, we execute the filtering algorithm multiple times until we get the possible solution indices i in T. Again, these are indices which have marks $\geq q-d$. In Amir *et al.*[7] the remaining indices in T after the filtering phase will be at most $\frac{N}{d}$. Based on this bound our quantum filtering algorithm will have at most $\frac{N}{q-d}$ valid indices remaining after the filtering phase.

Lemma 4.1. *The number of remaining candidate solution indices in T after the quantum filtering phase will be at most $\frac{N}{q-d}$.*

Proof. For each index i in T there corresponds a possible starting index of P in index $i-i_j$ of T. The total number of marks which will be accounted for all indices $i-i_j$ in the quantum filtering phase will be $\sum_{k=1}^{m} c_{l_k} = N$. Each of the indices in T which need to be discarded have fewer than d marks while the remaining indices will have marks $\geq q - d$. The upper bound on the number of remaining candidate solution indices after the filtering phase will then be $\frac{N}{q-d}$. □

We will execute the quantum filtering algorithm $\frac{N}{q-d}$ times to identify all $\frac{N}{q-d}$ candidate solution indices in T. We remove each resulting index from every iteration to make sure that the remaining indices with marks $\geq q-d$ will have higher probability as compared during the previous iteration. The quantum filtering phase will thus require $O\left(\frac{N}{q-d}\log_2(N)\right)$ time complexity.

Lemma 4.2. *The quantum filtering subroutine outputs $\frac{N}{q-d}$ indices i in T such that $H\left(T[i, i + M - 1], P\right) \leq d$ in quantum time $O\left(\frac{N}{q-d}\log_2(N)\right)$*

with lower bound probability

$$\frac{q-d}{N}$$

for each candidate index and a probability of ≈ 1 for all such indices.

Proof. Each iteration of the filtering algorithm is dominated by the application of the U_{Sub} operator which requires $O\left(\log_2(N)\right)$ time complexity. We search for $\frac{N}{q-d}$ highly probable solution indices in T as per Lemma 4.1. We iterate the quantum filtering subroutine $\frac{N}{q-d}$ times to get $\frac{N}{q-d}$ distinct candidate indices. The filtering subroutine will thus require $O\left(\frac{N}{q-d}\log_2(N)\right)$ time complexity. The amplitude of each state corresponding to starting indices in T with number of marks $\geq q-d$ is at least $\sqrt{\frac{q-d}{N}}$. The probability for each such state will thus be at least $\left|\sqrt{\frac{q-d}{N}}\right|^2 = \frac{q-d}{N}$. The number of indices in T we expect will remain as result of the filtering phase is at most $t = \frac{N}{q-d}$ by Lemma 4.1. The probability total probability for all t candidate indices will thus be ≈ 1. $\qquad\square$

4.2. *Verification phase*

In this phase we verify the resulting candidate $\frac{N}{q-d}$ indices in T from the filtering phase. Let $Loc = \{i$ where i is a result of filtering subroutine$\}$. We allot six registers for computation in this phase. The first register will be composed of $\log_2(N)$ qubits and we denote as *index register* for representing all $i \in Loc$. The second register will be composed of $M\log_2(|\Sigma|)$ qubits for representing all substrings $\text{T}[i, i+M-1], i \in Loc$, and we denote as *substring register*. The third register will also be composed of $M\log_2(|\Sigma|)$ qubits for representing P and we denote it as *pattern register*. The fourth register will serve as a binary indicator vector composed of M qubits for representing mismatches between the corresponding symbols of each substring and that of P and we will denote it as *mismatches register*. The fifth register will hold the value $H\left(\text{T}[i, i+M-1], P\right)$ and will be composed of $\log_2(M)$ qubits. We will denote this register as the *distance register*. The last register will be composed of $\log_2(M)$ qubits and will hold the value d and we denote it as the *threshold register*.

The initial state of our allotted set of registers for the verification phase will be the superposition state

$$|\delta_{\text{init}}\rangle = \sqrt{\frac{q-d}{N}} \sum_{i \in Loc} |i\rangle|\text{T}[i, i+M-1]\rangle|\text{P}\rangle|0\rangle^{\otimes M}|0\rangle^{\otimes \log(M)}|d\rangle \qquad (7)$$

4.2.1. *Identifying mismatches*

To identify mismatches between substrings of T and the pattern P we compare each of their corresponding symbols and we perform this comparison using operations on binary strings. Let $|\Sigma| = \sigma$. The state of each of the M contiguous $\log_2(\sigma)$ qubits of the substring register represents a symbol in Σ. Let ϕ be the set of all binary strings of length $\log_2(\sigma)$. Let $\Sigma^\phi(\cdot)$ be an arbitrary one-to-one mapping between Σ and ϕ, $\Sigma^\phi : \Sigma \to \phi$. Let $\Sigma_j^\phi(\cdot)$ be the state of the j-th bit of a binary string in ϕ. We extend the definition of Σ^ϕ into a sequence of symbols in Σ such that $\Sigma^\phi(\alpha_i, \ldots, \alpha_k) = \Sigma^\phi(\alpha_i), \ldots, \Sigma^\phi(\alpha_k)$. Thus, the binary string representation of a substring $\text{T}[i, i+M-1]$ with respect to Σ^ϕ will be

$$\Sigma^\phi(\text{T}[i, i+M-1]) = \Sigma^\phi(\text{T}[i], \ldots, \text{T}[i+M-1])$$
$$= \Sigma^\phi(\text{T}[i]), \ldots, \Sigma^\phi(\text{T}[i+M-1])$$

When comparing two corresponding symbols $\text{T}[i+j]$ and $\text{P}[j]$ we compare the binary strings mapped to them via Σ^ϕ. The result of the comparison will either be a 0 for a match and 1 otherwise. A cascade of a quantum comparator network can be configured such that each of the M comparisons for corresponding symbols of $\text{T}[i+M-1]$ and P can be executed in parallel. We denote the unitary operator for the identification of the mismatches as U_{Mis} and the resulting state after its application to the initial state $|\delta_{\text{init}}\rangle$ to be the state

$$|\delta_{\text{mis}}\rangle = U_{\text{Mis}}(|\delta_{\text{init}}\rangle)$$
$$= U_{\text{Mis}}\left(\sqrt{\frac{q-d}{N}} \sum_{i \in Loc} |i\rangle|\text{T}[i, i+M-1]\rangle|\text{P}\rangle|0\rangle|0\rangle|d\rangle \right)$$
$$= \sqrt{\frac{q-d}{N}} \sum_{i \in Loc} |i\rangle|\text{T}[i, i+M-1]\rangle|\text{P}\rangle|i_{\text{mis}}\rangle|0\rangle|d\rangle$$

The execution of a quantum comparator circuit will require $2\log_2(\sigma) + 1 \in O(\log_2(\sigma))$ time complexity. A parallel comparison of the M corresponding symbols in each substring and P will then also require $O(\log_2(\sigma))$.

4.2.2. *Computing Hamming distance*

We compute for each of the Hamming distance $H\left(\mathrm{T}[i, i + M - 1], \mathrm{P}\right), i \in$ *Loc*, by counting the number of mismatches in i_{mis}. We denote the unitary operator for this step as U_{Ham}. This operator will be a cascade of quantum full adders applied to qubits of the mismatches register. Let $i_{\mathrm{ham}} = H(\mathrm{T}[i, i + M - 1], \mathrm{P})$. Applying the U_{Ham} operator into the mismatches register will result to the quantum state

$$|\delta_{\mathrm{ham}}\rangle = U_{\mathrm{Ham}}\left(|\delta_{\mathrm{mis}}\rangle\right)$$
$$= \sqrt{\frac{q - d}{N}} \sum_{i \in Loc} |i\rangle |\mathrm{T}[i, i + M - 1]\rangle |\mathrm{P}\rangle |i_{\mathrm{mis}}\rangle |i_{\mathrm{ham}}\rangle |d\rangle \qquad (8)$$

A quantum full adder will require only a constant amount of time when adding two qubits of data. The mismatches register is composed of M qubits. The addition can be executed in a binary tree fashion to cut the time complexity down into $O(\log_2(M))$ instead of $O(M)$.

4.2.3. *Identifying valid indices* $|i\rangle$

We identify all solution indices from *Loc* by comparing each computed Hamming distance i_{ham} against d. A valid solution index i is one in which $i_{\mathrm{ham}} \leq d$. We thus need a reversible comparator network to compare each value i_{ham} with d. A possible quantum circuit for this operation is that in Ref. 16 which makes use of a binary tree for comparing two n-qubit numbers x and y. We set a controlled indicator bit from state $|0\rangle$ to state $|1\rangle$ if the output of the tree satisfies the control condition $\neg(x > y)$. We then apply a Pauli-Z operator to this indicator bit which rotates the phase of the state $|i\rangle$ by π if the controlled indicator bit is in state $|1\rangle$. This sets the sign of the amplitude of the indicator bit $|1\rangle$ from positive $(+)$ to negative $(-)$.

We denote the quantum marking operator as U_{Mark} and its application to the superposition state $|\delta_{\mathrm{ham}}\rangle$ will result to the new superposition state

$$|\delta_{\mathrm{mark}}\rangle = U_{\mathrm{Mark}}\left(|\delta_{\mathrm{ham}}\rangle\right)$$
$$= U_{\mathrm{Mark}}\left(\sqrt{\frac{q - d}{N}} \sum_{i \in Loc} |i\rangle |\mathrm{T}[i, i + M - 1]\rangle |\mathrm{P}\rangle |i_{\mathrm{mis}}\rangle |i_{\mathrm{ham}}\rangle |d\rangle\right)$$
$$= \sqrt{\frac{q - d}{N}} \sum_{i \in Loc} (-1)^{f(i_{\mathrm{mis}}, d)} |i\rangle |\mathrm{T}[i, i + M - 1]\rangle |\mathrm{P}\rangle |i_{\mathrm{mis}}\rangle |i_{\mathrm{ham}}\rangle |d\rangle$$

$$\qquad (9)$$

where $f(\cdot, \cdot)$ is defined as

$$f(a, b) = \begin{cases} 1 & , a \leq b \\ 0 & , otherwise \end{cases}$$

The binary comparator tree will require $O(\log_2(\log_2(M)))$ time steps while the rotation of phase operation is assumed to require a single time step only.

4.2.4. *Amplitude amplification of solution states $|i\rangle$*

After identifying the solution indices $|i\rangle$ in $|\delta_{\text{mark}}\rangle$ we amplify the amplitudes of the marked states. This step amplifies the amplitude of the marked states in $|\delta_{\text{mark}}\rangle$ to above the average amplitude and decreases the amplitude of non-marked states to below the average amplitude. We denote the operator for this step as U_{Amp} and define it as

$$U_{\text{Amp}} = 2|\delta_{\text{ham}}\rangle\langle\delta_{\text{ham}}| - I$$

where I is the identity operator. Operator U_{Amp} can also be defined with an $N \times N$ matrix with element $\alpha_{ij} = \frac{2}{N}$ if $i \neq j$ and $\alpha_{ij} = \frac{2}{N} - 1$ otherwise. We denote the superposition quantum state resulting from application of operator U_{Amp} to state $|\delta_{\text{mark}}\rangle$ as the state $|\delta_{\text{amp}}\rangle$. The increase in amplitude assures us that with high probability we get a solution starting location i when we measure the state $|\delta_{\text{amp}}\rangle$ of the first register.

The amplification of amplitude is performed in parallel into each of the candidate solution states in state $|\delta_{\text{mark}}\rangle$ and the changes are applied to each of the qubits in each state. The operation is applied to each qubit in the index register and so will require $\Omega(\log_2(N))$ time steps.

The unitary operation $U_{\text{Amp}}U_{\text{Mark}}$ is applied $O\left(\sqrt{\frac{N}{q-d}}\right)$ in iterations to the state $|\delta_{\text{ham}}\rangle$. The marking and amplitude amplification operations will thus require $O\left(\sqrt{\frac{N}{q-d}}\left(\log_2(\log_2(M)) + \log_2(N)\right)\right)$ time complexity.

4.2.5. *Measurement of state $|i\rangle$*

When we measure the state of the index register we only get one of the superpositioned quantum states $|i\rangle$ in $|\delta_{\text{amp}}\rangle$. We need to iterate the verification algorithm multiple number of times to get all solution indices. First, we need to have an idea about the number of solution states $|i\rangle$ there are in $|\delta_{\text{amp}}\rangle$. We can use the quantum counting algorithm in Ref. 17 for this purpose. Let us denote the resulting count as t. We iterate the quantum verification algorithm until we get t distinct indices i from the measurement operations. The quantum counting algorithm will require $O\left(\sqrt{\frac{N}{t}}\right)$ iterations of the marking step which has $O\left(\log_2(\log_2(M))\right)$ time complexity. t is bounded above by $\frac{N}{q-d}$ and so the counting subroutine will require $O\left(\sqrt{q-d}\log_2(\log_2(M))\right)$ time steps.

Lemma 4.3. *The verification subroutine outputs all indices $i \in$ Loc such that $H(T[i, i+M-1], P) \leq d$ with time complexity $O\left(\sqrt{\frac{N}{q-d}}\log(N)\right)$ with probability ≈ 1.*

Proof. The total time complexity for the verification phase as discussed in this section is

$$O\left(\log(\sigma) + \log(M) + \sqrt{\frac{N}{q-d}}\left(\log\log(M) + \log(N)\right) + \sqrt{q-d}\log\log(M)\right)$$

which is in

$$O\left(\sqrt{\frac{N}{q-d}}\log(N)\right)$$

where the logarithm is of base 2. For each iteration of $U_{\text{Amp}}U_{\text{Mark}}$ the amplitude of each state corresponding to a verified solution index in T is $\approx \sqrt{\frac{1}{t}}$ where t is the current count of remaining solution index to be found. The total probability of the solution indices at each iteration ≈ 1 due to optimality of the count of amplitude amplification. For each iteration of the verification subroutine the probability of getting as measurement outcome a solution index is thus ≈ 1. □

4.3. *Quantum algorithm for string matching*

Theorem 4.1. *There exists a quantum algorithm which outputs all starting indices i in T such that $H(T[i, i+M-1], P) \leq d$ with time complexity $O\left(\frac{N}{q-d}\log_2(N) + \sqrt{\frac{N}{q-d}}\log_2(N)\right)$.*

Proof. As per Lemma 4.2 and Lemma 4.3 the time complexity of the filtering phase is $O\left(\frac{N}{q-d}\log_2(N)\right)$ while that of the verification phase is $O\left(\sqrt{\frac{N}{q-d}}\log_2(N)\right)$, respectively. The complexity of the whole algorithm then is $O\left(\frac{N}{q-d}\log_2(N) + \sqrt{\frac{N}{q-d}}\log_2(N)\right)$. □

5. Conclusion

In this paper we have shown a quantum algorithm which outputs all starting indices of approximate copies of a pattern in a text which satisfy an input distance threshold under the Hamming distance metric with high probability. The algorithm is more suited to problem instances in which the size of the alphabet is large with respect to the input threshold distance d. It performs in time complexity $O\left(\frac{N}{q-d}\log_2(N) + \sqrt{\frac{N}{q-d}}\log_2(N)\right)$ where N is the size of the text, M is the size of the pattern, q is the number of distinct symbols of the alphabet in the pattern and d is the distance threshold. The filtering subroutine used in the algorithm is a basic one and succeeding works will be dedicated to studying whether we could bring down its time complexity to $O\left(\sqrt{\frac{N}{q-d}}\log_2(N)\right)$. Also, the verification subroutine in our algorithm performs exact counting of mismatches in each candidate solution substring resulting from the filtering phase. Further works can also be dedicated to studying an approximation approach to verification which could still provide the solution indices in a much lesser time.

References

1. D. E. Knuth, J. H. Morris, JR. and V. R. Pratt, Fast Pattern Matching in Strings *, *SIAM J. Comput.* **6**, 323 (1977).
2. R. S. Boyer and J. S. Moore, A fast string searching algorithm, *Commun. ACM* **20**, 762 (1977).
3. U. Vishkin, Deterministic Sampling-A New Technique for Fast Pattern Matching, in *Proc. twenty-second Annu. ACM Symp. Theory Comput. - STOC '90*, (ACM Press, New York, New York, USA, 1990).
4. R. A. Baeza-Yates and G. H. Gonnet, Fast String Matching with Mismatches, *Inf. Comput.* **108**, 187 (1994).
5. G. Navarro, A guided tour to approximate string matching, *ACM Comput. Surv.* **33**, 31 (March 2001).
6. M. Atallah and P. Dumas, *A Randomized Algorithm for Approximate String Matching*, tech. rep., Center for Education Research in Information Assurance and Security (2001).
7. A. Amir, M. Lewenstein and E. Porat, Faster algorithms for string matching with k mismatches, *J. Algorithms* **50**, 257 (February 2004).
8. R. Feynman, Simulating Physics with Computers, *SIAM J. Comput.* **26**, 1484 (1982).
9. R. Feynman, Quantum Mechanical Computers, *Found. Phys.* **16**, 507 (1985).

10. D. Deutsch and R. Jozsa, Rapid Solution of Problems by Quantum Computation, *Proc. R. Soc. A Math. Phys. Eng. Sci.* **439**, 553 (December 1992).
11. L. K. Grover, A fast quantum mechanical algorithm for database search, in *Proceedings, STOC 1996*, 1996.
12. M. Boyer, G. Brassard, P. Høyer and A. Tapp, Tight bounds on quantum searching, *Fortschritte der Phys.* **46**, 493 (1998).
13. P. W. Shor, Polynomial-Time Algorithms for Prime Factorization and Discrete Logarithms on a Quantum Computer, in *Proc. 35th Annu. Symp. Found. Comput. Sci.*, 1994.
14. D. Deutsch, A. Barenco and A. Ekert, Universality in quantum computation, in *Proc. R. Soc. Lond. A*, 1995.
15. A. Barenco, A. Ekert, K.-A. Suominen and P. Törmä, Approximate quantum Fourier transform and decoherence., *Phys. Rev. A* **54**, 139 (July 1996).
16. H. Thapliyal, N. Ranganathan and R. Ferreira, Design of a comparator tree based on reversible logic, in *Proc. 10th IEEE Int. Conf. Nanotechnol. Jt. Symp. with Nano Korea 2010*, (IEEE, August 2010).
17. G. Brassard, A. Tapp and P. Hoyer, Quantum counting, in *Autom. Lang. Program.*, eds. K. G. Larsen, S. Skyum and G. Winskel (Springer Berlin Heidelberg, 1998) pp. 820–831.

Modification and Parallelization of the qPMS7 Algorithm

Klarizze Romero, Henry Adorna, Jhoirene Clemente and Jan Michael Yap*

*Department of Computer Science, University of the Philippines Diliman,
Quezon City, Philippines*
E-mail: jcyap@dcs.upd.edu.ph
www.aclab.dcs.upd.edu.ph

Repeating subpatterns in DNA sequences are called motifs and finding them is important in the field of biology. There are many algorithms to solve the Planted Motif Search like PMS1, PMSPrune, and PMS5 but Planted Motif Search (PMS) is shown to be a NP-Hard problem. In this study, we modified an exact algorithm, qPMS7 , to be able to design a parallel algorithm. Then, we designed a parallel algorithm based on the modified qPMS7 algorithm to speedup the finding of motifs. Using the parallelized modified algorithm, we found out that the ratio of the time complexity of the original qPMS7 algorithm to the parallelized modified qPMS7 algorithm given a binary alphabet is at most $\frac{2^l}{l}$ which is significantly high.

Keywords: Planted Motif Search, qPMS7, Parallelization, Computational Biology.

1. Introduction

There are repeating patterns that are long enough found in DNA sequences[7]. These patterns are called Motifs[7]. Motifs are important so that one would know what DNA pattern would cause a certain gene expression, immunity response and other biological process[4]. Each motifs has its location in the DNA sequence[7]. Though we are aware that there are motifs in the DNA sequences, we don't exactly know what motifs we are searching for look like[7]. Not only do we search for those motifs, we also have to consider the mutations in motifs in the DNA sequences which further complicates the finding of the motifs[7].

There two kinds of algorithms being used in finding motifs- exact and approximate[5]. Approximate algorithms use heuristics to find motifs faster than exact algorithms but at a cost of the possibility of not being able to find the exact motifs. Whereas, exact algorithms[1,4,5,10] find the exact motifs which is why this study will focus on exact algorithms, specifically qPMS7.

qPMS7 is a fast exact motif finding algorithm in practice[5]. However, qPMS7's time complexity is still exponential[5], and one way to achieve speedup is to parallelize the algorithm as was done previously with the application[2,8,9]. This paper presents a modification and parallelization of the qPMS7 algorithm, which yields a better worst case time complexity than the original version.

2. Preliminaries

Before going to the discussion of the Motif Finding Problem, some foundational terms

- **DNA sequences** - A set of strings consisting of equal number of nucleotides each. Each nucleotide is an element of $\Sigma = \{$A, C, T, G$\}$.
- $l - mer$ - A string x of length l is called an $l - mer$. Given an $l - mer$ $x = (x[1] \ldots x[l])$ and a sequence $s = (s[1] \ldots s[m])$ with $l < m$, we use the notation $x \in_l s$ if x is an $l - mer$ in s.[5]
- **Hamming Distance**[7] - Given two strings x and y of equal length, the Hamming distance between x and y, denoted as $d_H(x, y)$, is the number of mismatches between them. If $|x| < |y|$, then $d_H(x, y)=$ min $\bigcup_{r \in_l y} d_H(x, r)$.
- (l, d, q)**-motif**[5] - Given a set of n strings S=$s_1, ..., s_n$ of length m each, a string M of length l is called an (l, d, q)-motif of the strings if there are at least q out of the n strings such that the Hamming distance between each one of them and M is no more than d.
- **d-neighborhood**[5] - Given a $l - mer$ x, the d-neighborhood of x, denoted as $B_d(x)$, is $\{y | d_H(x, y) \leq d\}$. $|B_d(x)| = \sum_{i=0}^{d} \binom{l}{i} (|\Sigma| - 1)^i$.

3. Motif Finding Problem

The Motif Finding Problem concerns itself with looking for a recurring subsequence of nucleotides within a number of genomes, and more so, what the recurring subsequences "look like"[7]. The process (or sometimes used as an equivalent terminology) by which this is solved is called Planted Motif

Search (PMS), or in its more general form, Quorum PMS (qPMS). The subtle difference between the two is in the cap on the assumed number of motifs found in the sequences: Given n (DNA) sequences upon which motifs are to be sought, qPMS assumes that the motif is found in at least q of the n sequences, while PMS assumes that the motif is found in all of the n sequences. Alternatively, it could be said that PMS is qPMS where q = n. qPMS is closer to the model of real data because not all motifs are in all DNA sequences[5], and as such is the preferred characterization of the Motif Finding Problem. Computationally, the Motif Finding Problem is known to be NP-Hard[5,6].

A more or less formal specification of the Motif Finding Problem is described by Jones and Pevzner[7]. Here, the input is a n x m matrix of DNA and l, the length of motif the user wants to find while the output is an array of n starting positions sp = $(sp_1, sp_2, ...sp_n)$, $1 \leq sp_i \leq$ m-l+1 that maximizes Score(sp,DNA)[7], a sample computation of which is shown in Figure 1. To further appreciate the computational hardness of the Motif Finding Problem, a look into a brute force method[7] of solving it is made. Given DNA, m, n and l, the brute force method of the Motif Finding algorithm, is as follows[7]:

Let bestScore=0.

(1) For each combinations of elements in sp, (1,1,1,...,1) to (m-l+1,m-l+1,m-l+1,...,m-l+1), denoted as sp[i]:

  (a) Compute Score(sp[i],DNA). To compute Score(sp[i],DNA), do the following steps:

    i. Align the n $l - mers$ from their corresponding sp_i in the DNA sequences. Count the number of A, C, G and T in each position of the $l - mers$, i.e. count the number of A, C, G and T in each position 1 to l of the $l - mers$.

    ii. The letter with the highest count in a corresponding position will be the letter in that position of the consensus motif.

    iii. Add of all the highest counts from positions 1 to l of the $l - mers$. The sum is denoted as Score(sp[i],DNA).

  (b) If Score(sp[i],DNA)>bestScore:

    i. bestScore=Score(sp[i],DNA)

    ii. bestMotif=sp[i]

(2) Output bestMotif.

Let n=3, m=4 and l=3. Given DNA sequences n x m {CATG,GCTG,ATGG}, and sp[i]=(2,2,1), compute Score(sp[i],DNA).

The starting positions of l-mers in the DNA sequences are 2,2 and 1, i.e. the l-mer starts at the 2nd position of the 1st sequence and so on {C<u>ATG</u>,G<u>CTG</u>, <u>ATG</u>G}.

Align the n l-mers from their corresponding sp_i. Count the number of A, C, G and T in each position.

l-mer of sequence 1	A	T	G
l-mer of sequence 2	C	T	G
l-mer of sequence 3	A	T	G
A	2	0	0
C	1	0	0
T	0	3	0
G	0	0	3
Consensus	A	T	G

Score(sp[i],DNA)=2+3+3=8

Fig. 1.   Example of the Computation of Score(sp[i],DNA).

The brute force method considers all $(m-l+1)^n$ combinations of starting positions sp and each starting position, and as such, the computation of Score(sp[i],DNA) takes $O(l)^7$. Therefore, brute force method of the Motif Finding Problem's overall complexity is $O(lm^n)^7$.

4. Existing Exact Algorithms

4.1. PMS5

PMS5 is an example of an exact algorithm[4]. It uses a neighborhood tree $T_d(x)$, where x $\in_l s_1$. $T_d(x)$, is $B_d(x)$ in tree form[4]. To construct a tree $T_d(x)$, the following are the rules:[4]

(1) Each node in $T_d(x)$ is a pair (t, p) where $t = t[1] \ldots t[l]$ is an $l-mer$ and p is an integer between 0 and l such that $t[p+1] \ldots t[l] = x[p+1] \ldots x[l]$. We refer to a node (t, p) as $l - mer\ t$ if p is clear.

(2) Let $t = t[1] \ldots t[l]$ and $t' = t'[1] \ldots t'[l]$. A node (t,p) is the parent of a node (t', p') if and only if

   (a) $p' > p$.

   (b) $t'[p'] \neq t[p']$ (From Rule 1, $t[p'] = x[p']$).

   (c) $t'[i] = t[i]$ for any $i \neq p'$

(3) The root of $T_d(x)$ is $(x, 0)$.

(4) The depth of $T_d(x)$ is d."

Because of the way the tree $T_d(x)$ is constructed, the following properties[4,5] are present:

(1) Given a child node (t', p') of a parent node (t, p), since there is only one character changed between them as mentioned in rule 2, $d_H(x, t') - d_H(x, t) = d_H(t, t') = 1$. As one goes deeper from $(x, 0)$, the $d_H(x, t)$ for a node (t, p) will get bigger. One character changed from a position p from x per level so $d_H(x, t) = h$ such that h is the level of the node (t, p) in the tree.

(2) Since a node (t', p') is one character changed from (t, p), all nodes are unique and, have their respective parent and descendants.

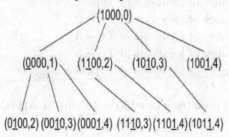

Fig. 2. A neighborhood tree of 1000, $T_2(1000)$[4].

$T_d(x)$ is where it gets the motifs from and it repeatedly gets the intersection of the motifs found so far with the intersection of motifs found in y $\in_l s_{2k}$ and z $\in_l s_{2k+1}$, for $1 \leq k \leq \lfloor \frac{n-1}{2} \rfloor$, until a certain threshold is met. After the threshold is met, for each candidate motifs r, it check whether $d_H(r, S*) \leq d$; S* are the remaining sequences $s_{2k+2}, s_{2k+3} \ldots s_n$[4].

To lessen the nodes being explored in the neighborhood tree, PMS5 uses Integer Linear Program (ILP) to determine whether to explore the descendants of the current node or not. The logic behind the ILP is discussed in a previous work[4]. For the ILP, the following variables are used:

(1) x which is the $l - mer$ x from the loop.
(2) y
(3) z
(4) t, where t is in (t,p), a node of $T_d(x)$

In a node (t,p), x, y, z and t are partitioned into two parts such that x is partitioned into x_1=x[1]..x[p] and x_2=x[p+1]..x[l], and so on. If p is 0, x_1="" while x_2=x; else if p=l, x_1=x while x_2=""[4]. Each location i in x_2, y_2 and z_2 are classified into one of these types[4]:

(1) Type 1: $x_2[i] = y_2[i] = z_2[i]$
(2) Type 2: $x_2[i] = y_2[i] \neq z_2[i]$
(3) Type 3: $x_2[i] = z_2[i] \neq y_2[i]$
(4) Type 4: $x_2[i] \neq y_2[i] = z_2[i]$
(5) Type 5: $x_2[i] \neq y_2[i], x_2[i] \neq z_2[i], y_2[i] \neq z_2[i]$

Then let[4]:

(1) n_1 be the number of locations of Type 1
(2) n_2 be the number of locations of Type 2
(3) n_3 be the number of locations of Type 3
(4) n_4 be the number of locations of Type 4
(5) n_5 be the number of locations of Type 5

When n_1, n_2, n_3, n_4 and n_5 are added, its sum is l-p; also, $(l\text{-p})=|x_2| = |y_2| = |z_2|$[4].

For any $(l$-p$)$-mer w= w[1]... w[l-p], w is a possible $(l$-p$)$-mer in t'=t_1w[4]:

(1) $N_{1,a}$ be the number of locations i of Type 1 such that w[i] $= x_2[i]$. $N_{1,a} \leq n_1$.
(2) $N_{2,a}(resp.N_{2,b})$ be the number of locations i of Type 2 such that w[i] $= x_2[i](resp.$w[i] $= z_2[i])$. $N_{2,a} + N_{2,b} \leq n_2$.
(3) $N_{3,a}(resp.N_{3,b})$ be the number of locations i of Type 3 such that w[i] $= x_2[i](resp.$w[i] $= y_2[i])$. $N_{3,a} + N_{3,b} \leq n_3$.
(4) $N_{4,a}(resp.N_{4,b})$ be the number of locations i of Type 4 such that w[i] $= y_2[i](resp.$w[i] $= x_2[i])$. $N_{4,a} + N_{4,b} \leq n_4$.
(5) $N_{5,a}(resp.N_{5,b}, N_{5,c})$ be the number of locations i of Type 5 such that w[i] $= x_2[i](resp.$w[i] $= y_2[i], $w[i] $= z_2[i])$. $N_{5,a} + N_{5,b} + N_{5,c} \leq n_5$.

Node (t,p)'s descendants won't be pruned if there is a solution (at least one w satisfying the constraints) in Ref. 4:

(1) $N_{1,a} + N_{2,a} + N_{3,a} + N_{4,b} + N_{5,a} \geq l - p - d + d_H(x_1, t_1)$.
(2) $N_{1,a} + N_{2,a} + N_{3,b} + N_{4,a} + N_{5,b} \geq l - p - d + d_H(y_1, t_1)$.
(3) $N_{1,a} + N_{2,b} + N_{3,a} + N_{4,a} + N_{5,c} \geq l - p - d + d_H(z_1, t_1)$.
(4) $N_{1,a} \leq n_1$.
(5) $N_{2,a} + N_{2,b} \leq n_2$.
(6) $N_{3,a} + N_{3,b} \leq n_3$.
(7) $N_{4,a} + N_{4,b} \leq n_4$.
(8) $N_{5,a} + N_{5,b} + N_{5,c} \leq n_5$.
(9) All of the variables are non-negative integers.

According to the literature[4], the ILP has only ten variables and depends on eight parameters $n_1, n_2, n_3, n_4, n_5, d - d_h(x_1, t_1), d - d_H(y_1, t_1)$ and $d - d_H(z_1, t_1)$[4]. Checking whether the ILP has a solution can be done in O(1) time[4].

4.2. *PMSPrune*

PMSPrune also uses a neighborhood tree, which is also the one used in PMS5, as a data structure to get motifs from. This time, each $l - mers$ from s_1 has its neighborhood tree and compares it with the rest of the sequence to see the motif has n-1 instances.

PMSPrune also uses incremental distance so that the distance of the descendant is -1,0 or 1 from the distance of the parent given the conditions similar to a previous work[3]. For $l - mers$ x, x' and z, where x' is an $l - mer$ t' from (t',p') and a descendant of $l - mer$ t x from (t,p), the following are the cases:

(1) $d_H(x', z) = d_H(x, z) - 1$ if x'[i]=z[i]
(2) $d_H(x', z) = d_H(x, z)$ if x'[i] $\neq$ z[i] and x[i] $\neq$ z[i] (5)
(3) $d_H(x', z) = d_H(x, z) + 1$ otherwise[3]

Since $d_H(x', S)$ is the maximum among the $d_H(x', s_i)$ for i=1 to n and $d_H(x', s_i)$ is the minimum among $d_H(x', z)$ where z is an $l - mer$ of s_i, the algorithm (Update Distance version 1) goes[3]:

Input: x, x', S, $\{D_i\}_{i=1}^{n}$ with $D_i = d_{i,1}, ...d_{i,m-l+1}$ where $d_{i,j}$ is the distance between the jth $l - mer$ of s_i and x

Output: $d_H(x', S)$ and $\{D'_i\}_{i=1}^n$

(1) For i=1,....n:

    (a) For j=1,....,m-l+1: calculate $d'_{i,j}$ using (5) knowing x'[i], $d_{i,j}$ and x[i].

    (b) Calculate the minimum of D'_i and call it D'_i.

(2) Output the maximum of D'_i with i=1,...,n.

According to the literature[3], this version of update distance, part of the PMSPrune algorithm, has the time complexity of O(nm) where n is the number of sequences and m is the length of each sequence.

4.3. qPMS7

While PMSPrune processes one $l - mer$ at a time and uses a tree as its data structure, qPMS7 processes two $l - mers$ at a time and uses an acyclic graph. The two $l - mers$ namely x and y are from sequences s_i and s_j respectively such that $x \in_l s_i$ and $y \in_l s_j$. Since these two $l - mers$ should be motifs of the sequences, the possible motifs should come from $B_d(x)$ and $B_y(y)$. Therefore, the nodes for the Acyclic graph $G_d(x, y)$ should come from $B_d(x) \cap B_d(y)$. To make the Acyclic graph $G_d(x, y)$ after getting $B_d(x) \cap B_d(y)$:[5]

(1) Each node in $G_d(x, y)$ is a pair (t,p) where t is an l-mer and p is an integer between 0 and l. A node (t,p) is referred to as l-mer t if p is clear. Let $t=t_1 t_2, x=x_1 x_2$ and $y=y_1 y_2$ where p= $|t_1| = |x_1| = |y_1|$ and $l - p=|t_2| = |x_2| = |y_2|$. Node (t,p) must satisfy the following constraints:

    (a) $t_2 = x_2$ if $d_H(t_1, x_1) > d_H(t_1, y_1)$, otherwise, $t_2 = y_2$.

    (b) $d_H(t, x) \le d$ and $d_H(t, y) \le d$.

(2) Let t=t[1]...t[l] and t'=t'[1]...t'[l]. There is an arc from a node (t,p) to a node (t',p') if and only if

    (a) p'>p.

    (b) t'[p']≠t[p']

    (c) t'[i]=t[i] for any i<p'.

Its traversal starts from (x,0) so, (x,0) should be in $B_d(x) \cap B_d(y)$[5]. Since (x,0) is in $B_d(x) \cap B_d(y)$, (y,p), if p is clear, should be a node in $G_d(x, y)$ too.

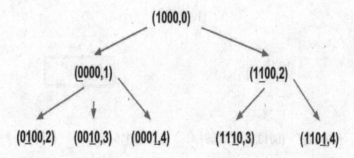

Fig. 3.   Acyclic graph $G_d(1000, 0100)$ given $x = 1000$, $y = 0100$, $l = 4$ and $d = 2$.

Since qPMS7 uses the same update incremental distance method as in the PMSPrune[5], there will be adjustments in (5) used in the method. In PMSPrune which uses $T_d(x)$, the difference between a parent node (t,p) and child node (t',p') is one character as stated in rules 2.b and 2.c in $T_d(x)$. However, in qPMS7 which uses $G_d(x, y)$, the difference between (t,p) and (t',p') is not necessarily one character as seen in rules 2.b and 2.c in making $G_d(x, y)$. To remedy that, let x be the parent $l - mer$, x' be the child $l - mer$, z be an $l - mer$ from s_k and, let's have a variable d" which is initially $d_H(x, z)$.

(1) For every i locations, $p' \leq i \leq l$, do:

    (a) d" = d" + 1 if x'[i] $\neq$ x[i]=z[i]

    (b) d" = d" - 1 if x'[i] = z[i] $\neq$ x[i] (modified 5)

    (c) d" = d" otherwise

After the iteration, $d_H(x', z) = $ d". By changing (5) to (modified 5), we can maintain the correctness of the incremental distance method.

qPMS7 also has a condition of whether or not to explore the descendants of the current node. It counts the number of input strings that has surviving $l - mers$, those that satisfy these conditions[5]:

(1) $t = t_1 t_2$, $x = x_1 x_2$, $y = y_1 y_2$ and $z = z_1 z_2$ where $p = |t_1| = |x_1| = |y_1| = |z_1|$ and l-$p = |t_2| = |x_2| = |y_2| = |z_2|$

(2) z be an $l - mer$ in s_k such that $s_k \neq s_i \neq s_j$.

(3) If $B_{d-d_h(t_1, x_1)}(x_2) \cap B_{d-d_h(t_1, y_1)}(y_2) \cap B_{d-d_h(t_1, z_1)}(z_2)$ is not empty, then it has surviving $l - mers$. If it is, the $l - mers$ in z can be safely ignored.

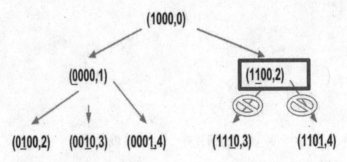

Fig. 4. Given $S = \{1000, 0100, 0011\}$, $q = 3$, $d = 2$, $l = 4$, $x = 1000$ and $y = 0100$. At the current node, $(1100,2)$, the descendants are pruned since $B_{d-d_h(11,10)}(00) \cap B_{d-d_h(11,01)}(00) \cap B_{d-d_h(11,00)}(11)$ is empty.

As pointed out in the literature[5], there is another way to find out whether $B_{d-d_h(t_1,x_1)}(x_2) \cap B_{d-d_h(t_1,y_1)}(y_2) \cap B_{d-d_h(t_1,z_1)}(z_2)$ is empty by using the ILP[4] that takes $O(1)$. The algorithm of qPMS7[5] is as follows:

For each $x \in_l s_i$, $y \in_l s_j$, $1 \leq i < j \leq n - q + 2$ do:

(1) Traverse the graph $G_d(x, y)$ in a depth-first manner starting from node $(x,0)$. At each node (t,p) do the following steps.

   (a) Incrementally compute $d_H(t, s_k)$ from its parent for $1 \leq k \leq n, k \neq i, k \neq j$.
   (b) Let q' be the number of input strings s_j such that $d_H(t, s_j) \leq d$. If q' $\geq q - 2$, output t.
   (c) Let q" be the number of input strings whose lists of surviving $l-mers$ are not empty. If q" $< q - 2$, then backtrack. Otherwise, explore its children.

DFS traversal is used so that the process will use less memory. However, parallelization with DFS is cumbersome because each node (t,p) to be processed in the algorithm needs its parent for the incremental computation of Hamming distance. Parallelizing by levels in this case would simply be the same as sequentially processing each node.

5. Modified qPMS7 Algorithm

As mentioned before, parallelization with DFS is cumbersome, so we need to change the traversal of the graph $G_d(x, y)$ such that parallelization will be more doable and the output is still correct. We propose to traverse the

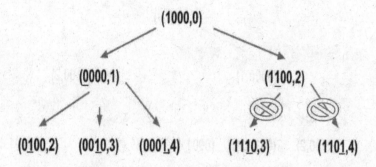

Let S={1000,0100,0011}, q=3, l=4 and d=2.
Given that s_i=1000 and s_j=0100, x=1000 and y=0100.

Using DFS, the order of nodes visited in the graph above is {(1000,0), (0000,1),(0100,2),(0010,3),(0001,4),(1100,2)}

Note: Pruning happens while traversing the graph.

After traversing the graph, the outputs, in order of traversal are {0000,0010,0001}.

Fig. 5.   An example of how the algorithm works.

graph in BFS and the algorithm is as follows:

For each x $\in_l s_i$, y $\in_l s_j$, $1 \leq i < j \leq n - q + 2$ do:

(1) Traverse the graph $G_d(x, y)$ in a **breadth-first** manner starting from node (x,0). At each node (t,p) do the following steps.

  (a) Incrementally compute $d_H(t, s_k)$ from its parent for $1 \leq k \leq n, k \neq i, k \neq j$.
  (b) Let q' be the number of input strings s_j such that $d_H(t, s_j) \leq d$. If $q' \geq q - 2$, output t.
  (c) Let q" be the number of input strings whose lists of surviving $l-mers$ are not empty. If q"$< q - 2$, **then do not include the children to the queue. Otherwise, include the children to the queue.**

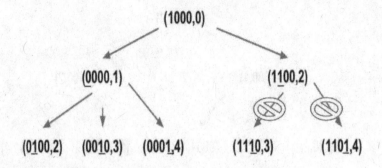

Let S={1000,0100,0011}, q=3, l=4 and d=2.
Given that s_i=1000 and s_j=0100, x=1000 and y=0100.

Using BFS, the order of nodes visited in the graph above is {(1000,0), (0000,1),(1100,2),(0100,2),(0010,3),(0001,4)}

Note: Pruning happens while traversing the graph.

After traversing the graph, the outputs, in order of traversal are {0000,0010,0001}.

Fig. 6. An example showing how the modified algorithm works and that, even in BFS and using the same graph, the output is still the same.

5.1. *Correctness of the Modified Algorithm*

BFS travels from the starting node (x,0) to the current node (t',p'). Let (t,p) be the parent node of (t',p'). The way the graph is built, starting from node (x,0), node (t,p) is nearer to (x,0) than (t',p') by the number of edges. In BFS, those nearer to the starting node are visited first before the farther ones (somewhat like a level far from (x,0)). Before visiting (t',p'), node (t,p) would have been visited which is the parent of the current node. So, $d_H(t, s_k)$ is already processed before $d_H(t', s_k)$. Incremental computation of $d_H(t', s_k)$ is possible. Therefore, even with BFS traversal, the $d_H(t', s_k)$ is the same as when DFS is used. The manner of traversal of graph wont affect the counting of the number of input strings s_j such that $d_H(t', s_j) \leq$ d denoted as q'. Therefore, even with BFS traversal, q' is the same.

In both traversals, each node is checked to determine whether to back-track or not. The difference is that in DFS, one will immediately visit its descendants and so on while in BFS, the nodes descendants will be visited later after all nodes in the current level are visited. Also, the process in ILP is local only to the node (t',p') and so, q" is also the same.

Therefore, both will eventually have visited the same set of nodes after the traversing the graph. Therefore, BFS traversal of the graph wont affect the output if it is used instead of DFS as stated in the algorithm. The difference between the two traversals is only in the sequence of the nodes they visited.

6. Parallelized Modified Algorithm

Each node (t,p) being visited is dependent only on its parents because of getting $d_H(t, s_k)$. Also, each node and its siblings are actually independent from one another - no process being done on one node has any influence to the processing of its siblings. In the BFS traversal of the modified qPMS7 algorithm, a node's siblings are visited before its descendants. Since a node and its siblings are independent from one another, and based on the modified qPMS7 algorithm, we can design a parallel algorithm wherein there can be two or more nodes being processed at the same time. Let:

(1) N(l,d) be the maximum number of nodes graph $G_d(x, y)$ can have which is also $B_d(x) \cap B_d(y) = B_d(x)$ and $B_d(x) \cap B_d(y) = B_d(y)$, or $B_d(x) = B_d(y)$, or $T_d(x) or T_d(y)$
(2) $k \in \mathbb{Z}$ be the number of processors where $1 \leq k \leq N(l, d) - 1$. The number of processors can be more than N(l,d)-1 but since there are at most N(l,d)-1 nodes to be processed, there will be some processors that won't be used which is wasteful.

The parallelized algorithm based on the modified qPMS7 algorithm is thus as follows:

For each x $\in_l s_i$, y $\in_l s_j$, $1 \leq i < j \leq n - q + 2$ do:

(1) Traverse the graph $G_d(x, y)$ in a **breadth-first** manner starting from node (x,0).

    (a) If the current node is (x,0), let one processor run.
    (b) Else, let each $k - k_I$ processors have the next $k - k_I$ nodes to be processed and k_I are the number of processors whose nodes aren't processed in the previous loop. If $k - k_I$ is greater than the

number of nodes to be processed, then let the number of additional
processors be the number of nodes left to be processed.

(2) At each node (t,p) do the following steps.

    (a) If a node (t,p)'s parent is not yet processed, let processor k_i hold
on to the node but skip the following steps.

    (b) Else, do the following steps.

        For all the processors, do the following in parallel:

        i. Incrementally compute $d_H(t, s_k)$ from its parent for $1 \leq k \leq n, k \neq i, k \neq j$.

        ii. Let q' be the number of input strings s_j such that $d_H(t, s_j) \leq d$. If q' $\geq q - 2$, output t.

        iii. Let q" be the number of input strings whose lists of surviving $l - mers$ are not empty. If q" $< q - 2$, then do not include the children to the queue. Otherwise, include the children to the queue.

6.1. *Correctness of the Parallelized Modified Algorithm*

Not processing the node (t,p) if its parent is not yet processed preserves
the correctness in computing $d_H(t, s_k)$. Since the parallelized algorithm is
based on the modified qPMS7 algorithm which uses BFS traversal and node
(t,p) is dependent only on its parent, the parallelized modified algorithm
will still yield correct output.

7. Analysis: Time Complexity

7.1. *Modified qPMS7 Algorithm*

According to the literature[5], the time complexity of the original qPMS7
algorithm is $O((n - q + 1)^2 nm^2 N(l, d))$. Starting from 0, there are (n-q+1)
sequences for the s_i and s_j combination. There are N(l,d) nodes to traverse
at most. Getting the incremental distance in each node is $O(nm)^3$ while
the ILP for s_k sequences takes $O((n\text{-}q+1)m)$ per loop.

It is noted that the manner of traversal does not affect the time complexity of the traversal, as the modification would still have to go through
N(l,d) nodes. Additionally, no modifications were done in the computation
for processing and pruning, and as such, the time complexity is still the
same for those processes. Therefore, the time complexity of the modified
qPMS7 algorithm is also $O((n - q + 1)^2 nm^2 N(l, d))$.

Let S={1000,0100,0011}, q=3, l=4, d=2 and k=4.
Given that s_i=1000 and s_j=0100, x=1000 and y=0100.

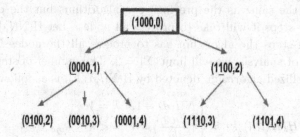

Since we are at (x,0), only processor is running

Output so far ={}

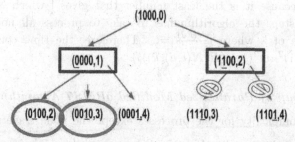

Nodes (0100,2) and (0010,3)'s parents are not yet processed so the
processors will hold on to their assigned node and do nothing for this
iteration. k_l=2

Output so far={0000}

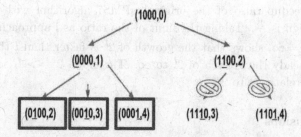

k-k_l=4-2=2 additional processors to get 2 more nodes. Since there is
only one node left, one processor won't be used.

Output so far={0000,0010,0001}, same as the modified algorithm's.

Fig. 7. Sample run of the parallelized modified qPMS7 algorithm. Boxes are processors
that are processing the enclosed nodes while ellipses are holding on to the node.

7.2. *Parallelized Modified qPMS7 Algorithm*

The computations needed for the $d_H(t, s_k)$ and, to expand and to prune a node is the same as the previous two algorithms but the difference is how many steps it will take to process all nodes. Let H(N(l,d),k) be the number of steps the algorithm has to process all the nodes N(l,d). For simplicity of analysis, we will limit $|\Sigma| = 2$. The number of steps taken by the parallellized algorithm, denoted by H(N(l,d),k), is as follows:

$$H(N(l,d),k) = \begin{cases} N(l,d) - 1, & k = 1 \\ \lceil \frac{N(l,d)}{k} \rceil, & 1 < k \le k_{opt} \\ l, & k_{opt} \le k \le N(l,d) - 1 \end{cases}$$

where k is the number of processors such that $k \in \mathbb{N}$, and $1 \le k \le N(l,d) - 1$. k_{opt} represents the ideal number of processors for parallelization because it is the least number that gives l which is the least number of steps the algorithm has to take to process all nodes and it is the value of k where $\lceil \frac{N(l,d)}{k} \rceil = l$. Therefore, the time complexity is $O((n - q + 1)^2 n m^2 (1 + (H(N(l,d), k))))$.

7.3. *Speedup of Parallelized Modified qPMS7 Algorithm*

The time complexity for the processes except the node traversal are the same. Given a binary alphabet, N(l,d) is at most $2^l \ge |B_d(x)| = \sum_{i=0}^{d} \binom{l}{i}$ and processing one at a time, the algorithm will do the processes in 2^l steps. With the parallelization, the algorithm will do the processes at best l times.

The speedup ratio of the original qPMS7 algorithm with the parallelized design is $\frac{2^l}{l}$. Taking the limit of the ratio as l approaches infinity, $\lim_{l \to \infty} \frac{2^l}{l} = \infty$, shows that the growth of 2^l is faster than l that l is too small to steady the growth of 2^l to ∞. Therefore, $2^l >> l$, so l steps is preferable relatively to 2^l.

8. Conclusions

With the proposed parallelized algorithm, the speedup is quite significant from 2^l to l when k_{opt} or more processors are used for the parallelization. Though the computation of the speedup is based on binary alphabet, for more than 2 alphabets, it can be said that the time complexity of the parallelized modified algorithm is still faster than the original algorithm.

The number of alphabet is directly proportional to the number of nodes and $N(l, d)$ is an increasing function. Therefore, the time complexity in both original and parallelized algorithm are bigger than the ones when binary alphabets are used and the parallelized algorithm's time complexity is still smaller than the original algorithm.

9. Recommendation

In this paper, the concerns are the parallelized simple multi-threaded design and speedup of the algorithm in theory so space and memory complexity, implementation and different parallel architecture are not considered.

BFS uses more memory than DFS because it stores nodes for the level in a queue before exploring the descendants. It is recommended to have further studies in the parallelized modified algorithm with space and memory constraint in mind. Along side, doing the implementation is of best interest since the modifications to the algorithm to comply the time and space complexity might make the implementation plausible.

The parallelized algorithm assumes that all processors to be used can communicate with each other. It is recommended to study the algorithm for other architecture where processor communication/signalling may be limited.

References

1. Bandyopadhyay, S., Sahni, S. and Rajasekaran, S. (2012). PMS6: A faster algorithm for motif discovery. *In: Proceedings of the second IEEE International Conference on Computational Advances in Bio and Medical Sciences (ICCABS 2012)*, 1–6.
2. Bandyopadhyay, S., Sahni, S. and Rajasekaran, S. (2013). PMS6MC: A multicore algorithm for motif discovery. *In: Proceedings of the second IEEE International Conference on Computational Advances in Bio and Medical Sciences (ICCABS 2013)*, 1–5.
3. Davila, J., Balla, S. and Rajasekaran, S. (2007). Fast and practical algorithms for planted (l, d) motif search. *IEEE/ACM Transactions on Computational Biology and Bioinformatics, 4(4)*, 544–552. doi:10.1109/TCBB.2007.70241.
4. Dinh, H., Rajasekaran, S. and Kundeti, V. (2011). PMS5: An efficient

exact algorithm for the (l,d)-motif finding problem. *BMC Bioinformatics, 12*, 410. doi:10.1186/1471-2105-12-410.

5. Dinh, H., Rajasekaran, S. and Davila, J. (2012). qPMS7: A Fast Algorithm for Finding (l,d)-Motifs in DNA and Protein Sequences. *PLoS ONE, 7(7)*, 1–8. doi:10.1371/journal.pone.0041425.

6. Evans, P. A., Smith, A. and Wareham H. T. (2004). On the complexity of finding common approximate substrings. *Theoretical Computer Science, 306*, 407–430. doi:10.1016/s0304-3975(03)00320-7.

7. Jones, N. and Pevzner, P. (2004). *An Introduction to Bioinformatics Algorithms.* Cambridge, USA: MIT Press.

8. Nicolae, M. and Rajasekaran, S. (2014). Efficient sequential and parallel algorithms for planted motif search. *BMC Bioinformatics, 15*, 34. doi:10.1186/1471-2105-15-34.

9. Nicolae, M. and Rajasekaran, S. (2015). qPMS9: An Efficient Algorithm for Quorum Planted Motif Search. *Scientific Reports, 5*, 7813. doi:10.1038/srep07813.

10. Rajasekaran S., Balla S. and Huang C. H. (2004). Exact Algorithms For Planted Motif Challenge Problems [PDF document]. Retrieved from http://www.researchgate.net/publication/221118162_Exact_algorithm_for_planted_motif_challenge_problems.

Location-aware Simple Abstract Machine of Call-by-Name RPC Calculus

Takatsugu Tamaizumi, Keishi Watanabe and Shin-ya Nishizaki

Department of Computer Science, Tokyo Institute of Technology,
Tokyo, 152-8552, Japan
E-mail:nisizaki@cs.titech.ac.jp

The remote procedure call (RPC) is a widely used technology for programming in distributed computation. Cooper and Wadler proposed the RPC calculus in order to model remote procedure calls. Araki and Nishizaki proposed call-by-name evaluation strategies of RPC calculus and studied correspondence between the call-by-name evaluation strategies of the RPC calculi. In this paper, we give an abstract machine semantics of call-by-name RPC calculi and study the theoretical relationship between the abstract machine semantics and the small-step structural operational semantics of the call-by-name RPC calculus. We then define an abstract machine semantics of call-by-value RPC calculus, which is simplified based on the method in the abstract machine for the call-by-name calculus.

Keywords: Lambda Calculus; Remort Procedure Call; RPC Calculus; Evaluation Strategy; Call-by-Name Evaluation.

1. Introduction

An *evaluation strategy* is a set of rules for evaluating expressions in a programming language, which defines in what order the arguments of a function are evaluated and when they are substituted into the function.

In *call-by-name* evaluation, an actual parameter expression is bound to the corresponding formal parameter variable before it is evaluated. In the lambda calculus, call-by-name evaluation is formulated as follows.

$$\frac{M \Downarrow \lambda x.M' \quad M'[x := N] \Downarrow V}{(MN) \Downarrow V}$$

$$\frac{}{x \Downarrow x,} \quad \frac{}{\lambda x.M \Downarrow \lambda x.M,} \quad \frac{M \Downarrow V}{(xM) \Downarrow (xV).}$$

This style of operational semantics is called, a *big-step* semantics, which was originally proposed by Kahn[1]. On the other hand, a *small-step semantics* is defined as a transition relation using *evaluation contexts*, which was given by Plotkin[2]. The evaluation context for the call-by-name semantics is defined inductively by the following grammar.

$$E[\ ] ::= x \mid (E[\ ]\, M).$$

The small-step semantics is defined by the following rules:

$$E\,[(\lambda x.M)N] \to E\,[M[x := N]].$$

In the above rule, we find that the actual parameter N is passed to the formal parameter x without evaluated.

In the *call-by-value* evaluation, an actual parameter expression is bound to the corresponding formal parameter variable *after* it is evaluated. The call-by-value evaluation is defined as follows.

$$V \Downarrow V$$

$$\frac{L \Downarrow \lambda x.N \quad M \Downarrow W \quad N[x := W] \Downarrow V}{(L\,M) \Downarrow V}$$

where V is a value, i.e. either a variable or a lambda abstraction.

The small-step semantics for the call-by-value evaluation is defined by the following evaluation context and the transition rules.

$$E[\ ] ::= [\ ] \mid (E[\ ]\, M),$$

$$E\,[(\lambda x.M)V] \to E\,[M[x::=V]].$$

In the call-by-value evaluation, an actual parameter is passed to a formal parameter as a resulting value after evaluation. Many functional and also procedural programming languages are based on the call-by-value evaluation since the actual parameters are evaluated just once, even if the formal parameter is not used during the evaluation. Call-by-name evaluation is occasionally preferable to call-by-value evaluation, since if a formal parameter is not used in a function body, then its actual parameter expression is not evaluated.

It is known that call-by-value evaluation is dual to call-by-name with respect to linear negation of Girard's linear logic[3][4][5].

In this paper, we firstly show the call-by-name RPC calculus given in the previous paper[6]. Secondly, we give a simple type theory for the calculus and then propose an abstract macine for the call-by-name calculus. The formalization of the abstract machine is much simpler than the one for the call-by-value calculus given in the previous work[7]. We also formulate an improved abstract machine for the call-by-calue calculus.

2. Call-by-Name RPC Calculus

We proposed the call-by-name RPC calculus in our previous work[6]. The call-by-value RPC calculus was developed by Cooper and Wadler[8]. Our culculus is an extended variant of the Cooper and Wadler's.

Definition 2.1. Sytax of the call-by-name RPC calculus *Terms* of the call-by-name RPC calculus are defined by the following grammar.

$$M ::= x \mid (\lambda^a x. M) \mid (MN) \mid (M)^a$$

where x is a variable and a is a location. The term $(M)^a$ was written as $\mathsf{eval}^a(M)$ in the previous work[6].

A location represents an identifier of a node in a distributed system, such as an IP address. In the following, we use locations such as c ("client") and s ("server").

The operational semantics of the call-by-name RPC calculus is given as a big-step semantics in the paper[6].

Definition 2.2 (Big-step Operational Semantics). *The big-step operational semantics of the call-by-name RPC caluclus is formulated as a ternary relation $M \Downarrow_a V$ among a term M, V and a location a.*

$$\frac{}{V \Downarrow_a V} \; \textit{Value}$$

$$\frac{L \Downarrow_a (\lambda^b x. N) \quad N[x := (M)^a] \Downarrow_b V}{(LM) \Downarrow_a V} \; \textit{Beta}$$

$$\frac{L \Downarrow_a (\lambda^b x. N) \quad N[x := (M)^c] \Downarrow_b V}{(L(M)^c) \Downarrow_a V} \; \textit{BetaEval}$$

$$\frac{M \Downarrow_a V}{(M)^a \Downarrow_b V} \; \textit{Eval.}$$

The relation $M \Downarrow_a V$ means that evaluation of a term M at a location a is termnated and its the resulting value is V.

Example 2.1 (Big-step Semantics for Call-by-name Evaluation). *The following example of call-by-name evaluation was mentioned in the previous paper[6].*

We consider evaluation of a term

$$(\lambda^s x.x(\lambda^s y.y))((\lambda^s z.z)(\lambda^c w.w)),$$

at a location c. *The deduction tree of its evaluation is as follows.*

$$\dfrac{\overline{(\lambda^s x.x(\lambda^s y.y)) \Downarrow_c (\lambda^s x.x(\lambda^s y.y))} \qquad \begin{matrix}\vdots\ \Sigma\\ ((((\lambda^s z.z)(\lambda^c w.w)))^c)(\lambda^s y.y) \Downarrow_s \lambda^s y.y\end{matrix}}{(\lambda^s x.x(\lambda^s y.y))((\lambda^s z.z)(\lambda^c w.w)) \Downarrow_c \lambda^s y.y}$$

where the subtree Σ *is as follows:*

$$\dfrac{\dfrac{\dfrac{\overline{\lambda^c w.w \Downarrow_c \lambda^c w.w}}{\lambda^s z.z \Downarrow_c \lambda^s z.z \quad ((\lambda^c w.w))^c \Downarrow_s \lambda^c w.w}}{\dfrac{((\lambda^s z.z)(\lambda^c w.w)) \Downarrow_c \lambda^c w.w}{((((\lambda^s z.z)(\lambda^c w.w))))^c \Downarrow_s \lambda^c w.w} \quad \dfrac{\lambda^s y.y \Downarrow_s \lambda^s y.y}{((\lambda^s y.y))^s \Downarrow_c \lambda^s y.y}}}{((((\lambda^s z.z)(\lambda^c w.w)))^c)(\lambda^s y.y) \Downarrow_s \lambda^s y.y} \ .$$

In the paper[9], we gave another operational semantics in the style of Plotkin, also called the small-step semantics.

Definition 2.3 (Small-Step Semantics). *We define a* small-step *semantics as a relation between pairs of an expression and a location,* $(M)^a$.

$$\begin{aligned}(E[(\lambda^b x.\, M)N])^a &\to (E_a[M[x := (N)^a]])^b \quad &\textbf{Beta}\\ (E[(\lambda^b x.\, M)(N)^c])^a &\to (E_a[M[x := (N)^c]])^b \quad &\textbf{BetaEval}\\ (E[(M)^b])^a &\to (E_a[M])^b \quad &\textbf{Eval}\\ (V)^a &\to V \quad &\textbf{EvalVal}\end{aligned}$$

The operation $E[\ ]_a$, called the *location restriction,* is defined as follows.

Definition 2.4 (Evaluation Context for Call-By-Name Evaluation). *An* evaluation context *for the call-by-value evaluation is defined by the following context.*

$$E[\ ] ::= x \mid (E[\ ]\, M).$$

We define a transformation of an evaluation context for imposing a location where the evaluation context should be evaluated.

Definition 2.5 (Location Restriction on Evaluation Context).
The location restriction *on an evaluation context $E_a[\ ]$ is defined inductively by the following equations.*

$$[\ ]_a = [\ ],$$
$$([\ ]\ V)_a = (E_a[\ ]\ V),$$
$$([\ ]\ (MN))_a = (E_a[\ ]\ (MN)^a),$$
$$([\ ]\ (M)^b)_a = (E_a[\ ]\ (M)^b).$$

We show a transition sequence of the term

$$(\lambda^s x.x(\lambda^s y.y))((\lambda^s z.z)(\lambda^c w.w)),$$

cited in Example 2.1 below.

Example 2.2 (Small-step Semantics of the Call-by-Name Evaluation).

$$\left((\lambda^s x.x(\lambda^s y.y))((\lambda^s z.z)(\lambda^c w.w)) \right)^c$$
$$\to \left((\ \underline{(\lambda^s z.\ z)(\lambda^c w.\ w)}\ )^c (\lambda^s y.\ y) \right)^s$$
$$\to \left(\underline{(\lambda^c w.\ w)^c}\ (\lambda^s y.\ y) \right)^s$$
$$\to \left(\underline{(\lambda^c w.\ w)(\lambda^s y.\ y)} \right)^c$$
$$\to \left(\underline{(\lambda^s y.\ y)^s}\ \right)^c$$
$$\to (\lambda^s y.\ y)^s$$
$$\to \lambda^s y.\ y$$

We can give a simple type theory[10] on the calculus, giving the following typing rules. The terms are independent.

Definition 2.6 (Simple Type Theory for the RPC Calculus).
Typing of the RPC calculus is given by a typing judgement $\Gamma \vdash_a M : A$, which is a relation among a typing assingment Γ, a location a, a term M, and a type A, defined inductively by the following rules.

$$\frac{\Gamma \vdash_a x : A}{\{x : A\} \in A}$$

$$\frac{\Gamma \vdash_b M : B}{\{x : A\}\Gamma \vdash_b M : B}$$

$$\frac{\Gamma \vdash_a M : A \to B \quad \Gamma \vdash_a N : A}{\Gamma \vdash_a (MN) : B}$$

$$\frac{\Gamma \vdash_a M : A}{\Gamma \vdash_b (M)^a : A}.$$

Subject reduction theorem for the small-step smantics and the simple type theory, which is consistent not only on the type but also on the location.

Theorem 2.1 (Subject Reduction Theorem). *If* $\Gamma \vdash_a M : A$ *and* $(M)^a \to (M')^{a'}$, *then* $\Gamma \vdash_{a'} : M' : A$.

This is easily proved using the following lemma.

Lemma 2.1. *If* $\{x : A\}\Gamma \vdash_a M : B$ *and* $\Gamma \vdash_c N : A$, *then* $\Gamma \vdash_a M[x := N] : B$.

3. Call-by-Name Location-aware Simple Abstract Machine

We proposed the call-by-name location-aware simple abstract machine, LSAM/CBN, which is an extension of the Simple Abstract Machine[11][7] for the Call-by-Name RPC calculus.

Definition 3.1. Syntax of LSAM/CBN A stack is a sequence of terms, written as

$$M_1 : M_2 : \cdots : M_n$$

and, if n equals 0, as [ ]. A *configuration* of LSAM/CBN is a triple of a term M, a stack S, and a location a, written as

$$(M, S)_a.$$

The configuration $(M, S)_a$ represents a current status of the abstract machine. The first component M of the configuration $(M, S)_a$ represents a current code part of the abstract machine, the second component S a current stack, and the third component a a current location in which the M is evaluated.

Definition 3.2 (Transition of Abstract Machine). *The transition relation of the LSAM/CBN-configuration*

$$(M, S)_a \to (M', S')_{a'}$$

is defined inductively by the following rules:

$$((MN), S)_a \to (M, N : S)_a$$
$$((\lambda^b x. M), N : S)_a \to (M[x := (N)^a], (S)^a)_b$$
$$((M)^b, S)_a \to (M, (S)^a)_b$$

We show a theorem that computation of the call-by-name RPC calculus corresponds to that of LSAM/CBN.

Before showing the theorem, we prepare an interpretation of an evaluation context in LSAM/NAME.

Definition 3.3. We define an *interpretation mapping* $[\![-]\!]$ of an evaluation context inductively as follows.

$$[\![\,[\,]\,]\!] = [\,]$$
$$[\![(E[\,]\,N)]\!] = [\![E[\,]\,]\!]{:}N.$$

We have a lemma on the interpretation of an evaluation context.

Lemma 3.1. $([\![E[\,]\,]\!])^a = [\![E^a[\,]\,]\!].$

Theorem 3.1 (Correspondence Theorem). *If*

$$(E[M])_a \to (E'[M'])_b,$$

then

$$(M, [\![E[\,]\,]\!])_a \overset{*}{\to} (M', [\![E'[\,]\,]\!])_b.$$

Proof. We make case analysis on the transition $(E[M])_a \to (E'[M'])_b$.
Case 1. We assume that

$$\left(E\left[(\lambda^b x. N)M\right]\right)_a \to \left(E^a\left[N[x := (M)^a]\right]\right)_b.$$

Then, we check a transition starting from the term correspoinding to the left-hand side of the assumption.

$$\left(((\lambda^b x. N)M),\ [\![E[\,]\,]\!]\right)_a$$
$$\to \left((\lambda^b x. N),\ M{:}[\![E[\,]\,]\!]\right)_a$$
$$\to \left(N[x := (M)_a],\ ([\![E[\,]\,]\!])\right)_a$$

Case 2. We assume that

$$\left(E[(M)^b]\right)_a \to \left(E^a[M]\right)_b.$$

Then, we have

$$((M)^b,\ \llbracket E[\ ]\rrbracket)_a$$
$$\to (M, (\llbracket E[\ ]\rrbracket)^a)_b$$
$$= (M, \llbracket E^a[\ ]\rrbracket)_b.$$

4. Single-Threading Abstract Machine for the Call-By-Value RPC Calculus

In the previous paper[7], we proposed an abstract machine of the call-by-value RPC calculus, which formalizes parallel computation with multi-threads. The abstract machine formulated as a transition between sets of multiple configurations. The following rule, app-lam-rpc[7], is a remote procedure call from a locaion a to b.

$$\{(V : \mathbf{lam}(b, x, C'){:}S_1,\ \mathsf{app}{:}C_1)_a, (S_2,\ C_2)_b\} \cup A$$
$$\to \{(S_1,\ \mathsf{wait}(m){:}C_1)_a, (S_2,\ C'[x := V]{:}\mathsf{ret}(a){:}C_2)_b\} \cup A$$

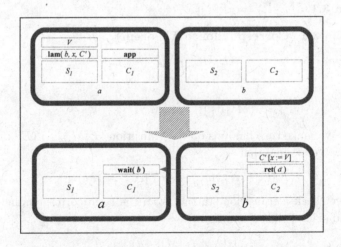

Fig. 1.   Rule app-lam-rpc.

On the other hand, the abstract machine defined in the previous section is formalized as a transition not between sets of configurations but between configurations. In other words, the computation on the abstract machine is single-threading. We can define a single-threading version of the abstract machine.

A code of the LSAM/CBN is given as a same tree structure as the call-by-name RPC calculus but a code of the call-by-value version, LSAM/CBV, is defined as a sequence of instructions.

Definition 4.1 (Syntax of LSAM/CBV). *A value V, an instruction I and a code C are defined by the following grammar.*

$$V ::= x \mid \mathsf{lam}(l, x, C)$$
$$I ::= V \mid \mathsf{app}$$
$$C ::= I_1 : \cdots : I_n$$
$$S ::= V_1 : \cdots : V_m$$

A configuration C is a triple of a stack S, a code C, and a location l, that is,

$$M ::= (S, C)_l$$

A single-threading abstract machine for the call-by-value abstract machine is formalized as follows.

Definition 4.2 (Call-By-Value Single-Threading Abstract Machine). *The transition relation between the configurations of LSAM/CBV*

$$(S, C)_a \to (S', C')_{a'}$$

is defined inductively by the following rules.

$$(S, x : C)_a \to (x : S, C)_a$$
$$(S, \mathsf{lam}(b, x, C') : C)_a \to (\mathsf{lam}(b, x, C') : S, C)_a$$
$$(V : \mathsf{lam}(b, x, C') : S, \mathsf{app} : C)_a \to (S, C'[x := V] : \mathsf{ret}(a) : C)_b$$
$$(S, \mathsf{ret}(b) : C)_a \to (S, C)_b$$

In the following, we give the definition of the call-by-value RPC calculus[8 7].

Definition 4.3 (Evaluation Context for the Call-By-Value Evaluation). *We define an evaluation context for the call-by-value evaluation is defined by the following grammar.*

$$E[\,] ::= [\,] \mid (E[\,])\, M) \mid (V\, E[\,]),$$

where V means a value, which is defined as follows.

$$V ::= x \mid (\lambda^a x. M).$$

The small-step semantics of the calculus is given by the following transition relation between terms.

Definition 4.4 (Small-step Semantics of Call-by-Value Evaluation). *The small-step semantics for the call-by-value evaluation of the RPC calculus is defined as a transition $(M)^a \to (M')^{a'}$ between eval-terms by the following rules.*

$$\left(E\left[(\lambda^b x. M)V\right]\right)^a \to \left(E_a\left[M[x := V]\right]\right)^b$$
$$\left(E[(M)^b]\right)^a \to \left(E_a[M]\right)^b$$
$$(V)^a \to V.$$

A term of the call-by-value RPC caluclus is translated into a code of LSAM/CBV. This translation can be thought as a "compilation" which generates bytecodes of LSAM/CBV.

Definition 4.5 (Term Translation). *The translation $T[\![-]\!]$ of terms of the call-by-value RPC calculus into codes of LSAM/CBV is defined inductively by the following equations.*

$$T[\![x]\!] = x,$$
$$T[\![\lambda^a x. M]\!] = \mathsf{lam}(a, x, T[\![M]\!]),$$
$$T[\![(MN)]\!] = T[\![M]\!] : T[\![N]\!] : \mathsf{app}.$$

We next show an example of the translation and an execution of the translated code.

Example 4.1. We consider the term

$$((\lambda^s x. x(\lambda^s y. y))((\lambda^s z. z)(\lambda^c w. w)))^c$$

mentioned in Example 2.1. This term is computed by the small-step semantics as follows.

$$((\lambda^s x. x(\lambda^s y. y))((\lambda^s z. z)(\lambda^c w. w)))^c$$
$$\to ((\lambda^s x. x(\lambda^s y. y))(\lambda^c w. w))^s$$
$$\to ((\lambda^c w. w)(\lambda^s y. y))^s$$
$$\to ((\lambda^s y. y))^c$$

This term can be translated as

$$T[\![(\lambda^s x.\, x(\lambda^s y.\, y))((\lambda^s z.\, z)(\lambda^c w.\, w))]\!]$$

$$=\mathsf{lam}\,(\mathsf{s}, x, (\mathsf{s}, y, y) : \mathsf{app}) : \mathsf{lam}(\mathsf{s}, z, z) : \mathsf{lam}(\mathsf{c}, w, w) : \mathsf{app} : \mathsf{app}.$$

Next we show the transition sequence staring with the translated code.

$$([\,], \mathsf{lam}\,(\mathsf{s}, x, (\mathsf{s}, y, y) : \mathsf{app}) : \mathsf{lam}(\mathsf{s}, z, z) : \mathsf{lam}(\mathsf{c}, w, w) : \mathsf{app} : \mathsf{app.})_\mathsf{c}$$
$$\to (\mathsf{lam}\,(\mathsf{s}, x, (\mathsf{s}, y, y) : \mathsf{app}),\ \mathsf{lam}(\mathsf{s}, z, z) : \mathsf{lam}(\mathsf{c}, w, w) : \mathsf{app} : \mathsf{app})_\mathsf{c}$$
$$\to (\mathsf{lam}(\mathsf{s}, z, z) : \mathsf{lam}\,(\mathsf{s}, x, (\mathsf{s}, y, y) : \mathsf{app}),\ \mathsf{lam}(\mathsf{c}, w, w) : \mathsf{app} : \mathsf{app})_\mathsf{c}$$
$$\to (\mathsf{lam}(\mathsf{c}, w, w) : \mathsf{lam}(\mathsf{s}, z, z) : \mathsf{lam}\,(\mathsf{s}, x, (\mathsf{s}, y, y) : \mathsf{app}),\ \mathsf{app} : \mathsf{app})_\mathsf{c}$$
$$\to (\mathsf{lam}\,(\mathsf{s}, x, (\mathsf{s}, y, y) : \mathsf{app}),\ \mathsf{lam}(\mathsf{c}, w, w) : \mathsf{app})_\mathsf{s}$$
$$\to (\mathsf{lam}(\mathsf{c}, w, w) : \mathsf{lam}\,(\mathsf{s}, x, (\mathsf{s}, y, y) : \mathsf{app}),\ \mathsf{app})_\mathsf{s}$$
$$\to ([\,], \mathsf{lam}(\mathsf{c}, w, w) : \mathsf{lam}(\mathsf{s}, y, y) : \mathsf{app})_\mathsf{s}$$
$$\to (\mathsf{lam}(\mathsf{c}, w, w),\ \mathsf{lam}(\mathsf{s}, y, y) : \mathsf{app})_\mathsf{s}$$
$$\to (\mathsf{lam}(\mathsf{s}, y, y) : \mathsf{lam}(\mathsf{c}, w, w),\ \mathsf{app})_\mathsf{s}$$
$$\to ([\,], \mathsf{lam}(\mathsf{s}, y, y))_\mathsf{c}$$
$$\to (\mathsf{lam}(\mathsf{s}, y, y),\ [\,])_\mathsf{c}$$

From the evaluation sequence of the small-step semantics and the transition sequence of LSAM/CBV, we think of the following conjecture.

If $(M)^a \to^* (V)^{a'}$, then we have

$$([\,],\ T[\![M]\!])_a \to^* (V,\ [\,])_{a'}.$$

5. Conclusions

In this paper, we propose the abstract machine LSAM/CBN for the call-by-name RPC calculus and studied a relationship between the calculus and the abstract machine. Then, we reconsider the abstract machine for the call-by-value RPC calculus proposed in the previous work, which is formulated as a parallel computation model. The parallel abstract machine can provide multi-threading computation. However, each evaluation path of the RPC calculus is not multi-threading but single-threading. In this paper, we give a simplified abstract machine LSAM/CBV for single threading computation and show an example of the computation.

At the moment, the relationship between the call-by-value RPC calculus and the abstract machien LSAM/CBV is not studied yet, which is our primary future work to be finished.

References

1. G. Kahn, Natural semantics, in *Proceedings of STACS 1987*, Lecture Notes in Computer Science Vol. 247 (Springer-Verlag, Berlin Germany, 1987).
2. G. Plotkin, Call-by-name, call-by-value, and the λ-calculus, *Theoretical Computer Science* **1**, 125 (1975).
3. P. Wadler, Call-by-value is dual to call-by-name – reloaded, in *Proceedings of the 16th RTA 2005*, (Springer-Verlag Berlin Heidelberg, 2005).
4. S. Nishizaki, Programs with continuations and linear logic, *Science of Computer Programming* **21**, 165 (1993).
5. J.-Y. Girard, Linear logic, *Theoretical Computer Science* **50**, 1 (1987).
6. S. Araki and S. Nishizaki, Call-by-name evaluation of rpc and rmi calculi, *Proceedings of the Third Workshop on Computation: Theory and Practice, WCTP2013, Proceedings in Information and Communication Technology* (2014).
7. K. Narita and S. Nishizaki, A Parallel Abstract Machine for the RPC Calculus, in *Informatics Engineering and Information Science*, Communications in Computer and Information Science Vol. 253 (Springer-Verlag, Berlin Germany, 2011).
8. E. Cooper and P. Wadler, The RPC calculus, in *Proceedings of the 11th ACM SIGPLAN Conference on Principles and Practice of Declarative Programming, PPDP 2009*, (ACM Press, 2009).
9. K. Watanabe and S. Nishizaki, Call-by-name evaluation of rpc calculus, in *Proceedings of International Conference on Advances in Information Technology and Mobile Communication – AIM 2015*, (Narosa Publishing House, 2015).
10. C. A. Gunter, *Semantics of programming languages: structures and techniques* (The MIT Press, 1992).
11. K. Narita, S. Nishizaki and T. Mizuno, A Simple Abstract Machine for Functional First-class Continuations, in *Proceedings of 2010 International Symposium on Communications and Information Technologies (ISCIT)*, (IEEE, 2010).

Parallelizing the Searching for K-mers and the Alignment of Reads to Edges to Speedup the Pregraph Construction in SOAPdenovo2

Grace Magno, Lovely Santos, Henry Adorna, Jhoirene Clemente and Jan Michael Yap*

Department of Computer Science, University of the Philippines Diliman, Quezon City, Philippines
*jcyap@dcs.upd.edu.ph
www.aclab.dcs.upd.edu.ph

For the past decade, there has been a high demand for low cost, high quality genome sequence of species that has led to the advancements in sequencing technologies, known as next-generation sequencing (NGS). Current sequencing techniques are marked by increase in throughput and reduction in cost and time as compared to previous sequencing methods. SOAPdenovo, an all-purpose genome assembler, has been used to successfully assemble genomes of variety of species that have been published. SOAPdenovo2, the successor of SOAPdenovo, has exceeded its predecessor greatly in terms of error correction algorithm, memory consumption on graph construction, coverage and scaffold length. Despite these notable improvements on SOAPdenovo, the time and space used in the de Bruijn graph construction still remains an issue. In this study, we describe a method that parallelizes the graph construction of the de novo assembly in SOAPdenovo2 to improve the time efficiency. In the method applied, the time complexity of two functions has been reduced from $T(n) = 4n+4$ to $T(n) = 5\frac{n}{m} + 7m + 12$, where n is the size of the hash table and m is the no. of partitions, and from $T(n) = 15n + 17$ to $T(n) = 22\frac{n}{m} + 5m + 23$, where n is the no. of kmers in a read and m is the no. of partitions.

Keywords: SOAPdenovo2, De Novo Assembly, de Bruijn Graphs, Pregraph Construction, Parallelization, Computational Biology.

1. Introduction

Deoxyribonucleic acid (DNA) sequencing, the process of determining the precise order of the four nucleotide bases – adenine(A), cytosine(C), guanine(G) and thymine(T) – in the DNA strand[8], is essential to different fields, especially in biology. It is vital in the field of medicine, agriculture and gene therapy. It helps researchers to fully understand the genetic makeup of the organisms being studied, as it is being aimed in the field of bioinformatics. Over the years, there have been notable advancements in sequencing techniques, but with current sequencing technologies, it still remains unfeasible to sequence a complete genome in one read, which gave rise to the genome assembly problem[20]. Genome assembly stitches together a genome from a large number of short sequenced fragments of DNA generated by shotgun assembly and then connecting them to assemble into the original sequence[1]. Given a family of reads which may contain errors and can be paired, the assembly problem's goal in constructing contigs consists of the following: (a) the breadth of coverage, which indicates how much the genome is represented, is maximal, (b) the number of assembly errors, such as chimeric contigs, mismatches, insertions and deletions, is minimal, and (c) the number of contigs is minimal, wherein redundancy has been indirectly reduced[2].

The first sequencing method that was used and for almost 30 years, the leading sequencing technology, is the Sanger sequencing method, developed by Fred Sanger in the 1970's. In this method, the double-stranded DNA sequence is separated into two strands – the template strand and the complementary strand. Four mixtures are created for replication, wherein a primer is first attached to one end of the template strand, which is the strand to be sequenced, to signal the starting point for the DNA replication. Replication continues as deoxyribonucleotides are added into the mixture. It stops every time a chemically altered base, called dideoxyribonucleotide, is added to the mixture and is inserted into the growing chain. The products of these four mixtures are then transferred to electrophoresis gel which separates the nucleotides according to size and nucleotide type. The shortest moves down the electrophoresis gel and DNA sequence is obtained by reading the output of electrophoresis from bottom to top[18].

Even though Sanger sequencing technology can provide a highly accurate genome sequence, due to its high cost and slow speed, it limits genome projects. This instigated a need for researchers to develop low-cost and faster sequencing methods that would still be able to obtain a genome sequence with the same accuracy as the Sanger-based. Since there is a great demand, high throughput DNA sequencing technology that is non-Sanger based, collectively known as next-generation sequencing (NGS), has been introduced, characterized by parallel sequencing of DNA strands, causing major impacts on genome research[7,12].

The challenge now in next-generation sequencing is how to build a genome assembler considering that most of the produced data is distorted by high frequencies of sequencing errors and multiple copies of short DNA sequences called genomic repeats, and that there is limited computational resources. Existing NGS assemblers have implemented different stages such as preprocess filtering, graph construction process, graph simplification process and post process filtering, where some of these steps take too much time to be executed[7].

2. Preliminaries

In genome assembly, we call the the identified short fragment strings of nucleotide bases that are assembled as *reads*. Sequences representing a region in the DNA, called *contigs*, are then obtained from these reads generated from their overlaps and overlapping contigs separated by gaps of known length comprise what is known as *scaffolds*.

There are two approaches in the assembly of the genome: the *reference-based assembly* and the *de novo assembly*. The reference-based assembly is the sequencing of new genome sequence by mapping it onto a reference genome[16], while de novo assembly is the sequencing of unknown genome from short DNA fragments called reads, to form overlapping reads called contigs, combined to form long DNA sequences called scaffolds, wherein there is no reference sequence used in the assembly[15].

The de novo assemblers are further classified into three: (1) assemblers that use overlap layout consensus (OLC), (2) assemblers that make use of greedy algorithms and (3) assemblers that use de Bruijn graphs. The framework of assemblers that use overlap layout consensus (OLC) is a three-step process: (a) computing the overlap between reads, (b) determining the order and orientation of the reads in the assembly, and (c) determining the nucleotide at each position in the contigs. The greedy assemblers use an algorithm that iteratively grows contigs by choosing the best overlap first. The de Bruijn assemblers, on the other hand, make use of k-mer, a sequence of length k generated from the alphabet of nucleotides (A, C, T, G) and k-mer graphs, a de Bruijn graph constructed from k-mers[17]. One k-mer is connected to another k-mer with a directed edge if the suffix of the former k-mer node is equal to the prefix of the second k-mer node – such that, given an alphabet $\Sigma = \{A, C, T, G\}$ and an integer k, a full

READS

ACTGA	TTTAC
TGAAT	TACGG
CTGAA	ACGGA

CONTIGS

ACTGAAT

TTTACGGA

SCAFFOLD

FIGURE 1

Fig. 1.   Reads, contigs and scaffolds.

de Bruijn graph has vertices $V(G) = \Sigma^*$ and arcs $E = \{< x, y >| \ x, y \in V(G), x[2..k] = y[1..k - 1]\}$, that is, if the two k-mers completely overlap except for one nucleotide base at each end.   Figure 2 shows examples for the three approaches in de novo assembly.

3. De Bruijn Graph in Genome Assembly

With the use of the de Bruijn graph, the difficult challenge of assembling contiguous genome from billions of short sequencing reads has been reduced into a tractable computational problem, transforming questions involving Hamiltonian cycles, an NP-complete problem, into a different question regarding Eulerian path, a path in a graph that visits every edge exactly once, and Eulerian cycle, an Eulerian that starts and ends on the same node, which can be solved in polynomial time[4]. The de Bruijn graph originated from the'superstring problem' that has the goal of finding a shortest circular 'superstring' that contains all possible 'substrings' of length k over a given alphabet[5]. Most short read assemblers make use of the de Bruijn graph. The graph is constructed by, first, from a set of reads, make a node for every k-mers. Second, given a k-mer, its suffix is all its nucleotide bases except the first base and its prefix is all its nucleotide bases except the last base. There is a directed edge between two nodes if they have *k-1* overlap. Lastly, in the constructed directed graph, a node's in-degree is the num-

SEQUENCE: AAGACTCCGACACTTT

R1	R2	R3	R4	R5	R6	R7	R8
AAGA	AGAC	CACT	GACA	ACTT	CTCC	CCGA	CTTT

A

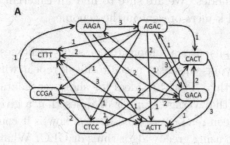

SEQUENCE: AAGACTCCGACACTTT

R1	R2	R3	R4	R5	R6	R7	R8
AAGA	AGAC	CACT	GACA	ACTT	CTCC	CCGA	CTTT

B

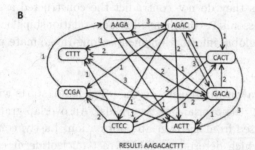

RESULT: AAGACACTTT

SEQUENCE: AAGACTCCGACACTTT

R1	R2	R3	R4	R5	R6	R7	R8
AAGA	AGAC	CACT	GACA	ACTT	CTCC	CCGA	CTTT
AAG	AGA	CAC	GAC	ACT	CTC	CCG	CTT
AGA	GAC	ACT	ACA	CTT	TCC	CGA	TTT

C

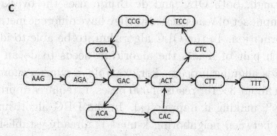

RESULT: AAGACTCCGACACTTT

Fig. 2.   Approaches to de novo assembly. Given the same set of reads: (A) Overlap graph constructed from the reads; (B) By using greedy algorithm on the overlap graph, complete sequence wasn't reconstructed; (C) de Bruijn graph with k = 4 constructed from the reads was able to reconstruct the complete sequence. Also, overlap graph construction is more complicated than constructing de Bruijn graph.

ber of edges entering it and its out-degree is the number of edges leaving it. Since the graph is balanced, there are equal numbers of in-degrees and out-degrees for all nodes. We are sure to find an Eulerian path as long as we have located all k-mers present in the genome.

De Bruijn graphs are appropriate to show genomes with repeats, whereas overlap layout consensus needs to mask repeat with length longer than the read length[4]. They are ideal for short read data sets with high coverage, which is the average number of times that a given nucleotide in the sequence has been read or sequenced. But how is it compared to other types of assemblers using greedy algorithms or OLC? What are the advantages of using de Bruijn graph algorithm over the other two algorithms?

Greedy assemblers, always choose to join the reads having the greatest overlap, as long as they do not contradict the constructed assembly thus far. This type of assemblers only consider local relationships between reads and does not use global information such as long-range mate pair links to resolve repetitive genomes.

Basic overlap layout consensus, on the other hand, starts with identifying and comparing the overlaps of two reads. An overlap graph will then be constructed based from the overlap information. Lastly, consensus step will take place, which determines the correct nucleotide at each specific position. This type of assembler can take into account global relationship between reads, just like the de Bruijn graph, with the development of complex assembly algorithms being applied to the overlap graph structure.

Even though, both OLC and de Bruijn uses the overlap information among the input set of reads globally, they have different methods to exploit overlap information. In the OLC algorithm, to be able to identify overlap between each pair of reads, the algorithm needs to do an all-against-all pairwise reads aligning process. For example, a whole genome shotgun assembly with about 3×10^6 reads of 500 bases, it requires approximately 10^{13} comparisons[6], making it impractical. In the DBG algorithm, the overlap relationship between neighboring k-mers is already established implicitly. They also differ in the algorithm complexity and computational efficiency, because in OLC, the layout step needed a Hamiltonian path, leading to the NP-Hard Hamiltonian path problem. In DBG, on the other hand, getting the contig sequence is an Eulerian path problem which is easier to resolve.

Hence, the main advantage of DBG is transforming the assembly problem to an easier problem in algorithm theory. In OLC, after the overlap and the layout steps, there is a need for the consensus step. In DBG, the consensus step is already disregarded after its construction process since k-mers already include consensus information [12].

During data processing both OLC and de Bruijn could implement a pre-assembly error correction, either by using read alignment probabilities or by using k-mer frequency spectrum. During contig construction, which is the core step in assembly, the main problem is dealing with repeats. Repeat reads in OLC are all placed as nodes in the graph, while in DBG repeat k-mers are collapsed into a single node. In OLC, since repeat regions have many areas of overlap with other reads there will be an increase in the computational time needed for pair-wise reads alignment and will require a very intensive memory to store the overlap relationships. A solution for OLC is to mask repeats pattern, first, before finding overlaps and then, recover it after contig construction. In contrary, DBG will not experience the same problem because, it has no pair-wise reads alignment step and the k-mer nodes from repeats are collapsed together during construction of DBG. In spite of intrinsic high computational efficiency of DBG in dealing with repeats. the major weakness of DBG is low-efficiency in utilizing longer reads because of the limited k-mer size, limiting also its potential to use long reads to overcome repeats, unlike OLC which works better with longer reads. During scaffold linkage, in OLC, repeat contigs can be identified by the number of reads they contain, because repeat contigs will surely have more reads than unique contigs, while in DBG, repeat contigs can be identified by the k-mer coverage depth of the contig, which is higher than that of the unique contig. Therefore, OLC is more suitable for low-coverage long reads and DBG is suitable for high-coverage short reads and especially for large genome assemblies [12].

3.1. *Choosing the k-mer length*

In de Bruijn-based assemblers, parameter k is significant, because this determines the size of the k-mers into which reads are partitioned and the choice of k represents a trade-off between many competing effects. Large value of k is desired so that repeats longer than k will not tangle the graph and will not break up contigs. But the larger the value of k the higher the chances that the k-mer will have an error in it, which decreases the number of correct k-mers present in the data. The size of k also has an effect when two reads overlap by less than k characters. They do not share a vertex in the graph and thus create a coverage gap that breaks up a contig. In practice, k is often chosen based on prior experience with similar datasets but this is very time consuming, since assembling a certain genome especially those with large sizes can take days.

A possible solution in choosing the k-mer length is to use the tool called KMERGENIE[3]. It generates abundance histograms for numerous common values of k, then fits a generative model to each histogram in order to estimate how many distinct k-mers in the histogram are genomic and lastly pick a value of k which maximizes the number of genomic k-mers. The method used can be integrated into assembly pipelines to choose k automatically. It is tested to be effective using three sequencing datasets: S. aureus, human chromosome 14 and B. impatiens, and KMERGENIE's choice leads to the best assemblies[3].

3.2. *Genome Assemblers*

For this study, five among the existing de Bruijn assemblers were compared and their performance and output results were used as measures for comparison and evaluation. The assemblers studied include Velvet, ABySS, Ray, SOAPdenovo and SOAPdenovo2. Table 1 shows a summary of these assemblers.

Velvet[22] is a set of algorithms that manipulate de Bruijn graphs, efficiently eliminating errors and resolving repeats. It hashes reads according to the chosen odd k-mer length and it uses graph simplification and compression without loss of information to save memory cost and make the assembly easier, while error removal is done after graph construction to allow for simultaneous operations over the whole set of reads, where in the center of interest is the removal of tips, bubbles that may be due to biological variants and erroneous connection brought about by cloning errors. Using Velvet, a large RAM is required. In assembling a bacterial genome, 2GB RAM was used[22].

Assembly By Short Sequencing (ABySS)[19], an assembler designed for short read sequences, has been developed for very large data sets such as the human genome. It has two stages: the sequence assembly and the paired end assembly. It uses parallel implementation of graph simplification used in Velvet and it distributes de Bruijn graphs across a cluster of computers and allows parallel implementation of assembly algorithms on billions of short reads. ABySS is relatively slow and it also requires a large amount of RAM. It was able to assemble the human genome using 16GB RAM[19].

Ray[2], on the other hand, is an assembler that run in parallel and distribute data across computers with message passing interface. It also makes use of de Bruijn graph but it does not rely on Eulerian walks. It defines specific subsequences, called seeds, to be able to generate an assembly and it uses heuristics to extend these seeds to contigs. Ray values the quality more than the length of contigs[2].

SOAPdenovo[11], an all-purpose genome assembler, starts with a preassembly sequencing error correction, which is important for large datasets to reduce memory consumption in the graph construction. It consists of processes such as removal of erroneous connections, mapping of reads to contigs and closing of gaps. SOAPdenovo also consumes a large amount of memory, being able to assemble human genome using 140GB amount of memory in the construction of de Bruijn graph[11].

SOAPdenovo2[14] is an improvement of the SOAPdenovo. It has enhanced error correction algorithm, reduced memory consumption in graph construction, increased coverage length and length in scaffold construction, and improved gap closure in SOAPdenovo. SOAPdenovo2 supports memory efficient long k-mer error correction and it uses a new space k-mer scheme to improve accuracy and sensitivity. SOAPdenovo2 uses a multiple k-mer strategy to make use of the advantages of both using small k-mers and large k-mers. First, small k-mers are used to remove sequencing errors and then graph is rebuilt using longer k-mers to resolve longer repeats by mapping the reads back to the previous de Bruijn graph[14]. Improvement in scaffold construction from SOAPdenovo includes detection of heterozygous contig pairs using contig depth and local contig relationships. The contig with higher depth was retained in the scaffold. Chimeric scaffolds are corrected using information from a larger insert size library[14]. The GapCloser module of SOAPdenovo was also improved by developing a new method that considers all reads aligned during previous cycles resolving conflicting bases and thus improving the accuracy of gap closure[14].

In all these assemblers under study, the common bottleneck is found to be the graph construction, which make use of de Bruijn graphs. Finding an alternative way of implementing the part which causes the bottleneck could help solve these problems. We want to look for the feasibility of establishing a parallel way of implementing the part which causes the bottleneck and investigate the effect to the efficiency and accuracy of the assembler.

Among the assemblers used today, SOAPdenovo2, an all-purpose assembler, can handle a variety of genomes, even the large ones, such as the human genome and it is one of the leading assemblers used in terms of speed and accuracy, as compared to other assemblers. This study will, therefore, focus on SOAPdenovo2. This study aims to provide an algorithm on how SOAPdenovo2 can parallelize its graph construction without sacrificing the accuracy.

4. Methods

4.1. *Identifying Bottlenecks in SOAPdenovo2's Pregraph Construction*

Despite the improvements from SOAPdenovo, SOAPdenovo2 generally still runs slowly as compared to other assemblers, Velvet 1.2.07 for example, which uses multi-threads. SOAPdenovo2 runs on a longer time than Velvet, and it also runs slow especially for those with larger genome size and contains greater number of repeats[10].

SOAPdenovo2 has four modules: the pregraph, the contig, the map and the scaffold, which can be run step by step or all at once. Figure 3 shows a summary of the code of SOAPdenovo2.

Using a sample data set from the 3000 Rice Genomes Project Data from GigaDB Dataset website (http://gigadb.org/dataset/200001) on SOAPdenovo2 with the default number of threads, output and results show that the most time-consuming part is its pregraph step. Figure 4 shows an example of how the pregraph step works.

First, the reads will be chopped into k-mers, in our example, k=3. Each k-mer is assigned a 128-bit integer *int_val*, and as for our example, the k-mers are randomly assigned an integer value. These k-mers will then be stored in a corresponding hash table called *kmerset*, which implements open

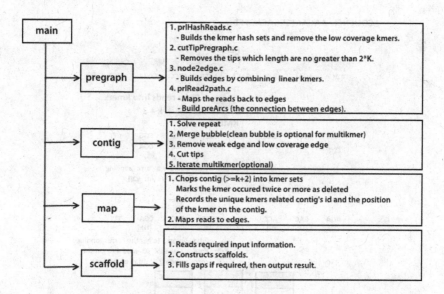

Fig. 3.   Modules in SOAPdenovo2 with corresponding major files used in each step.

addressing. In SOAPdenovo2, the number of hash tables depends on the number of threads defined before running the code, but the default is 8 threads. For our example, we will have $a = 3$, where a is the number of hash tables and $b = 4$, where b is the size of each hash table. A k-mer is stored in the kmerset $c = int\_val \bmod a$, and its position p in the kmerset is $p = int\_val \bmod b$. After storing the k-mers in the hash table, k-mers with low coverage will be removed and linear k-mers will be marked. Linear k-mers are k-mers whose in-degree and out-degree are both 1. To get the in-degree and out-degree of a k-mer, the left coverage, which is the number of bases that precedes the (k-1)-mer, and right coverage, which is the number of bases that proceeds the (k-1)-mer, are being taken. As for our example, AGA, CCG, CTC, TCC, CAC, ACA, CTT and CGA are linear k-mers. Then the frequencies of the k-mers will be counted. Single and minor tips having 2*k length will be removed and then linear k-mers will be marked again. Finally, edges are built by combining linear k-mers. (See Figure 5)

Output results from the rice genome datasets show that the searching for k-mers and the alignment of reads to edges, which are done after the marking of linear k-mers, are the bottleneck in SOAPdenovo2. By tracing down which functions within the standard pregraph are responsible for

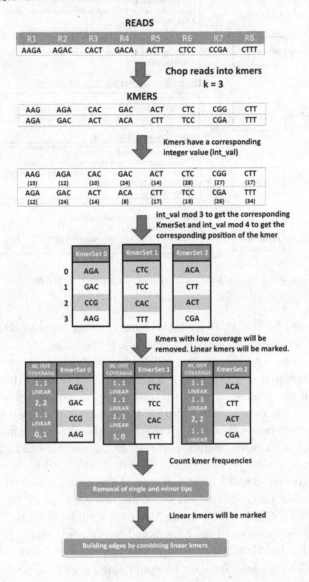

Fig. 4. SOAPdenovo2's pregraph step.

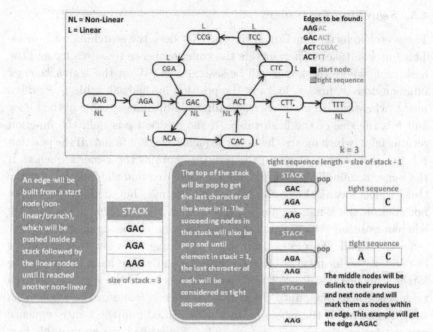

Fig. 5. Building edges by combining linear nodes.

these, we found out that the *search_kmerset* function in *newhash.c* and the *parse1read* function in *prlRead2path.c* consume much of the running time of SOAPdenovo2.

Since the searching for k-mers and the alignment of reads to edges make the pregraph construction of the assembly slow, we studied the behavior and processes of these functions, as well as the functions related to it, and looked for what can be done to speed up the processes, hence speeding up SOAPdenovo2's pregraph construction. SOAPdenovo2 implements parallel threading with shared memory, but this does not mean that the processes found within this function runs simultaneously with each other.

4.2. Parallelizing the Bottlenecks of SOAPdenovo2

Since we have found out that the bottleneck of SOAPdenovo2 is in searching for k-mers and aligning the reads to edges, we take a closer look to the parts of SOAPdenovo2 responsible for these, which, as mentioned, are the *search_kmerset* function and the *parse1read* function, respectively.

4.3. *Searching for k-mers*

The *search_kmerset* function is the one that does the searching for k-mers. This function takes as parameters the k-mer sequence to search for and the hash table where the k-mer will be searched on. What the *search_kmerset* function does is, first, it looks at the position in the hash table $p = int\_val$ mod b, where *int_val* is the corresponding 128-bit integer value of the k-mer and b is the size of the hash table. If the position p is null, the function returns false, which means the k-mer sequence was not found. If the position p is not null, it then checks if the position contains the k-mer sequence. If the k-mer is found in position p, a node is created and the function returns true, which means the k-mer sequence is found, but if position p does not contain the k-mer sequence, the function will perform linear probing wherein position p increments, and the function checks again if the k-mer sequence is null. It iterates until the k-mer sequence is found or it reaches the end of the hash table. If it reached the end of the hash table and the k-mer sequence is still not found, position p is set to the start of the hash table, then it iterates until the k-mer sequence is found or the whole hash table is visited. If the whole hash table is visited and the k-mer sequence was not found, the function returns false. Figure 6 shows an example how the *search_kmerset* works. This process can consume so much time if the k-mer sequence is not found at once, because it has to perform iterations in the hash table until the k-mer sequence is found, and the worst case would be searching through the whole hash table. Pseudocode for this function can be in Figure 8 in the Appendix section.

To handle this problem, we modified the algorithm to parallelize the searching of k-mers using threads. The hash table will be partitioned if the k-mer sequence is not found at once. Each thread will do the searching on a certain partition of the hash table (i.e. thread1 will do the searching on the first partition of the hash table, thread2 will do the searching on the second partition and so on). Figure 6 also shows an example how the modified algorithm works, and a pseudocode for it can be seen in Figure 9.

4.4. *Alignment of Reads to Edges*

The *parse1read* function is the one responsible for the alignment of reads to edges. *parse1read* takes a read as parameter. It processes the k-mers of the read stored as nodes in a node buffer. The function checks if a k-mer is not marked as deleted or if a k-mer is not found in any edge. Then, the function

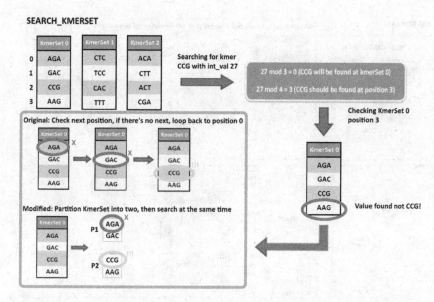

Fig. 6.   How the original and modified search_kmerset functions work.

will decide whether a k-mer should be retained or not. It also checks if k-mers in the read are linear. If a k-mer is linear, the function gets the edge index for that specific k-mer and store it in the node. But if the k-mer is not linear, it checks the connections leading to and from it directly. Firstly, it sets the found nonlinear k-mer as the current k-mer, then, checks if the current k-mer has a k-mer pointing to it which is also nonlinear (which we will term within the context of this procedure as the previous k-mer). If it has a previous k-mer, the function combines the previous k-mer to the last character of the current k-mer, thus creating (k+1)-mer, then, the current k-mer will be set as previous k-mer. But if the current k-mer has no previous k-mer, the function sets the current k-mer as previous k-mer and execute the same process with the succeeding nodes, as shown in Figure 7. This can also consume so much time since k-mers are processed one after the other and this is done for all reads. Figure 10 shows the pseudocode for the parse1read function.

To improve this, we modified the algorithm to parallelize the alignment of reads to edges, again, by using threads. The part of the node buffer which contains the k-mers for the input read will be partitioned. Each thread will work on a certain partition in the node buffer. Instead of processing the

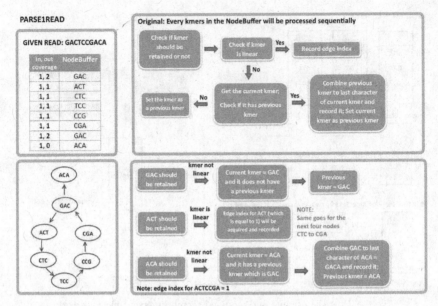

Fig. 7. How parse1read works.

k-mers one at a time, this algorithm processes two or more k-mers at the same time, depending on the number of partitions. Pseudocode for the modified function can be seen in Figure 11.

To avoid inconsistencies with the process, we took note of the dependecies for each function. For *search_kmerset* there is no dependency to be handled. For the alignment of reads to edges, the process being done is not being affected by the partitioning since we considered the dependency of storing the current k-mer as previous k-mer. Since the nodes being processed are taken from a node buffer, previous k-mer can be taken from there instead.

5. Algorithmic Analyses

5.1. *Proof of Correctness*

In proving the correctness of the parallelized functions, we first note that parallelization was done in each of the modified functions by partitioning the data structure each thread handles into disjoint substructures, i.e. each substructure has no common element. Furthermore, each thread performs the same procedures, and once a thread is successful, signals the other threads to halt. Therefore, the succeeding proof of correctness will proceed by viewing the modified functions as plain sequential algorithms.

To prove the correctness of each modified functions, we show that the invariant provided is true for all iterations — invariant is true before the first iteration of the loop (initialization), if the invariant is true for iteration n, it is true for iteration $n+1$ (maintenance) and when the loop terminates, the invariant is true on the entire input (termination).

5.1.1. *Searching for k-mers*

Given the following: v as the k-mer value to look for ; i, which starts from 0 and $j \geq 0$.

---

search_kmerset loop invariant

At the start of each iteration of the for loop,
we have set[j] $\neq$ v for all j < current iteration i.

For the **initialization**, the invariant holds before the first for loop iteration, since the if conditional statement is not yet encountered. For the **maintenance**, the loop invariant is maintained at each iteration, otherwise there should exist some j < i-th iteration such that set[j] = v. However, if in j-th iteration of the loop, such that set[j] = v, true value will be returned and there will be no i-th iteration of the loop, which shows contradiction. As for the **termination**, there are two possible cases when the loop terminates — one is that it terminates after i < set->size iterations, and returns true, in which case the if conditional ensures that set[j] = v. The other case is that i is equal to the set->size, and return false, meaning for all j < set->size set[j] $\neq$ v, therefore the invariant still holds.

5.1.2. *Aligning of Reads to Edges*

Given the following: *start*, which is the starting node of a particular partition, *finish*, which is the last node of a particular partition, and *nodeBuffer*, which contains all the k-mer nodes of the read being processed.

> parse1read loop invariant
>
> *At iteration i, the sub-array of k-mers nodeBuffer[start..i-1] is processed*

For the **initialization**, For i = start, the invariant is respected: since, trivially there is no previous node to be processed. For the **maintenance**, Given the sub-array nodeBuffer[start..i-1] processed. Iteration i processes node i, which is the succeeding node, as computed by the j loop. nodeBuffer[start..i-1] contains only processed elements, therefore the invariant is preserved. As for the **termination**,At the last iteration, nodeBuffer[start..finish-2] is processed, and the finish-1 is the only node to be processed. Hence nodeBuffer[start..finish-1] is processed.

5.2. *Time Complexity*

The original search_kmerset function takes 4n + 4 number of steps, where n is the size of the hash table, while the algorithm we described for searching of k-mers takes $\frac{5n}{m} + 7m + 12$ steps, where n is the size of the hash table and m is the number of partitions. If m=2, the algorithm described will take 2.5n + 26 steps.

$$f(m) = \frac{5n}{m} + 7m + 12$$
$$y = \frac{5n}{m} + 7m + 12$$
$$\frac{dy}{dm} = \frac{-5n}{m^2} + 7$$

To get the minimum, $\frac{dy}{dm}$ is set to 0

$$0 = \frac{-5n}{m^2} + 7$$
$$-7 = \frac{-5n}{m^2}$$
$$m^2 = \frac{5n}{7}$$
$$m = \sqrt{\frac{5n}{7}}$$

Substituting the value of m to the equation $f(m) = \frac{5n}{m} + 7m + 12$

$$f(m) = \frac{5n}{m} + 7m + 12$$

$$y = \frac{5n}{\sqrt{\frac{5n}{7}}} + 7 * \sqrt{\frac{5n}{7}} + 12$$

$$y = \frac{5\sqrt{7n}}{\sqrt{5}} + \frac{7\sqrt{5n}}{\sqrt{7}} + 12$$

$$y = \frac{70\sqrt{n}}{\sqrt{35}} + 12$$

Therefore, m should be equal to $\sqrt{\frac{5n}{7}}$, which is the number of partitions needed to get the minimum number of steps. To be able to maintain the constant value within the equation y should be equal to $\frac{70\sqrt{n}}{\sqrt{35}} + 12$.

The original parse1read function, on the other hand, takes $15n + 17$ steps, where n is the number of k-mers in a read, while the algorithm we described for the alignment of reads to edges takes $\frac{22n}{m} + 5m + 23$, where n is the number of k-mers in a read and m is the number of partitions. If m=2, the algorithm described will take $11n + 33$ steps.

$$f(m) = \frac{22n}{m} + 5m + 23$$

$$y = \frac{22n}{m} + 5m + 23$$

$$\frac{dy}{dm} = \frac{-22n}{m^2} + 5$$

To get the minimum $\frac{dy}{dm}$ is set to 0

$$0 = \frac{-22n}{m^2} + 5$$

$$-5 = \frac{-22n}{m^2}$$

$$m^2 = \frac{22n}{5}$$

$$m = \sqrt{\frac{22n}{5}}$$

```
1    function search_kmerset ( KmerSet * set, Kmer seq, kmer_t ** rs ) (3 + 4n) -- (4n+4)
2      // variable declaration (1)
3      ** for if else statement (3)
4      #ifdef MER127 (1) -- (2)
5          variable assignment (1)
6      #else (1) -- (3)
7          // variable declaration (1)
8          variable assignment (2)
9      #endif
10     while ( 1 ) (n) where n is the size of the hashtable worst case -- (4n)
11         ** for if else statement (4)
12         if ( is_kmer_entity_null ( set->flags, hc ) ) (1) -- (2)
13             return statement (1)
14         else (1) -- (4)
15             if ( KmerEqual ( get_kmer_seq ( set->array[hc] ), seq ) ) (1) -- (3)
16                 variable assignment (1)
17                 return statement (1)
18             // else would be those outside this else statement (3)
19             variable assignment (1)
20         if ( hc == set->size ) (1) -- (2)
21             variable assignment (1)
22     return 0; (1)
```

Fig. 8.   Original search_kmerset.

```
1    function *threaded_search(void* sparam) -- (5 + 5n/m)
2      // variable declarations (3)
3      variable assignments (5)
4      for (j=start; j<finish; j++){ (n/m) where n is the no. of kmers and m is the no. of threads/partitions -- (5n/m)
5          ** for if else -- (5)
6          if(!set->found) (1) -- (5)
7              ** for if else -- (4)
8              if ( is_kmer_entity_null ( set->flags, j ) ) (1) -- (3)
9                  variable assignment (1)
10                 break statement (1)
11             else if(KmerEqual ( get_kmer_seq ( set->array[j] ), seq )) (1) -- (4)
12                 variable assignments (2)
13                 break statement (1)
14         else (1) -- (2)
15             break statement (1)
16   PUBLIC_FUNC int search_kmerset ( KmerSet * set, Kmer seq, kmer_t ** rs ) -- (3 + 7m + 4) -- (7m + 7)
17     // variable declaration (1)
18     ** for if else (3)
19     #ifdef MER127 (1) -- (2)
20         variable assignment (1)
21     #else (1) -- (3)
22         // variable declaration (1)
23         variable assignments (2)
24     #endif
25     ** for if else -- (7m+4)
26     if ( is_kmer_entity_null ( set->flags, hc ) ) (1) -- (2)
27         return statement (1)
28     else (1) -- (7m+4)
29         ** for if else -- (7m+3)
30         if ( KmerEqual ( get_kmer_seq ( set->array[hc] ), seq ) ) (1) -- (3)
31             variable assignment (1)
32             return statement (1)
33         ** else would be those outside this else statement (6m + m + 3) -- (7m +3)
34     // variable declarations (4)
35     for (i = 0; i < nthreads; i++) { (m) where m is the no. of threads/partitions -- (6m)
36         variable assignments (5)
37         function call (1)
38     for (j = 0; j < nthreads; j++) { (m) where m is the no. of threads/partitions -- (m)
39         function call (1)
40     ** for if else -- (3)
41     if (set->found){ (1) -- (3)
42         variable assignment (1)
43         return statement (1)
44     else (1) -- (2)
45         return statement (1)
```

overall (5 + 5n/m + 7m + 7) -- (5n/m + 7m + 12)
** if m == 2: (2.5n + 26)

Fig. 9.   Modified search_kmerset.

```
1    function parse1read ( int t, int threadID ) -- (6 + 15n + 11) -- (15n + 17)
2        // variable declarations (10)
3        variable assignments (6)
4        for ( j = start; j < finish; j++ ) (n) where n is the no. of kmers in a read -- 17n)
5            variable assignment (1)
6            ** for if else -- (16)
7            if ( ( node->deleted ) || ( node->linear && !node->inEdge ) ) (1) -- (5)
8                ** for if else statement -- (4)
9                if ( retain < 2 ) (1) -- (4)
10                   variable assignments (2)
11                   // add the continue statement to number of steps
12               else (1) -- (2)
13                   break statement (1)
14               continue statement (1)
15           ** the next lines serve as the else of the previous if
16           ** else would be -- (16)
17           variable assignment (1)
18           ** for if else -- (15)
19           if ( node->linear ) (1) -- (10)
20               ** for if else -- (2)
21               if ( isSmaller ) (1) -- (2)
22                   variable assignment (1)
23               else (1) -- (2)
24                   variable assignment (1)
25               ** for ifdef else -- (7)
26 #ifdef MER127 (1) -- (7)
27               ** for if else -- (6)
28               if ( retain == 0 || IsPrevKmer ) (1) -- (6)
29                   variable assignments (5)
30               else if ( edge_index != mixBuffer[pos - 1].low2 ) (1) -- (5)
31                   variable assignments (4)
32 #else (1) -- (7)
33               ** for if else -- (6)
34               if ( retain == 0 || IsPrevKmer ) (1) -- (6)
35                   variable assignments (5)
36               else if ( edge_index != mixBuffer[pos - 1].low ) (1) -- (5)
37                   variable assignments (4)
38 #endif
39           else (1) -- (15)
40               ** for if else -- (2)
41               if ( isSmaller ) (1) -- (2)
42                   variable assignment (1)
43               else (1) -- (2)
44                   variable assignment(1)
45               if ( IsPrevKmer ) (1) -- (10)
46                   variable assignments (3)
47                   ** for if else -- (4)
48                   if ( KmerSmaller ( wordplus, bal_wordplus ) ) (1) -- (4)
49                       variable assignments (3)
50                   else (1) -- (4)
51                       variable assignments (3)
52                   variable assignment (2)
53               variable assignments (2)
54       if ( retain < 1 ) (1) -- (2)
55           variable assignment (1)
56       if ( retain < 2 ) (1) -- (4)
57           variable assignments (2)
58           return statement (1)
59       if ( ( pos - start ) != retain ) (1) -- (2)
60           print statement (1)
61       if ( pos < finish ) (1) -- (3)
62           variable assignments (2)
```

Fig. 10.   Original parse1read.

```
1    static void *threaded_parse (void *param) { (8 + 2 + 2 + 22n/m + 11) -- (22n/m + 23)
2        // variable declarations (10)
3        variable assignments (8)
4        ** for if else -- (2)
5        if (thread_id = 0) (1) -- (2)
6            variable assignment (1)
7        else (1) -- (2)
8            variable assignment (1)
9        variable assignments (2)
10       for ( j = start; j < finish; j++ ) (n/m) where n is the no. of kmers in a read and m is the no. of threads/partitions (22n/m)
11           variable assignment (1)
12           if (node->flag == 0) { (1) -- (21)
13               variable assignment (1)
14               **for if else -- (19)
15               if ( ( node->deleted ) || ( node->linear && !node->inEdge ) ) (1) -- (5)
16                   if ( retain < 2 ) (1) -- (4)
17                       variable assignments (2)
18                       ** include continue statement
19                   else (1) -- (2)
20                       break statement (1)
21                       continue statement (1)
22                   ** the code that follows will serve as the else of previous if
23                   ** else would be -- (19)
24                   variable assignment (1)
25                   ** for if else -- (18)
26                   if ( node->linear ) (1) -- (11)
27                       ** for if else (2)
28                       if ( isSmaller ) (1) -- (2)
29                           variable assignment (1)
30                       else (1) -- (2)
31                           variable assignment (1)
32                       ** for ifdef and else -- (7)
33   #ifdef MER127 (1) -- (7)
34                       ** for if elseif -- (6)
35                       if ( retain == 0 || IsPrevKmer ) (1) -- (6)
36                           variable assignments (5)
37                       else if ( edge_index != mixBuffer[pos - 1].low2 ) (1) -- (5)
38                           variable assignments (4)
39   #else (1) -- (7)
40                       ** for if elseif -- (6)
41                       if ( retain == 0 || IsPrevKmer ) (1) -- (6)
42                           variable assignments (5)
43                       else if ( edge_index != mixBuffer[pos - 1].low ) (1) -- (5)
44                           variable assignments (4)
45   #endif
46                   else (1) -- (18)
47                       ** for if else statement -- (2)
48                       if ( isSmaller ) (1) -- (2)
49                           variable assignment (1)
50                       else (1) -- (2)
51                           variable assignment (1)
52                       if ( IsPrevKmer ) (1) -- (13)
53                           variable assignment (1)
54                           if (j == indexArray[t] + ((readlen/numthread)*thread_id) - 1) (1) -- (3)
55                               ** for if else -- (2)
56                               if ( smallerBuffer[j-1] ) (1) -- (2)
57                                   variable assignment (1)
58                               else (1) -- (2)
59                                   variable assignment (1)
60                           variable assignments (2)
61                           ** for if else -- (4)
62                           if ( KmerSmaller ( wordplus, bal_wordplus ) ) (1) -- (4)
63                               variable assignment (3)
64                           else (1) -- (4)
65                               variable assignment (3)
66                               variable assignments(2)
67                       variable assignments(2)
68           if ( retain < 1 ) (1) -- (2)
69               variable assignment (1)
70           if ( retain <   2 ) (1) -- (4)
71               variable assignment (3)
72           if ( ( pos - start ) != retain ) (1) -- (2)
73               print statement (1)
74           if ( pos < finish ) (1) -- (3)
75               variable assignment (2)
76   function parse1read ( int t, int threadID ) -- (4m + m) -- (5m)
77       // variable declarations (4)
78       for (i = 0; i < numthread; i++) { (m) where m is the no. of threads/partitions -- (4m)
79           variable assignments (3)
80           function call (1)
81       for (j = 0; j < numthread; j++) { (m) where m is the no. of threads/partitions -- (m)
82           function call (1)
```

Fig. 11.   Modified parse1read.

Substituting the value of m to the equation $f(m) = \frac{22n}{m} + 5m + 23$

$$f(m) = \frac{22n}{m} + 5m + 23$$

$$y = \frac{22n}{\sqrt{\frac{22n}{5}}} + 5 * \sqrt{\frac{22n}{5}} + 23$$

$$y = \frac{22\sqrt{5n}}{22} + \frac{5\sqrt{22n}}{\sqrt{5}} + 23$$

$$y = \frac{220\sqrt{n}}{\sqrt{110}} + 23$$

Therefore, m should be equal to $\sqrt{\frac{22n}{5}}$, which is the number of partitions needed to get the minimum number of steps. To be able to maintain the constant value within the equation y should be equal to $\frac{220\sqrt{n}}{\sqrt{110}} + 23$.

Both modified algorithms have asymptotic time complexity for their minimum number of steps of $O(\sqrt{n})$ compared to their original which have asymptotic time complexity of $O(n)$. Therefore, the time complexities of original algorithms grows faster than the time complexities of modified algorithms as the number of n increases.

6. Conclusions and Recommendations

The study of the genome is very significant in the field of bioinformatics to better understand and improve not only the lives of humans, but also the lives of other species, as well as understanding microorganisms. Genome assemblers have become available and with the existence of numerous high throughput sequencing algorithms and technologies, improvements are still needed for faster and more accurate output. Even, SOAPdenovo2, being one of the leading assemblers today, is evaluated as relatively slow, especially when dealing with larger genomes.

The algorithm that we described in this study implements parallelization to solve the bottleneck in SOAPdenovo2. Improving the execution time of SOAPdenovo2, which means, being able to produce the output faster, is significant for researchers to be able to come up with other possible methods to improve the accuracy of the output of the assembly algorithm.

Extensions of improving SOAPdenovo2's execution time are to study different partitioning methods applied to the functions and to study the behavior of SOAPdenovo2 with respect to the number of partitions made. Another one is to focus on accuracy and repeat handling, which will be important for sequencing genomes with many repeats, like rice genome.

References

1. Baker, M. (2012). De novo genome assembly: what every biologist should know. *Nature Methods, 9(4)*, 333–337.
2. Boisvert, S., Laviolette, F. and Corbeil, J. (2010). Ray: simultaneous assembly of reads from a mix of high-throughput sequencing technologies. *Journal of Computational Biology, 17(11)*, 1519–1533.
3. Chikhi, R. and Medvedev, P. (2014). Informed and automated k-mer size selection for genome assembly. *Bioinformatics, 30(1)*, 31–37.
4. Compeau, P., Pevzner, P. and Tesler, G. (2011). How to apply de Bruijn graphs to genome assembly. *Nature Biotechnology, 29(11)*, 987–991.
5. de Bruijn, N. G. (1946). A Combinatorial Problem. *Koninklijke Nederlandse Akademie v. Wetenschappen, 49*, 758–764.
6. Deonier, R., Tavare, S. and Waterman, M. (2005). Computational genome analysis. New York, USA: Springer.
7. El-Metwally, S., Hamza, T., Zakaria, M. and Helmy, M. (2013). Next-Generation Sequence Assembly: Four Stages of Data Processing and Computational Challenges. *PLoS Computational Biology, 9(12)*, e1003345. doi:10.1371/journal.pcbi.1003345.
8. Genome.gov (2014). Human Genome Project Completion. [online] Available at: http://www.genome.gov/11006943 [Accessed 6 Dec. 2014].
9. Georganas, E., Buluc, A., Chapman, J., Oliker, L., Rokhsar, D. and Yelick, K. (2014). Parallel De Bruijn Graph Construction and Traversal for De Novo Genome Assembly. *In: Proceedings of the International Conference for High Performance Computing, Networking, Storage and Analysis*, 437–448.
10. Kajitani, R. *et al.* (2014). Efficient de novo assembly of highly heterozygous genomes from whole-genome shotgun short reads. *Genome Research, 24(8)*, 1384–1395. doi:10.1101/gr.170720.113.
11. Li, R., Zhu, H., Ruan, J., Qian, W., Fang, X., Shi, Z., Li, Y., Li, S., Shan, G., Kristiansen, K. *et al.* (2010). De novo assembly of human genomes with massively parallel short read sequencing. *Genome Research, 20(2)*, 265–272. doi:10.1101/gr.097261.109.

12. Li, Z., Chen, Y., Mu, D., Yuan, J., Shi, Y., Zhang, H., Gan, J., Li, N., Hu, X., Liu, B., Yang, B. and Fan, W. (2012). Comparison of the two major classes of assembly algorithms: overlap–layout–consensus and de-bruijn-graph. *Briefings in Functional Genomics, 11(1)*, 25–37. doi:10.1093/bfgp/elr035.

13. Lu, B., Zeng, Z. and Shi, T. (2013). Comparative study of de novo assembly and genome-guided assembly strategies for transcriptome reconstruction based on RNA-Seq. *Science China Life Sciences, 56(2)*, 143–155. doi:10.1007/s11427-013-4442-z.

14. Luo, R., Liu, B., Xie, Y., Li, Z., Huang, W., Yuan, J., He, G., Chen, Y., Pan, Q., Liu, Y. *et al.* (2012). SOAPdenovo2: an empirically improved memory-efficient short-read de novo assembler. *Gigascience, 1(1)*, 18. doi: 10.1186/2047-217X-1-18.

15. Miller, J., Koren, S. and Sutton, G. (2010). Assembly algorithms for next-generation sequencing data. *Genomics, 95(6)*, 315–327. doi:10.1016/j.ygeno.2010.03.001.

16. Pop, M. (2004). Comparative genome assembly. *Briefings in Bioinformatics, 5(3)*, 237–248.

17. Pop, M. (2009). Genome assembly reborn: recent computational challenges. *Briefings in Bioinformatics, 10(4)*, 354–366.

18. Sanger, F. and Coulson, A. (1975). A rapid method for determining sequences in DNA by primed synthesis with DNA polymerase. *Journal of Molecular Biology, 94(3)*, 441–448. doi:10.1016/0022-2836(75)90213-2.

19. Simpson, J., Wong, K., Jackman, S., Schein, J., Jones, S. and Birol, I. (2009). ABySS: a parallel assembler for short read sequence data. *Genome Research, 19(6)*, 1117–1123. doi:10.1101/gr.089532.108.

20. Sovic, I., Skala, K. and Sikic, M. (2013). Approaches to DNA de novo assembly. *In: 2013 36th International Convention on Information & Communication Technology Electronics & Microelectronics (MIPRO)*, 351–359.

21. Wang, B., Ekblom, R., Bunikis, I., Siitari, H. and Höglund, J. (2014). Whole genome sequencing of the black grouse (Tetrao tetrix): reference guided assembly suggests faster-Z and MHC evolution. *BMC Genomics, 15(1)*, 180. doi: 10.1186/1471-2164-15-180.

22. Zerbino, D. and Birney, E. (2008). Velvet: algorithms for de novo short read assembly using de Bruijn graphs. *Genome Research, 18(5)*, 821–829. doi:10.1101/gr.074492.107.

Design and Implementation of an Advanced Source Code Reading Tool for Framework-based Software

Yuu Ohmura[1] and Takuo Watanabe[2]

Department of Computer Science, Tokyo Institute of Technology,
2-12-1 Ookayama, Meguroku, Tokyo 152-8552, Japan
E-mail: [1]yuu@psg.cs.titech.ac.jp, [2]takuo@acm.org

We propose an advanced reading aid tool that targets source code using frameworks. This tool helps programmers by displaying abstraction level and code level views that automatically synchronize with each other. For example, the tool can be configured to display UML class/sequence diagram views and a code level view with debugging information, where each view shows the current execution point of the target code. One does not get lost after switching views from one to another since the tool provides properly synchronized views. The goal of this work is to show by experiments that the use of this tool increases the comprehensibility of framework-based codes. This paper reports our current research progress in the development of the tool.

Keywords: Source Code Reading, Program Comprehension, Software Visualization, Computer Science Education, Software Development Tool.

1. Introduction

A considerable number of modern software systems are developed using rich application frameworks and libraries. Thus, before being involved in the development (or maintenance) of a system, an engineer should gain a good grasp of the underlying frameworks or libraries. The documents and code samples accompanying with them are, however, sometimes not enough for the purpose; they are often incomplete, imprecise, and/or obsolete. Also, writing accurate and comprehensible documents of an application framework is not an easy task in general. For example, a sort of *inversion of control*, which is often observable in typical frameworks, may complicate the documentation due to its dynamic (behavioral) nature. Such a situation leads the engineer to read the source code of the frameworks or libraries.

When engineers check the source code of frameworks or libraries, they read it from two perspectives: at an abstraction level, such as a UML[1] class/sequence diagram, and at the source code level. At the abstraction level, engineers use UML class/sequence diagrams that reverse the source code. At the source code level, engineers use type information, lists of variables and methods using an integrated development environment (IDE) and a debugging tool. Engineers can read and understand source code by switching between views using the debugging tool.

However, there is no tool that shows abstraction level and code level views that automatically synchronize with each other. Therefore, engineers have to synchronize the abstraction level and code level views themselves.

The remainder of this paper is organized as follows: we present our proposed method and its expected effect in Section 2. The implementation of our tool is explained in Section 3. In Section 4, we present a case study. We discuss related work in Section 5. In Section 6, we summarize this work and describe future work.

2. Proposed Method and Expected effect

We propose a tool to solve the above problem. This tool automatically synchronizes abstraction level and code level views. Specifically, the tool shows users the current location of program execution on UML class/sequence diagrams. A UML class/sequence is generated from source code. Users should be able to understand the location of the UML class/sequence diagrams corresponding to the site of program execution correctly.

We believe that this tool has two main effects: users do not lose sight of the current program execution in the source code; and they can rebuild UML class/sequence diagrams while executing a program.

When users generate UML class/sequence diagrams from source code, the diagrams are enormous. However, users need program module diagrams that they can follow. This tool helps them to delete unnecessary figures from the enormous UML class/sequence diagrams generated from source code. This function is useful when users understand a framework and framework-based code.

Since the relationships among modules in frameworks and framework-based code are complicated, users have to determine these relationships through program execution. Using our tool, users can achieve this easily. In this paper, we implemented Eclipse[2] Plugin, which includes the above-mentioned functions.

3. Implementation

In this paper, we targeted the programming language Java and developed Eclipse Plugin, which contains the proposed functions. We used AmaterasUML[3], which is the UML editor in Eclipse, the open source software provided by The Eclipse Foundation. Generally, Eclipse is used as Java IDE. AmaterasUML (Eclipse Plugin) is provided as a UML class/sequence diagram editor.

In this tool, we modified the source code in Eclipse Java Debug Perspective. Stepping through the execution of a Java program, this tool displays the location of program execution with a red background for the source code and a UML class/sequence diagram synchronously. First, we obtain debug information (class name, method name) from Eclipse Java Debug Perspective during debugging execution. Next, we change the background color on the UML class/sequence diagrams corresponding to the debug information to red.

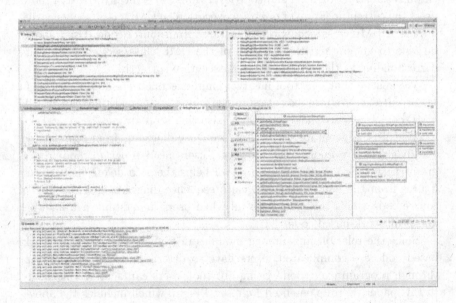

Fig. 1.   Execution screenshot.

4. Short Case Study

To assess the effectiveness of this tool, we performed a short case study in which we searched for the place in the source code where Eclipse changes the Stack Trace Window on debugging. We identified three positive effects of our tool using this short case study.

4.1. *Inner Class, Anonymous Class on UML Class Diagrams*

The first positive effective is that when users track program execution, they do not lose sight of which class it is in the UML class diagrams. This is more useful when multiple classes are in a file, such as an inner class, because users are not able to identify the class as a current execution class using a file name. In our tool, users can identify the class using UML class diagrams. Our tool was effective with anonymous classes. AmaterasUML is not able to generate an anonymous class on UML class/sequence diagrams from source code. Therefore, users must add a class diagram to the UML class diagrams corresponding to an inner class in the source code. In this short case study of "DebugPlugin.java" the file involved one public class, four inner classes, and one anonymous class. Our tool is useful in this situation.

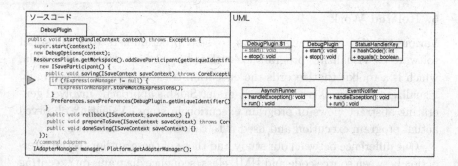

Fig. 2.   Execution image.

4.2. *Improve Class Diagrams Dynamically*

The second positive effect is that AmaterasUML can generate enormous UML class diagrams from the target source code. However, users want only the UML class diagrams that they need. Therefore, they delete unnecessary classes from the generated UML class diagrams. In our tool, they are able to perform this operation while they execute the program. For example, the "IDDebugEventSeListener" Interface has various sub-classes. Therefore, AmaterasUML displays enormous class diagrams. Users can delete unnecessary classes from the UML class diagrams effectively, while they execute the program.

4.3. *UML Sequence Diagrams*

The third positive effect is that the UML Sequence diagrams combine the first and second effects. In the generated UML Sequence diagrams, an execution sequence is not restored completely. Specifically, when the execution sequence includes an interface, the execution sequence on UML Sequence diagrams is cut off. However, users can improve UML Sequence diagrams dynamically just as they do UML class diagrams. Therefore, they are able to link abstract classes and interfaces to concrete classes using debug information. For example, while processing events on a graphical user interface, developer register concrete an event listener class which extends some interface. When an event occurs, the event listener class is executed. In this case, it is easy for users to restore all of the execution sequences that they need.

5. Related Work

Various studies have devised ways to help programmers to understand software by visualizing program execution[4–6]. Ishio[4] developed Amida, which is a toolkit that records the execution trace of a Java Program and visualizes the trace as a sequence diagram. Salah's approach[5] involved generating abstract views of program execution in steps. Valentin[6] observed actual program execution and used it to construct state machines.

One difference between our study and those of these authors is the interaction between source code and UML class/sequence diagrams on executing a program.

6. Concluding Remark

In this paper, we proposed and implemented a tool that helps programmers by displaying abstraction level and code level views that automatically synchronize with each other. We also demonstrated three positive effects of the tool in a short case study.

In the future, we will improve and evaluate our tool. Three improvements to our tool enable it to 1) delete unnecessary classes from generated UML class diagrams automatically, 2) link abstract classes and interfaces to concrete classes automatically, and 3) function such that it supports asynchronous processing. There is much asynchronous processing in Eclipse Debug Perspective. When tracking asynchronous processing, users are not able to track the program execution sequence because the program is executed by another thread.

We will also attempt to confirm that our tool helps programmers to read source code, including the number of executions of a target program, and the number of changes in the breakpoint of a target program.

We assume that the number of evaluation items decreases. To understand software, programmers execute target software and change the breakpoint for a target source code many times when they get lost in the code. Using our tool, we think that programmers will avoid these situations.

We believe that our tool will also be useful for computer science instructors. Generally, when instructors teach program behaviors, such as Stack or Queue, they use diagrams or animations, which are difficult to prepare. Our tool should help the instructor to create these easily.

References

1. UML http://www.uml.org
2. Eclipse http://www.eclipse.org
3. AmaterasUML http://amateras.osdn.jp
4. T. Ishio, Y. Watanabe and K. Inoue, AMIDA: A sequence diagram extraction toolkit supporting automatic phase detection, in *30th International Conference on Software Engineering*, (ACM, 2004).
5. M. Salah and M. Spiros, A hierarchy of dynamic software views: From object-interactions to feature interactions, in *20th International Conference on Software Maintenance*, (IEEE, 2004).
6. D. Valentin, L. Christian and W. Andrzej, Mining object behavior with ADABU, in *4th International Workshop on Dynamic Analysis*, (ACM, 2006).

Blackhole Rogue Access Point Detection and Disassociation

J. M. Barrientos, K. G. D. Dy, T. J. L. Mandap, K. B. Nagano and G. Cu

College of Computer Studies, De La Salle University,
Manila, Philippines
jilliane_barrientos@yahoo.com, kimberlydy@ymail.com,
tiffanymandap@yahoo.com, kaye_balce@yahoo.com,
greg.cu@delasalle.ph
www.dlsu.edu.ph

Blackhole rogue access points cause critical threats to the network by replicating SSIDs of legitimate access points. Several commercial products were already made to mitigate rogue access points however these products are highly technical and involve tedious work for the network administrator for he/she is the one who decides whether an access point is rogue or not. In this paper, we propose a solution for blackhole rogue access point clients to be automatically disassociated. This paper proposes a solution for the blackhole rogue access points where the clients of the blackhole rougue access point are automatically disassociated. By sending disassociation frames to the blackhole rogue access point, its clients are disconnected from the device. However, this solution requires the blackhole rogue access point to have at least 1 client to be able to send disassociation frames to it. Also, rogue access points with spoofed MAC addresses can neither be detected nor disassociated.

Keywords: rogue access point detection, black hole rogue access point, rogue access point disassociation.

1. Introduction

A rogue access point is a wireless access point installed on a wired enterprise network without authorization from the network administrator [1]. A rogue access point may be a wired rogue access point or a blackhole rogue access point. A wired rogue access point is an access point that is directly connected to a network and is usually installed by a legitimate user who is unaware of the threat he is going to put at stake [2]. On the other hand, a blackhole rogue access point is an access point outside the network but may pose as a legitimate network to encourage clients to connect to it and steal sensitive information. Also, a blackhole rogue access point may involve an outsider who has an agenda to penetrate a wireless network.

A previous research in the university was conducted with regards to detecting and preventing rogue devices on the network. This research used techniques such as site survey, MAC list checking, and deauthentication. This approach uses a sensor to monitor the network and then gather inputs from the detected devices which will be used to pinpoint which APs are rogue.

Another research uses a Denial-of-Service (DoS) attack so future clients will not be able to connect to the rogue access point [2]. These methods conducted were able to mitigate rogue access points but it was not implemented into a system.

2. Detection System

The system developed in this research detects both wired rogue access points and blackhole rogue access points. It terminates a wired rogue access point by disabling its switch ports and it disassociates clients connected to it if it is a blackhole rogue access point.

The hardware system setup is shown in Fig. 1 and is composed of three important components:

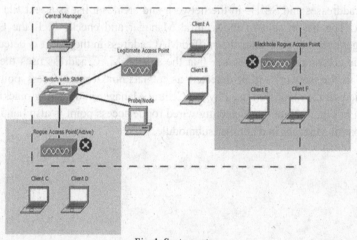

Fig. 1. System setup.

- Central Manager   The central manager is the main controller of the system. It contains all of the functions. These functions involve sending and receiving data, passing and communicating to the probe in order to analyze data, classify rogue access points, and for disassociation.

- Probe/Node

  The probe/node serves as both a sniffer and a tool for disassociation in one device. The probe/node can be a client in order to connect to access points and check their authentication. It can also sniff data through airmon [4], a software that can sniff access points around an area. Another feature of it as a node is the disassociation of blackhole rogue access points' clients through aireplay [5], which is a software that disassociates clients from an access point. The probe/node is a raspberry Pi computer.

- Manageable Switch

  The switch to be used must have SNMP support in order to locate and terminate the wired rogue access points. It should also have port mirroring feature to gather traffic from the network

The system in the research mainly checks the list of MAC addresses of legitimate access points in the network. The Probe/Node in the network sniffs MAC addresses and SSIDs in the network and creates a list as a text file in csv format. The list in sent to the Central Manager and checks it. If the Central Manager does not encounter the sniffed MAC address in the list, it is detected as a rogue access point. If does see that the sniffed MAC address uses the same SSID in the network, it is detected as a blackhole rogue access point. An overview of the algorithm used by the Central Manager in detecting blackhole is shown in Fig. 2. Note that detecting wired rogue access point is also handled by the Central Manager in a another submodule.

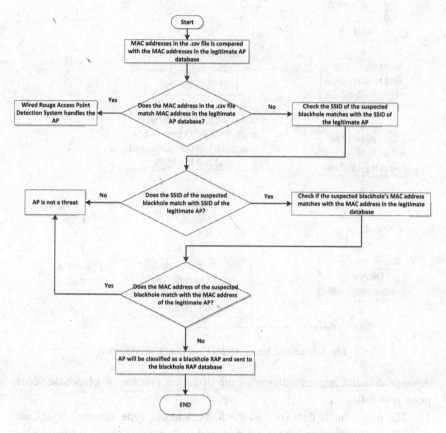

Fig. 2. Algorithm used by the Central Manager in the system in detecting blackhole access points.

2.1. *Blackhole Rogue Access Point Detection Algorithm*

The Blackhole Rogue Access Point Detection starts with the sniffing of data from access points using the Probe/Node that are present and within the range of the probe as shown in Fig. 3. If the sniffed MAC address of access point matches in the legitimate list, the access point is considered as a legitimate access point. If the sniffed MAC address of access point is not in the list, it is compared with the list of legitimate SSIDs. When there is a match, the access point is considered a blackhole access point.

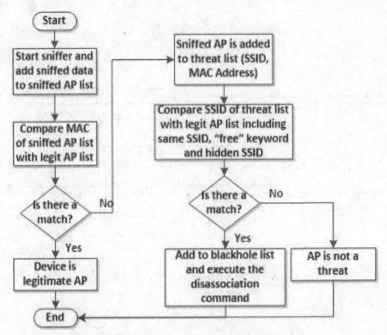

Fig. 3. Blackhole Rogue Access Point Detection Algorithm.

A more detailed implementation of the detection process of blackhole access point is as follows:

1. The probe sniffs data such as the MAC address, type, channel, SSID, and encapsulation from APs or hotspots and is then saved to a csv file which is shown in Fig. 4 which is then sent to the central manager via FTP.

BSSID	channel	Speed	Privacy	Cipher	Auth	Power	#beacons	#IV	LAN IP	ID-length	ESSID
00:16:86:A5:F1:7E	6	54	WEP	WEP		-84	1177	925	0. 0. 0. 0	15	Trojan_Virus3.0
00:27:22:C0:61:41	6	54	OPN			-83	2614	6665	10.128.168. 1	14	Pinoy_Telekoms
00:18:25:01:60:80	6	54	OPN			-82	981	2978	10. 10. 10. 1	18	One Archer's Place
00:18:25:12:7C:20	6	54	OPN			-78	2772	15980	10. 10. 3. 40	18	One Archer's Place
00:26:3E:48:C9:40	6	54	WEP	WEP	OPN	-78	2262	841	0. 0. 0. 0	6	myWiFi
00:26:3E:47:F4:C0	6	54	WEP	WEP	OPN	-74	2706	4300	0. 0. 0. 0	6	myWiFi
C0:C1:C0:E7:D6:49	6	54	WPA2	CCMP	PSK	-42	3480	71	0. 0. 0. 0	10	BlackWidow

Fig. 4. Sample of sniffed data output.

2. Once the central manager receives the csv file, it is then parsed to get only the necessary information as shown in Fig. 5.

BSSID	ESSID
00:16:B6:A5:F1:7E	Trojan_Virus3.0
00:27:22:C0:61:41	Pinoy_Telekoms
00:18:25:01:60:B0	One Archer's Place
00:18:25:12:7C:20	One Archer's Place
00:26:3E:48:C9:40	myWiFi
00:26:3E:47:F4:C0	myWiFi
C0:C1:C0:E7:D6:49	BlackWidow

Fig. 5. Sample csv file containing normalized data.

3. The Central Manager detects whether an AP is a blackhole or not based on an algorithm where the steps are explained as follows:

   a. The MAC address from the sniffed data is compared with the MAC address table of the SNMP database which was obtained through the SNMP command. If there is a match, it means that it is a possible wired rogue access point thus, it will fall under the Wired Rogue Access Point Detection system. If there is no match, it will proceed to the next step.

   b. When there is no match, it will then check if the SSID of the suspected blackhole matches the SSID of the legitimate AP, as shown in Fig. 3. If it matches, then the device is a legitimate AP. If there is no match, the access point will be added to the threat list. If the AP stored in the threat list has the same SSID as the legitimate AP, has the word "free" in its SSID, or has a hidden SSID then its data will be stored in the blackhole access point database for the disassociation process. If there is no match, it means the AP is not a threat and no action will be taken.

2.2. *Blackhole Rogue Access Point Disassociation*

With the algorithm used, it can detect the blackholes, whether it is NAT or not, and put their information in a file. Thus, the central manager can invoke a command to the node to send disassociation frames to the blackholes as shown in Fig. 6.

```
13:41:46  Sending DeAuth to broadcast -- BSSID: [C0:C1:C0:E7:D6:49]
13:41:47  Sending DeAuth to broadcast -- BSSID: [C0:C1:C0:E7:D6:49]
13:41:47  Sending DeAuth to broadcast -- BSSID: [C0:C1:C0:E7:D6:49]
13:41:48  Sending DeAuth to broadcast -- BSSID: [C0:C1:C0:E7:D6:49]
13:41:48  Sending DeAuth to broadcast -- BSSID: [C0:C1:C0:E7:D6:49]
13:41:49  Sending DeAuth to broadcast -- BSSID: [C0:C1:C0:E7:D6:49]
```

Fig. 6. Sample of real-time disassociation activity.

3. Results

3.1. *Test Setup*

The first setup is shown in Fig. 7. It contains a legitimate AP, Computer with Central Manager, Wireless Client, one Blackhole RAP, switch, and a probe/node.

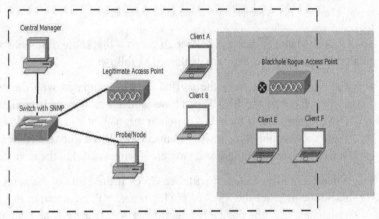

Fig. 7. Network setup for first experiment.

The second setup is illustrated in Fig. 8. It consists of a legitimate AP, Computer with Central Manager, Wireless Client, one Blackhole RAP, one wired Rogue Access Point, switch, and a probe/node.

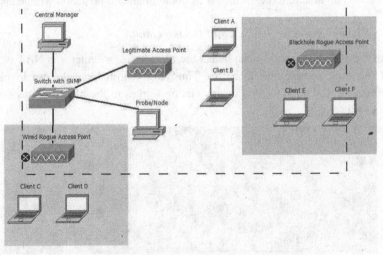

Fig. 8. Network setup for second experiment.

3.2. *Blackhole Rogue Access Point Detection and Disassociation for First Setup*

Six test cases were conducted for the first setup to test the system performance in sniffing and disassociating different kinds of blackhole rogue access point in this kind of setup. These test cases are scenarios how blackhole rouge access points are used in the network. The test cases also show how the algorithm fares in different scenarios. The test cases are as follows:

Test Case 1: One active blackhole rogue access point with at least one client is in the network.

Test Case 2: One active blackhole rogue access point with at least one client and does not have broadcasted SSID is in the network.

Test Case 3: One active laptop with enabled virtual access point (hotspot) with at least one client is in the network.

Test Case 4: One active laptop with enabled virtual access point (hotspot) with at least one client but does not have its SSID broadcasted in the network.

Test Case 5: One active blackhole rogue access point with NAT (network address translation) support and has at least one client is in the network.

Test Case 6: One active blackhole rogue access point with NAT support and has at least one client but does not have broadcasted SSID in the network.

Table 1. Blackhole rogue access point detection and disassociation result for First Setup.

Test Case	Sniffed/Detected	Disassociation
Test Case 1: One Active Blackhole RAP	✓	✓
Test Case 2: One Active Blackhole RAP without broadcasted SSID	✓	✓
Test Case 3: One active Laptop (with hotspot)	✓	✓
Test Case 4: One active Laptop (with hotspot) without broadcasted SSID	✓	✓
Test Case 5: One active Blackhole RAP with NAT support(pocket wifi)	✓	✓
Test Case 6: One active Blackhole RAP with NAT support(pocket wifi), without broadcasted SSID	✓	✓

Based from the results from the test cases shown in Table 1, it is found out that when the probe sniffs an access point, through the device's MAC Address, the probe can also disassociate it. Meanwhile, for the disassociation, it is required that at least one client is connected to the device to be considered active and for the system to be able to send disassociation frames to it otherwise the device is considered inactive and no disassociation frames could be sent to it.

3.3. *Blackhole Rogue Access Point and Wired Rogue Access Point Simultaneous Detection for Second Setup*

For this setup, both types of rogue access points were combined in one network in order to test the algorithm in classifying an access point to be wired or wireless. These test cases are scenarios how blackhole rouge access points are used in the network. The test cases also show how the algorithm fares in different scenarios.

In the process of testing, it was discovered that the Ping test was not effective because it cannot connect to a specific access point when there are a lot of access points with the same SSID, instead, it connects to the one which has the strongest signal. However, an alternative for the Ping test is the SNMP walk. The SNMP walk checks the devices connected to the switch. From there, it can be distinguished if an access point is wired to the network or is a wireless access point. A limitation, however, would be that with this method, spoofed MAC address cannot be detected.

Test cases:

Test Case 1: One wired rogue access point is active (with at least 1 client) in the network and one Blackhole rogue access point is active (with at least 1 client) in the network.

Test Case 2: One wired and active laptop with virtual AP and one pocket wifi as Blackhole rogue access point

Test Case 3: One wired and active rogue access point and one laptop with hotspot

Table 2. Blackhole and wired rogue access point detection result in a single network.

Test Case	Detected
Test Case 1: One wired rogue access point is active (with at least 1 client) in the network and one Blackhole rogue	✓
Test Case 2: One wired and active laptop with virtual AP and one pocket wifi as Blackhole rogue access point	✓
Test Case 3: One wired and active rogue access point and one laptop with hotspot	✓

4. Conclusion

For the blackhole rogue access points, it should have at least one client to be active in order to be detected and disassociated for the proposed solution. Furthermore, unlike wired rogue access points, disassociation does not involve classifying a rogue access point to be with or without NAT. As long as an access point poses a threat by imitating the legitimate access point, it can be disassociated with the proposed solution. However, in order to disassociate the clients of a rogue access point, there must be one active client connected to the rogue access point. It is also found out that the wired rogue access points and the blackhole rogue access points should be on the same network as the Probe/Node and the Central Manager to be detected by them and to disassociate their clients. Another limitation of the system is that it is not able to detect MAC address spoofing. Currently, research is being done to detect this by checking the volume of frames detected from a spoofed MAC address.

References

1. "Wireless Networking Wi-Fi Advantages and Disadvantages to Wireless Networking," 14 February 2014. [Online]. Available: http://ipoint-tech.com/wireless-networking-wi-fi-advantages-and-disadvantages-to-wireless-networking/.
2. A. Venkataraman and R. Beyah, "Rogue-Access-Point Detection: Challenges, Solutions, and Future Directions," *IEEE Security & Privacy*, vol. 9, no. 5, pp. 56–61, 2011.
3. R. Cheema, D. Bansal and S. Sofat, "Deauthentication/Disassociation Attack: Implementation and Security in Wireless Mesh Networks," *International Journal of Computer Applications*, vol. 23, no. 7, pp. 7–15, 2011.
4. mister_x, "Airmon-ng," [Online]. Available: http://www.aircrack-ng.org/~~v/doku.php?id=airmon-ng. [Accessed 28 August 2015].
5. mister_x, "Aireplay-ng," [Online]. Available: http://www.aircrack-ng.org/doku.php?id=aireplay-ng. [Accessed 28 August 2015].

WSAN: Node Network Communication Protocol through Coordination Messaging

F. K. Flores and G. Cu

Computer Technology Department, De La Salle University,
Manila, National Capital Region, Philippines
fritz_kevin_flores@dlsu.edu.ph and greg.cu@delasalle.ph
www.dlsu.edu.ph

Wireless sensor and actuator networks or WSAN are comprised of spatially distributed autonomous devices, enabling a number of applications through sensing and actuating of components in an environment. Wireless sensor nodes have been a popular platform, however communication is constrained due to having a half-duplex medium and low bandwidth. Despite these constraints, these networks must still be able to handle traffic from nodes in the network while providing fair throughput. Protocols such as IEEE 802.15.4 does not have any form of traffic handling while protocols like ZigBee may contain too much overhead from features which may not be needed by all networks. Since these protocols are not specifically built for WSANs but rather for wireless sensor networks, a decrease in efficiency may be observed. The study aims to create a network communication protocol with traffic handling that uses messaging for node communication for WSANs.

Keywords: Ambient Intelligence, Wireless Sensor and Actuator Networks, Node Communication Protocol, Traffic Handling.

1. Background of the Study

Wireless sensor and actuator networks or WSAN are one of the popular systems branching from wireless sensor networks or WSNs. These networks are comprised of heterogeneous and autonomous devices containing sensors and actuators that communicating wirelessly in order to perform varying and distributed tasks in and for an environment. WSANs are essentially augmented WSNs that contain actuators, enabling them to interact with the environment through means such as environmental controls, appliance automation, alerts and others (Ngai *et al.*, 2006).

Though WSANs have been quite popular, the challenge on the communications channel remains (Chen *et al.*, 2011). This is because WSANs typically communicate using IEEE 802.15.4, a half-duplex, short ranged, and low bandwidth channel (Saifullah *et al.*, 2013). Since WSANs are coupled with actuators, these networks usually follow a four-step model from detection, reporting, coordination, and actuation, which takes a considerable amount of bandwidth and delay before the actuation occurs (Ngai *et al.*, 2006).

Even though WSANs has become a very popular platform, there are still a lot of areas for improvement. Once of which is the communication process. Currently there are no WSAN communication standards. Using protocols from WSN may yield a decrease in effectivity since these protocols do not take into account the factor of actuation of environments.

Protocols such as IEEE 802.15.4 and ZigBee are protocol standards for WSNs. IEEE 802.15.4 allow direct communication through the mac layer but does not provide any means of traffic handling. On the other hand, ZigBee enables higher functions such as network coordination, routing, security, an application framework and others but may have a large amount of overhead thus decreasing throughput and performance for reliability. However since these protocols are not specifically built for WSAN environments they may present a decrease in network effectiveness. The study aims to create a traffic handling protocol for WSAN environments by providing a means of coordination through message while maintaining high throughput on the network.

2. Wireless Sensor Network Protocols

2.1. *IEEE 802.15.4*

The IEEE 802.15.4 is a standard for low data rate wireless connectivity that comprises of the physical and the data link layers of a network, based on the OSI architecture. It is said to be able to provide communication for nodes within a ten (10) meter radius and may use the 2.4 GHz band for communication.

The two layers covered by the standard are the physical layer and the data link layer. The physical layer is the bottom most layer and is the interface between the data link layer and the radio channel. It handles the activation of the transceiver, link quality indication (LQI), clear channel assessment (CCA), channel selection, and data transmission.

The data link layer provides communication support such as beaconing, synchronizing, application of CSMA-CA, time slots or GTS handling, reliable connection and others. This layer is also called the medium-access control or mac layer. It is where addressing and communication handling is done.

Overall the standard has low power consumption as well as a fairly low data loss rate. Since the protocol is also on the lower layers of the communication stack, the throughput is relatively higher as opposed to complete protocols but because of this routing, security and other functions are not being handled by it. It also does not have any form of traffic handling or coordination to do tasks such as provide quality of service, classifying data types, or even communication intermediation.

2.2. *ZigBee Protocol*

The ZigBee standard is a high level full protocol standard for wireless communication build on top of the IEEE 802.15.4 standard. ZigBee utilizes the physical and mac layers of the low power low data rate IEE 802.15.4, while implementing its own network and application layer.

The ZigBee standard is the one responsible for providing the higher layers of the network and application layer allowing various features and capabilities to a network. The network layer of the standard is responsible for allowing features such as routing and hops while the application layer allows a framework which may be used for multiple application in various areas such as WSN, embedded computers, and others.

In IEEE 802.15.4, the nodes typically have two (2) roles, a node or end device and a coordinator. However in ZigBee, there are three (3) roles, the end device, coordinator, and the router with each one having their own functions. In ZigBee the router is capable of routing data from one node to another unlike the end device. The ZigBee standard has a lot more capabilities, however due to it being a high level protocol which multiple features, it may contain too many features for certain WSN or WSAN environments, rendering it unutilized.

2.3. *Protocol of the Study*

Wireless sensor networks focuses on topologies, which provide efficient and reliable delivery of sensor data from the sensor nodes to the sink node. WSN nodes contain sensors for monitoring situations such as lighting, temperature, movement, and other environmental phenomena. These networks also focus on energy conservation, minimalistic processing, and mobility, allowing both time-based and event-triggered monitoring of an environment (Chen *et al.*, 2011).

On the other hand, WSANs differ from traditional WSNs due to the actuating capability. Actuation in the sense that certain activities; both automatic and electronically controlled responses, from various actuators provide intervention or automation as responses in an environment based on particular phenomena observed by the nodes.

The purpose of the creating a communication protocol through coordination messaging is to provide a protocol specifically addressing the requirements of WSANs. This is because the added capability of actuation would present different requirements for communication in the network. As opposed on WSNs, where only sensing is done, WSANs provide controls depending on certain conditions and apply intervention depending on the environment.

The proposed protocol is currently built on top of IEEE 802.15.4. This is because the IEEE 802.15.4 low data rate wireless protocol is a widely used as well as already presents an effective means of allowing communication between nodes in a network. However, since the IEEE 802.15.4 protocol does not have any built in processing to provide a form of traffic handling, the proposed protocol of the study would build a traffic handling and coordinator layer on top it, effectively utilizing the physical and mac layer protocol.

3. Network Communication Protocol Design

The WSAN Network Communication Protocol of the study is composed of two parts; which are a coordinator topology and a communication design. These parts make up the entire network communication protocol, which would be evaluated based on the measure of effective data rate, packet loss rate, speed in communication, and effectiveness in addressing the needs of a WSAN.

3.1. *Coordinator Topology*

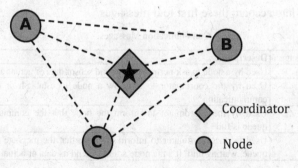

Fig. 1. Coordinator Topology used by the study.

The topology used in the study is a hybrid of the peer-to-peer and star topologies, which the study designates as the Coordinator Topology. This is to apply the capability of peer-to-peer topology in enabling direct communication of the different nodes in the WSAN and also that of the star topology to enable a coordinator responsible for organizing the node communication.

The topology contains four (4) entities comprised of three (3) nodes; designated by A, B, and C, as well as a coordinator designated by the star. The nodes used in the study may be equipped with either sensors, actuators, or both. This is to take into account WSANs with varying node functions. The coordinator is the one responsible for managing the coordinating process for node communication.

3.2. *Communication Design*

Through the Coordinator Topology of the study, communications would be intermediated and handled by the coordinator through a method of Coordination Messaging where the nodes establish communication with other nodes through the coordinator. The coordinator manages and informs the nodes if they are able or unable to send. Since the study uses messages in order to manage communications, there is no need to apply any form of time synchronization.

The table below shows the four common coordination messages used for the protocol; from Query to Send, Deny to Send, Queue Full, as well as Standby and Wait. These coordination messages require a confirmation reply from the recipient node, whether a sensing node, actuating node, or the coordinator to signal that the node has received it. There are other coordination messages, which may also be used in a network, however for this situation the protocol would only take into account these first four messages.

Table 1. Communication Messages.

Coordination Message	Description
Query to Send	Used by a node to ask permission to send sensor data or actuation
Deny to Send	Used by the coordinator to disallow a node to establish or continue communication
Queue Full	Used by the coordinator to inform the node that the communication queue is full
Standby and Wait	Used by the coordinator to inform the node that the message is in the queue, waiting until it's the node's turn to send its data or actuation

The Query to Send message is typically sent by the node in order to inform that the coordinator that the node would like to send sensor data or actuation commands. If accepted by the coordinator, it would reply an ACK – Send Message indicating that the node may send its message right away. This is only the case if the queue of the coordinator is empty.

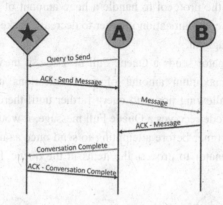

Fig. 2. Query to Send Coordination Messaging.

Once the sending node transmits its data to the recipient, the recipient must return a reply indicating that it has received the data and applied any actuation changes. After which, the sending node informs the coordinator that the conversation has concluded. Then the coordinator would listen for other nodes wanting to establish communication once again.

The Deny to Send message, as opposed to Query to Send, is a reply from the coordinator to the sending node. This is done when there is a problem at the destination node, where the sending node may not be allowed by the coordinator to send its data or command. A situation where this may be used is when recipient node experience connection problems such as being unreachable.

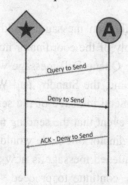

Fig. 3. Deny to Send Coordination Messaging.

The Queue Full message is also sent by the coordinator as a reply to the Query to Send message by the sending node. The implementation of the protocol of the study includes a queuing system. The purpose of the queuing system is to allow the protocol to handle a huge amount of network traffic by means of throttling communication in order to decrease packet loss with the cost of a decreased throughput.

When a coordinator sends a Queue Full message, it means the coordinator has reached the maximum amount of communications it can contain for throttling, thus disallowing nodes to query further until there is a space in the. Once the sending node receives a Queue Full message, it would have to wait for a random back off timer before attempting to send once again. This is to allow time for the coordinator to process the items in the queue, hopefully available when queued again.

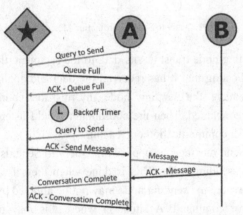

Fig. 4. Queue Full Coordination Messaging.

The last common coordination message would be the Standby and Wait message, which is also a reply of the coordinator node from the Query to Send message. As opposed to the Queue Full message wherein the sending node is tasked to resend at a later time, the Standby and Wait message is sent by the coordinator if the Query to Send message of the sending node is accepted and added into the queue. In the event that the sending node receives a Standby and Wait message from the coordinator, the node would have to wait for the signal of the coordinator that the queued message is now available to send. Once the wait is lifted the node may continue to proceed sending the message to the designated recipient.

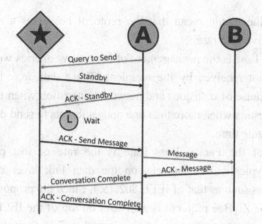

Fig. 5. Standby and Wait Coordination Messaging.

Another main difference of the Queue Full and the Standby and Wait messages is the back off or wait time. The back off time is used to signify that the sending node would have to wait for a random back off period before sending a Query to Send message again. This would mean that the node itself is counting for the duration of the wait. As opposed to that of the wait time used on the Standby and Wait message, wherein the node would not count or wait for a length of time, but rather wait until the coordinator sends the signal allowing the message to be sent.

4. Performance Testing and Results

In order to determine the effectiveness of the coordination applied by the protocol in the study. It would be compared to the base IEEE 802.15.4 protocol as well as that of ZigBee. The metrics measured would be effective data rate, packet loss rate, speed in communication, and effectiveness in addressing the needs of a WSAN.

The categories used would be Queries Sent, Queries Accepted, Queries Lost, Packet Loss Rate, and Average Sending Interval. The Queries Sent is the measurement of how many queries were sent during the test, the test duration is about 1 minute, however for the ZigBee test, the testing duration is different.

Queries Accepted are the measurement of queries, which were received by the recipient node from the number of Queries Sent. Having a high amount of Queries Accepted would mean that there is relatively lower packet loss rate.

Also a high value would mean that the protocol possesses a relatively high amount of effective data rate.

The Queries Lost is the measurement of how many queries were sent by the nodes but are not received by the recipient. These data may be lost during transmission because of collisions and network congestion when the packet data was sent. This results when more than one node attempts to send data in a shared medium at the same time.

The value of the Packet Loss Rate is the rate of lost packets during transmission. Typically this happens on the data link layer on shared and wireless mediums such as that of IEEE 802.15.4. Since the proposed protocol of the study and the ZigBee protocol is also built on top of the IEEE 802.15.4, all the protocols in the test are susceptible to packet loss from IEEE 802.15.4. However because the upper layers of the ZigBee protocol focuses on applying reliability to the communication, the upper layers are tasked to resend any lost packets from the lower layers.

Lastly the Average Sending Interval is the measurement on how long before another node packet is sent or able to be sent in a wireless network. Having a small interval would mean that more messages may be sent within a smaller time span. However having a fast data rate may render a network to experience a higher packet loss due to the amount of communications happening in a time frame as well as due to network congestion or collision. A slow interval would mean that nodes would have more time to process messages and may have lower packet loss because of fewer communications happening within a time frame.

4.1. *IEEE 802.15.4 Performance Testing*

The first test is the IEEE 802.15.4 Performance Test wherein WSAN nodes with basic communication capabilities are used to test the metrics for this protocol. For this test, the environment contains two nodes, a sensor/actuator node and a node sink. The sensor/actuator node is tasked to send sensor data while the node sink is tasked to reply with actuation commands to the sending node.

Table 2. IEEE 802.15.4 Performance Metrics.

	Test 1	Test 2	Test 3
Queries Sent	10545	10542	10542
Queries Accepted	10202	9757	10184
Queries Lost	343	785	358
Packet Loss Rate	3.25%	7.44%	3.39%
Average Sending Interval	19.57ms	17.57ms	16.25ms

It may be observed that based on the Queries Send and Queries Accepted, that using base IEEE 802.15.4 protocol results to having a data rate of 10500 queries per minute, which is a very high effective data rate. Having a high data rate with a low packet loss rate means that the protocol network is effective. However it must be noted that the measure of how effective a protocol is may be different for every test and environment. This is because each test and situation may have their own set of requirements and factors present in their network.

Using IEEE 802.15.4 also presents an excellent reliability count having about 3-7% packet loss rate. The average sending interval is about 16-19ms per packet. This would mean that the protocol also has a high transmission speed.

4.2. *ZigBee Performance Test*

The ZigBee test is similar to that of the IEEE 802.15.4 test parameters however, ZigBee decreases effective data rate for reliability, security and others. Also for this test since ZigBee already contains traffic handling as well as other features, it is understandable that using ZigBee may pose a significant decrease in the metrics resulted on top of the IEEE 802.15.4.

Table 3. ZigBee Performance Metrics.

	Low	Normal	High
Queries Sent	219	214	258
Queries Accepted	213	208	195
Queries Lost	6	6	63
Packet Loss Rate	2.74%	2.80%	24.42%
Average Sending Interval	1949ms	1359ms	625ms

Also the entire test duration is based on the amount of queries and the traffic levels from Low, Normal, and High. For the Low and Normal tests when using ZigBee, it may be seen that they relatively have a high sending interval with a low effective data rate. This is because ZigBee does plenty of traffic handling and preprocessing in order to provide its various services and features.

4.3. *Network Communication Protocol Query Testing*

This test is similar to that of the IEEE 802.15.4 Performance Test and the ZigBee test wherein there is a sending node and a node sink. The following data describes the sensor/actuator node tasked to send sensor data while the coordinator is tasked to reply with actuation commands to the sending node.

Table 4. Sending Node – Node Communication Protocol Metrics.

Sending Node	Test 1	Test 2	Test 3
Queries Sent	1478	1476	1478
Queries Accepted	1183	1182	1182
Queries Lost	295	294	296
Packet Loss Rate	19.95%	19.91%	20.03%
Average Sending Interval	28.96ms	26.21ms	25.91ms

The results show a relatively good enough effective data rate of 1100 communications per minute. However the cost of this is having an increase to the packet loss rate to about 20% packet loss. It may also be seen in the figure that the average sending interval is almost 10ms more than that of the IEEE 802.15.4, this is because of the additional overhead and preprocessing required when using the proposed protocol.

4.4. *Network Communication Protocol Full Message Test*

The Full Message Test is a test wherein the full proposed protocol is applied in a WSAN environment. This test attempts to mimic an actual environment by providing a high traffic test as well as a low traffic test. During the high traffic test, the average sending interval is higher as opposed to the moderate traffic test. The scenario of both tests is also that there are (3) devices in the network; a coordinator, sending node, and receiving node communicating with each other simultaneously.

For the first test, the High Traffic Test shows a fast interval of about 29-32ms. Because of this interval, the cost is a decrease in the effective data rate. This may be concluded that based on the figure below, using the proposed protocol may not be effective for network where the sending interval is short.

Table 5. High Traffic Query to Send – Coordination Messaging.

High Traffic Test	Test 1	Test 2	Test 3
Queries Sent	981	982	1026
Queries Accepted	475	476	371
Queries Lost	506	506	655
Packet Loss Rate	51.58%	51.52%	63.84%
Average Sending Interval	32.18ms	32.23ms	29.46ms

For the second test, the Moderate Traffic Test, reveals a moderately paced sending interval of about 78 to 97ms, which is about (3) times than that of the High Traffic Test. It may also be seen that since there was an increase in the sending interval, there have been a fewer queries which may be sent at a certain point in time.

Table 6. Moderate Traffic Query to Send – Coordination Messaging.

Moderate Traffic Test	Test 1	Test 2	Test 3
Queries Sent	475	501	411
Queries Accepted	452	480	392
Queries Lost	23	21	19
Packet Loss Rate	4.84%	4.19%	4.62%
Average Sending Interval	78.58ms	78.80ms	97.64ms

5. Conclusion and Recommendation

The Network Communication Protocol provided a way to establish a form of coordination within the nodes of the network through means of coordination messaging. The protocol uses a coordinator topology, which enables all nodes to have a centralized communication process. Because of this, coordination messaging was made possible, enabling a WSAN to handle traffic systematically as opposed to simply throwing data in the network.

As compared to IEEE 802.15.4 and ZigBee, the Network Communication Protocol through Coordination Messaging allows a relatively good data rate while still providing a form of traffic handling and coordination. IEEE 802.15.4 provides a high data rate but does not have any form of traffic handling while ZigBee has traffic handling and other features at the cost of a high data rate.

The study was able to achieve the centralization and coordination at the cost of decreasing throughput. This would mean that the protocol in the study sacrifices the amount of effective data rate in order to achieve a higher reliability rate and a low packet loss rate. This is because the Network Communication Protocol takes up an additional amount of overhead as compared to simply sending the data directly to the network. Also because of its centralization capability, the nodes were able to send their data in a systematic manner.

Currently the Network Communication Protocol through Coordination Messaging of the study, reveals a method on enabling a form of traffic handling. However there are still plenty of areas where the protocol may be improved. A few of which are to provide a means of security in the form of hashing and encryption of node information; traffic and data categorization with quality of service; a means of routing to extend beyond the IEEE 802.15.4 range of (10) meters since the protocol is built on top of that; as well as others.

References

1. Ong A. V. (2013) "Data Collection Protocol for Wireless Sensor Network-Based Home Automation." MS Thesis, De La Salle University, Manila, Philippines.
2. Boukerche, A., Araujo, R. B. and Villas, L. (2007, November). A novel QoS based routing protocol for wireless actor and sensor networks. In Global Telecommunications Conference, 2007. GLOBECOM'07. IEEE (pp. 4931–4935). IEEE.
3. Mahmood, A., Shi, K., Khatoon, S. and Xiao, M. (2013). Data Mining Techniques for Wireless Sensor Networks: A Survey. International Journal of Distributed Sensor Networks, 2013.
4. Molla, M. M. and Ahamed, S. I. (2006). A survey of middleware for sensor network and challenges. In Parallel Processing Workshops, 2006. ICPP 2006 Workshops. 2006 International Conference on (pp. 6–pp). IEEE.
5. Ngai, E. H., Zhou, Y., Lyu, M. R. and Liu, J. (2006, October). Reliable reporting of delay-sensitive events in wireless sensor-actuator networks. In Mobile Adhoc and Sensor Systems (MASS), 2006 IEEE International Conference on (pp. 101–108). IEEE.
6. Law, Y. W. and Havinga, P. J. (2005, December). How to secure a wireless sensor network. In Intelligent Sensors, Sensor Networks and Information Processing Conference, 2005. Proceedings of the 2005 International Conference on (pp. 89–95). IEEE.
7. Karl, H. and Willig, A. (2007). Protocols and architectures for wireless sensor networks. John Wiley & Sons.
8. Ucklemann D., Harrison M. and Michahelles F. (2011) Architecting the Internet of Things. Springer London.
9. Zhou, H. (2012). The internet of things in the cloud: A middleware perspective. CRC Press.
10. Xia, F. (2008). QoS challenges and opportunities in wireless sensor/actuator networks. Sensors, 8(2), 1099–1110.
11. Chen J., Johansson K., Olariu S., Paschalidis I. and Stojmenovic I. (October 2011) "Guest Editorial Special Issue on Wireless Sensor and Actuator Networks".
12. Baronti, P., Pillai, P., Chook, V. W., Chessa, S., Gotta, A. and Hu, Y. F. (2007). Wireless sensor networks: A survey on the state of the art and the 802.15. 4 and ZigBee standards. Computer communications, 30(7), 1655–1695.
13. Ganz, A., Ganz, Z. and Wongthavarawat, K. (2003). Multimedia Wireless Networks: Technologies, Standards and QoS. Pearson Education.

14. Chen, D. and Varshney, P. K. (2004, June). QoS Support in Wireless Sensor Networks: A Survey. In International Conference on Wireless Networks (Vol. 233, pp. 1–7).
15. Melodia, T., Pompili, D., Gungor, V. C. and Akyildiz, I. F. (2005, May). A distributed coordination framework for wireless sensor and actor networks. In Proceedings of the 6th ACM international symposium on Mobile ad hoc networking and computing (pp. 99–110). ACM.
16. Joint Conference of the IEEE Computer and Communications Societies. Proceedings IEEE (Vol. 4, pp. 2646-2657). IEEE.
17. Khan, M. A., Shah, G. A. and Sher, M. (2011). A QoS based multicast communication framework for wireless sensor actor networks (WSANs). International Journal of Innovative Computing, Information and Control, 7(12), 7003–7020.
18. Sharma, D., Verma, S. and Sharma, K. (2013). Network Topologies in Wireless Sensor Networks: A Review 1.
19. Alliance, Z. (2007). ZigBee 2007 specification. Online: http://www. zigbee. org/Specifications/ZigBee/Overview. aspx.
20. Lee, J. S., Su, Y. W. and Shen, C. C. (2007, November). A comparative study of wireless protocols: Bluetooth, UWB, ZigBee, and Wi-Fi. In Industrial Electronics Society, 2007. IECON 2007. 33rd Annual Conference of the IEEE (pp. 46–51). IEEE.
21. Kinney, P. (2003, October). Zigbee technology: Wireless control that simply works. In Communications design conference (Vol. 2, pp. 1–7).

Securing Health Information System with CryptDB

Nicole Anne D. C. Lopez

Department of Physical Sciences and Mathematics,
University of the Philippines Manila,
Manila, 1000, Philippines
E-mail: ndlopez@up.edu.ph
www.upm.edu.ph

Richard Bryann L. Chua

Department of Physical Sciences and Mathematics,
University of the Philippines Manila,
Manila, 1000, Philippines
* E-mail: rlchua@up.edu.ph
www.upm.edu.ph

Department of Computer Science (Algorithms and Complexity Laboratory),
University of the Philippines Diliman,
Quezon City, 1101, Philippines
www.upd.edu.ph

Due to the privacy concerns that come with health data, it is important that
data stored in health information system are encrypted. Homomorphic encryption has come into attention these past years as a method for storing confidential data. It allows us to perform computation over encrypted data without
the need to decrypt it. CryptDB is one tool that allows us to use homomorphic
encryption in MySQL. In our work, we developed a dental information system
using CryptDB and evaluated the differences in the development methods between CryptDB and regular PHP/MySQL development. We also noted the
changes in the development efforts needed when using CryptDB.

Keywords: CryptDB; Homomorphic Encryption; Health Information System.

1. Introduction

Information systems are gradually replacing paper-based records for years
now, including in the health industry, although it is not yet on the same
extent as that of finance and business industries. With the shift to digital health records, different confidentiality issues are popping out which
threaten its adoption. These confidentiality issues are usually present in
health information but not in the other fields[1]. To address these confiden-

tiality issues, we need to store health information in encrypted format while at the same time able to perform meaningful computation with it.

Encrypted databases are very rare in the industry. Some of those that need to encyrpt an entire database use packages like DBMS_CRYPTO[a] and SQLCipher API[b]. Another way is to use the *strawman* design[2]. With strawman design, certain sensitive fields are stored in encrypted form to protect the confidentiality of those fields. Computation on the encrypted fields are done by first decrypting it before performing the actual computation. This process is usually performed in a stored function with the secret key included inside the stored function. Unfortunately, this only gives the user an illusion of security, but actually provides very little real security[3]. A curious database administrator may gain access to this key and snoop on the sensitive data in the database.

A recent technique for encrypted database is the use of homomorphic encryption. In homomorphic encryption, we can perform computation on an encrypted data without decrypting it. Although homomorphic encryption is not a totally new concepts, its high computational cost prevents it from being used in most applications. It is only in the past few years that homomorphic encryption becomes practical. We introduce homomorphic encryption in Section 2 and CryptDB in Section 3. In Section 4, we discuss our development of a dental information system using CryptDB.

2. Homomorphic Encryption

Rivest, Adleman and Dertouzous first suggested the concept of homomorphic encryption in 1977[4]. *Privacy homomorphism* or *homomorphic encryption* is a special class of encryption function which allows the encrypted data to be computed on directly without needing any knowledge about the decryption function[5]. Suppose $E_K(\cdot)$ is an encryption function with key K and $D_K(\cdot)$ is the corresponding decryption function. Then $E_K(\cdot)$ is homomorphic with respect to the operator $\circ$ if there exists an efficient algorithm Alg such that

$$Alg(E_K(x), E_K(y)) = E_K(x \circ y).$$

Eventually, the RSA cryptosystem of Rivest, Shamir, and Adleman became the foundational concept of homomorphic encryption[6]. However, this

---

[a]http://docs.oracle.com/cd/B13789_01/network.101/b10773/apdvncrp.htm
[b]http://sqlcipher.net/about/

scheme is not secure from different attacks such as brute force, mathematical attacks, timing attacks, and chosen-ciphertext attacks[7].

The first homomorphic scheme that reached a remarkable rating of safety was the Goldwasser-Micali scheme[8]. However, it is only capable of encrypting one bit at a time[9]. This gives the scheme a low throughput and makes it impractical. Using the Goldwasser-Micali cryptosystem as basis, Chan revised two algorithms: Hill Cipher and Rivest's Scheme, which exhibit homomorphism but are prone to ciphertext-only attacks, to create his homomorphic encryption scheme[5]. Although Chan's scheme has a better throughput than the Goldwasser-Micali scheme, it uses symmetric encryption. Once an adversary gets hold of the key, unauthorized access and manipulation on private data will be possible. Another homomorphic scheme is the Paillier's scheme which uses public-key cryptography and block-cipher encryption algorithm[10]. However, this is proven to be unsecure from chosen-ciphertext attack[11]. Due to the difficulty in the construction of a homomorphic cryptosystem, some groups worked on somewhat homomorphic encryption (SWHE), which only works from some functions[6,12].

The first fully homomorphic encryption (FHE) scheme was the Gentry scheme which came out in 2009[13]. In a fully homomorphic encryption scheme, there are no limitations on the functions that can be performed. Although computation on encrypted data using homomorphic encryption is possible with Gentry scheme, it is still very expensive[2]. Gentry scheme has a complexity of $\tilde{O}(\lambda^7)$, where λ is the security parameter of the scheme[14]. In 2013, IBM came out with its homomorphic encryption library (HElib), which uses the Brakerski-Gentry-Vaikuntanathan (BGV) scheme and some optimizations to make it faster compared to Gentry's scheme and eventually making homomorphic encryption practical[15].

Even with its high cost, homomorphic encryption has been applied to different areas. Riggio et al. in 16 used homomorphic encryption in performing statistical analysis on data coming from wireless sensor netowrks. Zhu and Xiang in 17 used homomorphic encryption with data confusion to provide protection on mobile-based code. Han et al. in 18 used homomorphic encryption to delegate data computation from weak computational devices such as mobile phones to a more powerful computational device. Fujitsu even uses homomorphic encryption in its biometric authentication technology when performing statistical calculations and biometric authentication[19].

It can't be denied that homomorphic encryption has its most useful application on data security. Theft of private data is a very important problem to be addressed nowadays, especially for Internet-based applications[20]. An attacker can use the vulnerability points of a software to gain unathorized access to servers[21], curious administrators on a data provider may snoop on private data[22], and adversaries with physical access to servers can access all digital information on disk and on memory[23].

3. CryptDB

Most database management systems (DBMS) find it impractical to implement homomomorphic encryption. Hence, in 2011 Popa et.al developed CryptDB as a solution for homomorphic encryption in databases. CryptDB doesn't implement a fully homomorphic encryption, which makes it fast, but is able to address the confidentiality challenges in a database[2,24]. CryptDB's architecture is similar to that of Yuping et. al. in 25 which has an encryption framework over the different levels of a database management system. Here, instead of directly connecting the application to the DBMS, a new entity is added which is now responsible for encryption.

Figure 1 shows the structure of CryptDB. It consists of two parts: database proxy and an unmodified DBMS. It uses user-defined functions (UDFs) to perform cryptographic operations. The database proxy intercepts all the SQL queries and transforms those queries to execute on encrypted data. Since query processing is divided into two separate entities, the encryption and decryption processing to database information is done in the background and is transparent to the application and DBMS servers[25].

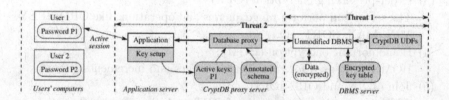

Fig. 1.   CryptDB's architecture[2].

CryptDB provides practical and provable confidentiality in the face of attacks on applications backed by SQL databases. It works by executing SQL queries over encrypted data using a collection of SQL-aware encryption schemes. To process a query in CryptDB:

(1) The application issues a query, which will be intercepted and rewitten by the proxy. The proxy anonymizes each table and column name and using the master key MK, encrypts each constant in the query with the scheme suited for the desired operation.

(2) The proxy checks if the server should be given keys to adjust the encryption layers before executing the query. If so, it issues UPDATE query that invokes a user-defined function (UDF) which in turn will adjust the encryption layers of the appropriate columns

(3) The proxy forwards the encrypted query to the DBMS server, which executes it using standard SQL.

(4) The DBMS server returns the encrypted query result which the proxy decrypts and sends back to the application.

To allow the processing of queries, CryptDB has four onion types which are built from the following encryption types which has varying types of query they can each support:

(1) Random (RND)

RND provides the maximum security and does not allow any computation to be performed efficiently on the ciphertext.

(2) Deterministic (DET)

DET allows the server to perform equality checks, meaning it can perform selects with equality predicates, equality joins, GROUP BY, COUNT, DISTINCT, etc.

(3) Order-preserving encryption (OPE)

The server can perform range queries and operations like ORDER BY, MIN, MAX, SORT, etc.

(4) Homomorphic encryption (HOM)

HOM can be used for computing averages and increments.

(5) Join (JOIN and OPE-JOIN)

JOIN supports all operations of DET and also enables the server to determine repeating values between two columns while OPE-JOIN enables joins by order relations.

(6) Word search (SEARCH)

SEARCH is used to perform searches on encrypted data to support operations like MySQL's LIKE operator.

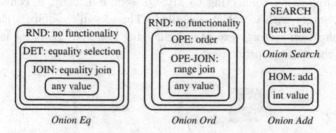

Fig. 2. Onion encryption layers and the classes of computations they allow [2].

4. Developing Health Information Application Using CryptDB

We developed a dental information system using CryptDB for the teaching dental clinic of the University of the Philippines, College of Dentistry. The dental information system has functions for the management of patient records and computing descriptive statistics for the clinic. These patient records can be accessed by both the student and faculty clinicians of the College. In order to comply with the Health Insurance Portability and Accountability Act (HIPAA) requirement of limiting access to and encrypting patient records in order to protect patient privacy, we need to limit the access of the patient records to only student and faculty clinicians. While this can be accomplished in the application system, we still need to prevent a malicious database administrator from viewing the patient records by directly accessing the database. To prevent a malicious database administrator from viewing our database and at the same time able to perform meaningful computation and processing of our data we decided to encrypt all the fields in the database through the use of CryptDB. Although encrypting only the sensitive fields will be enough the protect the privacy of the patients, properly identifying these sensitive fields can be hard as data identified as non-sensitive could be combined with data obtained from other databases to infer a patient's private information.

We used a virtual image of Ubuntu 12.04.5 (64-bit) in VirtualBox in our development. In this virtual image, we setup Apache 2.2.22 with PHP 5.3.10 as web server, MySQL 5.5.44 with MySQL Proxy as database server, and CryptDB Volume 5, Issue I.

The development method is almost similar to the usual development method for PHP and MySQL. We came up with an architecture that is similar to how we will do it in normal PHP development except that instead of our application connecting to MySQL server directly, it connected to MySQL proxy with CryptDB installed. This doesn't require a change in our application settings except for changing the MySQL database server port to the MySQL proxy port.

Fig. 3.   System architecture of the dental information system.

Database tables, including the table names, table fields and table data are encrypted when stored. For example, the unencrypted **patient** table shown in Fig. 4 when stored in the MySQL database will be encrypted by CryptDB into the one shown in Fig. 5.   However, the tables are encrypted

```
| UPCD_ID  | patientFName  | patientMName | patientLName | houseno | street
          | brgy                     | city         | province    | gender |
  bdate    | age | clinician | section            | date       | deceased | s
tatus     |
+----------+---------------+--------------+--------------+---------+------------
----------+--------------------------+--------------+-------------+---------+
----------+---------+-----------+--------------------+------------+----------+--
----------+
| 14-00001 | Michelle      | Velasco      | Dela Cruz    | 568     | Dela Cruz S
t.        | Canumay                  | Valenzuela City | Metro Manila | Female |
  1993-02-15 | 21  | 4        | Operative Dentistry | 2014-03-27 | No        | O
pen       |
| 14-00002 | Azeil Louisse | A            | Codizar      | 234     | Codizar St.
          | Dasma Heights            | Dasmarinas   | Cavite      | Female |
  1993-05-24 | 20  | 2        | Oral Diagnosis     | 2014-03-29 | No        | f
or approval |
| 14-00003 | Hainah Kariza | Avenido      | Leus         | 3423    | Marcelo Gre
en Village | Sucat                   | Paranaque    | Metro Manila | Female |
  1993-09-11 | 20  | 2        | Oral Diagnosis     | 2014-03-30 | No        | O
pen       |
```

Fig. 4.   Patient table view.

IPUQYVDUJEoEq	GFGMBWVIMQoOrder
737419dd0be316ea1ef4ec47cc7631781e62e824560bf5bb617b67df8e1a5e7b	2666881662546430040
2c47898830d027d91a25df2fa2cf7e3e56dcca815ac220488c07f0baa3e94fe3	3639489763157244356
611d0abf76ec5283b4ad17e1cbc751e3896ed000717e72b925498c020daa393a	15978174409738422366

Fig. 5. A portion of patient table view stored in MySQL in encrypted form.

with just a single key across all tables. Hence, if there are two rows with the same entries on a particular column in a database, their corresponding encrypted values are the same. Suppose the database has a table **users** whose actual contents are shown in Fig. 6. Here, users 7 and 9 have the same **userLName** entry. In Fig. 7, it can be seen that they have the same encrypted values. This is a potential security risk.

```
mysql> use DentISt;
Reading table information for completion of table and column names
You can turn off this feature to get a quicker startup with -A

Database changed
mysql> select * from users;
+--------+---------------+--------------+-----------+
| userID | userFName     | userMName    | userLName |
+--------+---------------+--------------+-----------+
| 1      | Nicole Anne   | Dela Cruz    | Lopez     |
| 2      | Liezl         | Del Rosario  | Santos    |
| 3      | Maristela     | Salvador     | Dela Cruz |
| 4      | Jezra         | Yerro        | Alcantara |
| 5      | Sherwin Keith | Ballestar    | Saringan  |
| 6      | Richard Bryann| L            | Chua      |
| 7      | Vincent Peter | C            | Magboo    |
| 8      | Geoffrey      | A            | Solano    |
| 9      | Ma. Sheila    | Abad         | Magboo    |
| 10     | Joser John    | Tinio        | Barron    |
+--------+---------------+--------------+-----------+
10 rows in set (0.16 sec)

mysql>
```

Fig. 6. Users table view.

There are some MySQL data types that are not yet supported in CryptDB. Among them are ENUM, DATE, TIME and DATETIME. We have to substitute all of them with VARCHAR data type and treat these types of data as string.

BoOrder	cdb_saltUHIOLRHACV	PVSFRATJPWoEq	IRNCFLGNSJoOrder	cdb_saltZXIJNVAUVF
49359095	12111128104500058418	70077dadce89b0d0707eca354629805c6547a84b34feda8f94c39cd7ca89c423	7267486519703892628	10944753827445148262
75396099	10262843523447396890	4e0e79a4c8c76a3b49d28f9fe597eba005d46e80b270c9a0b3971129af2a61e5	16996891779216194444	15161670677227455464
34532396	18343576481637645350	9b86a108472ae7e360bbd1193253d8c873a632b8200c407cce705b76ff4f315b	14248754189936148230	12857491272373898112
43911164	70890672410399814472	58f890f7ef93007703d4b7a2dc4c49954f2e4970254bc7cb2463fa38fa5be250	17523967764440954580	10849189210893766363
34868242	15368778603311250370	fa931bfb4034efdfe9bc9d2c17301245cec40570487a20ecf68a4e18766b2298	33804376383382887507	17106778954135480127
48766296	16503392749334214388	26a1c92d8cc28b6fc1a7a94d8665f1e3d0486998a08de086b6a52c97173d3cfb	6888339719685884479	1769566905357597210
34696731	35198236621292252510	dc578725459c48684770c72bff93c9618af408a7f0934582911ac62b6ec961c0	40250536152067432239	14684368310177238502
31807922	10533679286171735405	046ac8e7ed32625c4570f45e2c1f916ce93b4673e1e99344305932e11e836b80	15948789913721357493	5508773277586550371
28973515	11163687530872963359	dc578725459c48684770c72bff93c9618af408a7f0934582911ac62b6ec961c0	13219265647392015466	10883687118532227877

Fig. 7.   Users table view as stored in MySQL database.

There are MySQL commands which are not supported. Among the unsupported commands are CHANGE, MODIFY and RENAME under ALTER. To modify a table structure, we have to drop the table and recreate it with the new table structure. Hence, we need to export all rows in the old table, modify the corresponding SQL statements according to the new table structure, and insert it into the new table. This poses a problem when there are many rows in the table we want to modify.

Some MySQL SQL operators are not supported in CryptDB. Some of these are LIKE and CONCAT which are used in string searches. We have to substitute LIKE with an equality relation and case-sensitivity on search strings must be' considered. For example the normal query

SELECT * FROM users WHERE users_firstname LIKE '%string%'.

is implemented as

SELECT * FROM users WHERE users_firstname = 'string'.

In this query, the search results are exact matches and also case-sensitive. This is not a problem in our system since the standard practice in most health information system for searching a patient record is either by using the patient ID or the full patient name. The operator JOIN on two fields in which one field is auto-incremented is also not supported. To solve this, we didn't use auto-incremented fields in the database and instead, implemented the auto-incrementation in the application.

In terms of performance, we observed that queries run longer in CryptDB compare to running directly with MySQL, which is caused by the homomorphic encryption performed by CryptDB. However, the difference is not that big. Hence, we no longer measured the difference between their query execution times. We also observed that CryptDB consumes a relatively high amount of RAM (56% of memory) compared to other processes.

```
top - 03:30:08 up  1:03,  4 users,  load average: 3.50, 2.58, 1.87
Tasks: 162 total,   2 running, 160 sleeping,   0 stopped,   0 zombie
Cpu(s): 72.7%us, 22.5%sy,  0.0%ni,  0.0%id,  0.0%wa,  0.0%hi,  4.8%si,  0.0%st
Mem:   2061512k total,  1941812k used,   119700k free,    87812k buffers
Swap:  2095100k total,    18640k used,  2076460k free,   239156k cached

  PID USER      PR  NI  VIRT  RES  SHR S %CPU %MEM    TIME+  COMMAND
  938 root      20   0  116m  73m  14m R 37.5  3.6  6:17.50 Xorg
 2539 root      20   0 1560m 1.1g  11m S 30.7 56.0  5:43.91 mysql-proxy
 2458 nicole    20   0  189m  21m  12m S 15.5  1.1  1:46.11 gnome-terminal
 2387 nicole    20   0  566m 112m  37m S  4.8  5.6  6:18.12 firefox
  981 mysql     20   0  328m  38m 7628 S  3.9  1.9  0:25.48 mysqld
 1305 www-data  20   0 42688  11m 3408 S  2.6  0.6  0:01.20 apache2
  186 root      20   0     0    0    0 S  1.6  0.0  0:10.02 jbd2/sda1-8
 1844 nicole    20   0  142m  12m 9920 S  1.6  0.6  0:19.84 metacity
 2680 root      20   0     0    0    0 S  1.0  0.0  0:02.94 kworker/0:2
 2912 nicole    20   0  2852 1184  896 R  1.0  0.1  0:05.83 top
  620 messageb  20   0  4140 1780  880 S  0.3  0.1  0:03.37 dbus-daemon
 1036 root      20   0  9900 1344  992 S  0.3  0.1  0:03.57 VBoxService
 2933 root      20   0     0    0    0 S  0.3  0.0  0:01.00 kworker/0:3
    1 root      20   0  3672 1332 1312 S  0.0  0.1  0:01.42 init
    2 root      20   0     0    0    0 S  0.0  0.0  0:00.00 kthreadd
    3 root      20   0     0    0    0 S  0.0  0.0  0:00.31 ksoftirqd/0
    5 root      20   0     0    0    0 S  0.0  0.0  0:00.92 kworker/u:0
```

Fig. 8.   Memory Consumption of CryptDB.

5. Conclusions and Future Work

We have shown in the application we developed that it is practical and possible to use homomorphic encryption in the storage of health records with a system such as CryptDB. In our system, all the database records, including the table names, are encrypted. This allows us to comply with the HIPAA requirement. This also effectively prevents a malicious database administrator from getting confidential information from our database.

However, there are still limitations in the use of CryptDB. But since CryptDB is still an ongoing project, we could expect improvements in CryptDB. But even with the present limitations of CryptDB, it is still possible to develop a fully functional application system since there are ways to circumvent these limitations.

6. Acknowledgment

We thank Raluca Ada Popa of University of California, Berkeley and Aaron Burrows of Massachusetts Institute of Technology for responding to our inquiries on CryptDB. We also thank the anonymous reviewers for their careful and significant comments and suggestions on this paper.

References

1. S. Braghin, A. Coen-Porisini, P. Colombo, S. Sicari and A. Trombetta, Introducing privacy in a hospital information system, *Proceedings of the Fourth International Workshop on Software Engineering for Secure System*, 9 (2008).
2. R. A. Popa, C. M. S. Redfield, N. Zeldovich and H. Balakrishnan, CryptDB: Protecting confidentiality with encrypted query processing, *Proceedings of the Twenty-Third ACM Symposium on Operating Systems Principles* (2011).
3. E. Chickowski, Five worst practices in database encryption `http://www.darkreading.com/database/five-worst-practices-in-database-encrypt/231900083`, (2011), [Accessed on October 2013].
4. R. L. Rivest, L. Adleman and M. L. Dertouzous, On data banks and privacy homomorphisms, *Foundations of Secure Computation, Academic Press*, 169 (1978).
5. A. C.-F. Chan, Symmetric-key homomorphic encryption for encrypted data processing, *IEEE International Conference on Communications 2009* (2009).
6. C. Gentry, Computing arbitrary functions of encrypted data, *Communications of the Association of Computing Machinery* **53**, 96 (March 2010).
7. Y. Pan and Y. Deng, Cryptanalysis of the Cai-Cusick lattice-based public-key cryptosystem, *International Association for Cryptologic Research* (2011).
8. M. Tebaa, S. E. Hajji and A. E. Ghazi, Homomorphic encryption applied to the cloud computing security, *Proceedings of the World Congress on Engineering 2012* **I** (July 4-6, 2012).
9. J. Bringer, H. Chabanne, M. Izabachène, D. Pointcheval, Q. Tang and S. Zimmer, An application of the Goldwasser-Micali cryptosystem to biometric authentication, *The 12th Australasian Conference on Information Security and Privacy* (2007).
10. P. Paillier, Public-key cryptosystems based on composite degree residuosity classes, *Proceedings of EUROCRYPT 1999* **1592**, 223 (1999).
11. A. Dasa and A. Adhikari, An efficient IND-CCA2 secure Paillier-based cryptosystem, *Information Processing Letters Volume 112, Issue 22* (2012).
12. D. Boneh, C. Gentry, S. Halevi and F. Wang, Private database queries

using somewhat homomorphic encryption, *Proceedings of the 11th international conference on Applied Cryptography and Network Security* (November 30, 2012).

13. C. Gentry, A fully homomorphic scheme, PhD thesis, Stanford University 2009.

14. H.-M. Yang, Q. Xia, X.-F. Wang and D.-H. Tang, A new somewhat homomorphic encryption scheme over integers, *2012 International Conference on Computer Distributed Control and Intelligent Enviromental Monitoring* (2012).

15. P. Ducklin, IBM takes a big new step in cryptography: practical homomorphic encryption http://nakedsecurity.sophos.com/2013/05/05/ibm-takes-big-new-step-in-cryptography/, (May 5, 2013), [Accessed on October 2013].

16. R. Riggio, T. Rasheed and S. Sicari, Performance evaluation of an hybrid mesh and sensor network, *Global Telecommunications Conference (GLOBECOM 2011)* (2011).

17. P. Zhu and G. Xiang, The protection methods for mobile codebased on homomorphic encryption and data confusion, *2011 International Conference on Management of e-Commerce and e-Government* (2011).

18. Jing-Li, H. M. Yang, C.-L. Wang and S.-S. Xu, The implemention and application of fully homomorphic encryption scheme, *Second International Conference on Instrumentation and Measurement, Computer, Communication and Control* (2012).

19. F. L. Ltd., Fujitsu develops world's first homomorphic encryption technology that enables statistical calculations and biometric authentication http://www.fujitsu.com/global/news/pr/archives/month/2013/20130828-01.html, (August 28, 2013), [Accessed on October 2013].

20. P. R. ClearingHouse, Chronology of Data Breaches http://www.privacyrights.org/data-breach, (2005), [Accessed on September 2013].

21. N. V. Database, CVE Statistics http://web.nvd.nist.gov/view/vuln/statistics, (2011), [Accessed on September 2013].

22. A. Chen, GCreep: Google engineer stalked teens, spied on chats http://gawker.com/5637234/, (2010), [Accessed on September 2013].

23. J. A. Halderman, S. D. Schoen, N. Heninger, W. Clarkson, W. Paul, J. A. Calandrino, A. J. Feldman, J. Appelbaum and E. W. Felten, Lest we remember: Cold boot attacks on encryption keys, *Proceedings of the 17th Usenix Security Symposium* (July-August 2008).

24. R. A. Popa, N. Zeldovich and H. Balakrishnan, CryptDB: A practical encrypted relational DBMS, *Computer Science and Artificial Intelligence Laboratory Technical Report* (2011).
25. Z. Yuping and W. Xinghui, Research and realization of multi-level encryption method for database, *2010 2nd International Conference on Advanced Computer Control (ICACC)* (2010).

Spoken Dialogue Agent System for Writing Resumes while Practicing Job Interviews

Kaoru Sumi and Kodai Morita

The Graduate School of Future University Hakodate,
Hakodate, Hokkaido, Japan
E-mail: kaoru.sumi@acm.org

We propose a system that automatically generates a resume while an agent and a user interact. This research is a prototype for automatically generating dialogue questions without preparing a dialogue pattern in advance. The agent prepares the questions for a job interview from the format of a resume and practices a job interview. The system stores the user's information through an interview and finally creates the resume. The system provides both opportunities for practicing an interview and writing a resume.

Keywords: spoken dialogue agent, interaction, generating questions job interviews, resumes.

1. Introduction

This research aims at developing a spoken-dialogue agent system without the need to prepare a dialogue pattern in advance by a human. Most of previous spoken-dialogue agent systems have used dialogue patterns, where a human has to input all of the questions and answering patterns into the system[1]–[4]. For example, if the user says "What is your name?", the system then searches for its pattern from the question pattern and answers "My name is Eliza" from the answering template of the question pattern. This research is a prototype for automatically generating dialogue questions without preparing a dialogue pattern in advance.

The proposed system generates questions by studying the system developed by Avaz[*] for generating speech for people with speech disorders. According to Avaz, we can generate all questions by using when, where, who, what, why, how, whom, and so on (Fig. 1). The proposed system automatically generates a resume while an agent and a user interact as a prototype for automatically generating dialogue questions without preparing a dialogue pattern in advance. The agent is as an interviewer who asks a question, and the system aids the user

---

[*] A. Narayanan, Avaz, http://avazapp.com/freespeech/

in self-examination. The system finally outputs a resume using the information recorded by the interaction between the agent and the user.

We intend to use the dialogue during a job interview as our research domain because the characteristics of this dialogue is mostly questions and answers, and the domain of the dialogue is limited to the user's activities. The users have the advantage learning the dialogue during a job interview and obtaining a resume according to the interview.

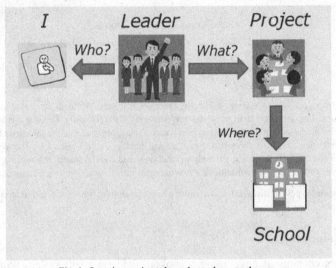

Fig. 1. Questions using who, what, where, and so on.

2. Spoken dialogue agent system for practicing job interviews and writing resumes

Figure 2 shows the conceptual diagram of the system. The system automatically generates a resume while an agent and a user interact.

Our character agent system (Fig. 3) consists of a three dimensional (3D) character agent display system, a speech recognition system, a speech synthesis system, a dialogue control system, and a facial-expression recognition system[5]–[9]. The 3D character agent display system displays a 3D character agent that can show the facial expressions for "smiling," "laughing," "anger," "sadness," "disgust," "frightened," and "surprised." These facial expressions can be digitally controlled in intensity. The system superimposes the mouth shapes of the vowels onto each facial expression, lip-synching with the sounds. Fluid movement of the facial expressions and lip-synching are possible using

Microsoft XNA morphing technology. Our system uses the Google speech API[†] as the speech recognition system and AITalk[‡] as the Japanese speech synthesis system. As a dialogue control system, we revised Artificial Intelligence Markup Language (AIML), which is based on Extensible Markup Language (XML) to use the Japanese language.

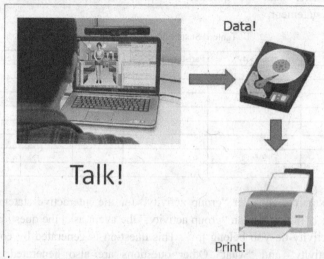

Fig. 2. The conceptual diagram of the system.

Fig. 3. System screenshot of the spoken dialogue agent system for practicing job interviews and writing resumes.

[†] Wind Craft, Wind-Craft, http://wind-craft.net/
[‡] AITalk, http://www.ai-j.jp/about

2.1. *Dialogue*

The proposed system will generate a question from a table using Perl. First, in Excel, the system creates a table such as Table 1 in the CSV format. Then, the system converts the language using Perl into a CSV format and generates a question. After that, the question is incorporated into the system as an interactive statement.

Table 1. Statements of questions.

	Group activity	Part-time job	Hobby	Project	Research
What					
What doing					
How long					
Where					
Advantage					
Why					
Troubles					
Resolution					

For example, consider "group activity" for the interactive statement that uses Table 1. In the column "group activity," the agent asks the question "What a group activity do you belong to?". This question is generated by combining "group activity" and "what" Other questions are also generated. For the combination of "circle" and "what doing," the system generates a question such as "What are you doing in there?". In the case of "how long," the agent asks the question "How long have you belonged to there?". Furthermore, for the combination of "part-time job" and "what," the question "What is your part-time job?" is generated. For the combination of "part-time job" and "where," "Where have you had a part-time job?" is generated. Finally, for "advantage," the agent asks "What did you obtain?"

The system creates a question for each column, if it is question column of "group activity," the group activities of "what," "what doing", "how long" is generated. After that, questions are generated for each column corresponding to "project," "part-time job," "hobby," and "research." For the questions in each column, the system starts with "what" and then goes to "what are you doing," "how long," "where," and "advantage." Then, a random question from "troubles" is asked. Questions related to "why" and "resolution" are asked after the "advantage" and "troubles" questions.

An example dialogue is as follows.

```
Agent: "What a group activity do you belong to?"
User:  "I belong to a baseball team"
Agent: "What are you doing in there?"
User:  "I was a pitcher."
Agent: "What did you struggle with the group
        activity?"
User:  "Because we did not have a sufficient number
        of people, we could not practice baseball
        very much."
Agent: "How did you overcome this obstacle?"
User:  "We decided the time that the most people
        could participate every week by talking
        with folks."
```

In this system, the agent is positioned as the interviewer. If the user and agent talk, it becomes interview practice for the user. We think that the system can provide the user with appropriate tension to avoid boredom by using the agent as an interviewer or a teacher. During interview training, the system generates a question from Table 1. After the agent questions the user, the table is gradually filled in with the user's answers that are saved in each column. The system creates each output item using the stored answers after the agent asks questions for all columns. After the last question, the system enters the sentences in the correct place in the resume if sentences were created for each output item. The sentences are output as the sentences of the resume using the stored text with some supplemental words.

2.2. *Resume writing*

The system shows a sentence summary based on the user's answers before outputting a resume to the user. The user can edit the sentences presented by the system. Because of this, the users can also manually edit typographical errors and omissions due to speech recognition. If the user does not like the text presented by the system, it can be modified impromptu to achieve a better resume.

The system sets the positions of new lines and the font sizes according to the number of characters of the text that has been modified when outputting to resume. The system outputs a resume in line with the format of Future University-Hakodate (Fig. 4). The resume sections are personality (strengths, weaknesses), research, projects, group and extracurricular activities, statement

154

of purpose, self-appeal, hobbies and specialties, accomplishments, and concentrated subjects. "projects" is , in a curriculum that takes place when Future University Hakodate three years, students and professors join in specific project that is something to achieve the goal.

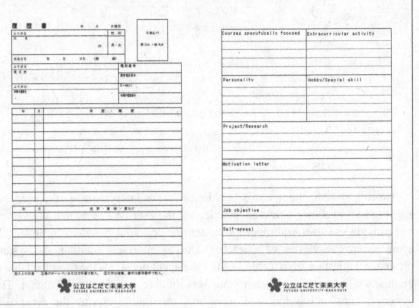

Fig. 4. Resume Format of Future University Hakodate.

As a recording method, the agent asks a question to the user for each output statement. The system saves the questions and answers with respect to each output statement in txt format. For example, for "group and extracurricular activities," the question "What a group activity do you belong to?" may be asked. If the user answers "I belong to a baseball team" this record is saved. After that, the system will ask questions such as "How long have you belonged to there?" and "What are you doing in there?".

The system generates a question on the basis of the table that combined the elements of each output item and question. The system can generate many different questions by using the table that summarizes the question contents and each output item from a small amount of initial information from the question. The agent will ask the user to fill in the table. The elements of a question can easily generate many questions by adding a column.

3. Experiment

We conducted an experiment to examine the problems of the dialogue system for practicing a job interview. The subjects were three university students; questions were asked in group activities. Each of the questions and answers are summarized in Table 2.

Table 2. Answers of Subjects in the experiment.

Group activity					
	What a group activity do you belong to?	What are you doing in there?	What did you obtain?	What did you struggle with the group activity?	How did you overcome this obstacle?
Subject 1	I belong to wind music circle	I was assigned to the trombone	I had a large lung capacity	I had a hard time because of the monotonous practice	I practiced every day
Subject 2	Drama club	I was assigned to the large props	Engineering skills and connections with other members	I didn't have know-how	I overcame this by having a talk with my fellow members

Subjects answered as follows.

Subject 1: My circle was the wind music circle. Therefore, I was assigned to the trombone. I had a large lung capacity because I practiced a long tone every day. I had a hard time because of the monotonous practice, but I practiced every day.

Subject 2: I was in a drama club. Thus, I was assigned to the large props. I have obtained engineering skills and connections with other members. However I didn't have know-how, I overcame this by having a talk with my fellow members.

After they used the system, we interviewed the subjects of the experiment.

· "What did you think of this system?"

I was puzzled because it asked almost immediately; I had to respond without thinking. I think I answered only uninterrupted words because the time between questions is very short. The system should ask more expansive and motivational questions.

· "What do you think it will be better: creating the resume from the beginning on your own or obtaining the resume automatically using the system?"

I think that it is good for people who are not accustomed to making sentences. However, I think that there is no need for people who are accustomed to making sentences.

I think it is better to have a function for revising sentences. If all sentences are automatically output, I do not feel it is mine.

The problem with this system is the typographical errors and omissions due to errors during voice recognition. It is difficult to talk in great detail when using the system. In addition, the time between questions asked by the agent is very short.

4. Discussion

We developed a spoken-dialogue agent system for practicing job interviews and writing resumes and conducted a preliminary experiment to find the problems of the dialogue system. As a result of the experiment, an investigation has revealed that we should consider additional methods of asking for more information on a certain topic. When we talk to each other, it is not in a style of "exchanging of questions and answers"; instead, we make up words if we cannot say words at one time. As an interviewer, for example, it is possible to follow up with "What do you mean?" or "Please explain it with concrete descriptions." In the case that the system has difficulties with voice recognition, it is possible to reply with "pardon me?" or "Please speak slowly." We will examine these replies from the agent.

Our system can easily generate and change questions by updating the table used in the system. For example, if the user adds "internship" to the table used in the system, the system automatically generates questions: "What was your internship? (what)," "What did you do there? (what are you doing)," "Where did you do your internship? (where)," "How long did you do your internship? (how long)," "What did you learn? (advantage)," "Why did you do? (why)," "What did you have trouble with? (trouble)," and "How did you resolve any problems? (resolution)."

According to the comment from a subject in the preliminary experiment, the system should ask more expansive and motivational questions. Asking follow-up questions and subordinate topics will be beneficial to construct more expansive and motivational questions. Additionally, "how" and "why" must be beneficial for these questions.

When considering the idea of a spoken-dialogue agent system for practicing job interviews and writing resumes, it is beneficial to the job hunter to learn interviewing techniques and write resumes. As an interview function, it will be helpful to learn interviewing alone, despite the fact that it is very difficult. As a writing resume function, it is beneficial to the job hunter to analyze their resume and conduct a self-examination. Revising a resume should be their training for writing a resume. Therefore, it is helpful for learning to explain and appeal their own.

5. Conclusion

In this paper, we proposed a spoken dialogue agent system that automatically generates a resume while an agent and a user interact in a practice job interview. As a result of the experiment, we found that further refinement of the questions generated by the system is necessary so that detailed questions are asked.

References

1. Weizenbaum, Joseph: ELIZA — A ComputerProgram For the Study of Natural Language Communication Between Man And Machine, Communications of the ACM 9 (1): pp. 36–45 (1966).
2. Güven Güzeldere; Stefano Franchi (1995-07-24). "dialogues with colorful personalities of early ai". Stanford Humanities Review, SEHR, volume 4, issue 2: Constructions of the Mind. Stanford University. Retrieved 2008-02-17.
3. Joshua, Quittner (1997-12-08). "WHAT'S HOT IN BOTS". Time Magazine. http://content.time.com/time/magazine/article/0,9171,987519,00.html
4. Chat between A.L.I.C.E and the chat bot Jabberwacky in Discover (May 03, 2007) http://discovermagazine.com/2007/brain/i-chat-therefore-i-am
5. Kaoru Sumi: Communication with a Virtual Agent via Facial Expressions, IJCAI Workshop on Empathic Computing, 4th International Workshopon Empathetic Computing (IWEC'13), Beijing, China (2013).
6. Kaoru Sumi, Ryuji Ebata: Human Agent Interaction for Learning Service-Minded Communication, iHAI2013, 1st International conference on Human-Agent Interaction, (2013).
7. Kaoru Sumi, Ryuji Ebata: A Character Agent System for Promoting Service-Minded Communication, Intelligent Virtual Agents, Lecture Notes in Computer Science, LNAI8108, pp. 438, Springer (2013).
8. Kodai Morita, Training on a Dialog System with a Character Agent for Communicating the Mind of Service, Graduation Thesis in Future University Hakodate (2013).
9. Kodai Morita and Kaoru Sumi, A Training System with a Character Agent for Communicating the Mind of Service. JSAI2014, The Japanese Society for Artificial Intelligence 2014. (in Japanese) 2014.

Building an English - Cebuano Tourism Parallel Corpus and a Named - Entity List from the Web

Lucelle L. Bureros, Zarah Lou B. Tabaranza and Robert R. Roxas

Department of Computer Science, University of the Philippines Cebu,
Gorordo Ave., Lahug, Cebu City, 6000, Philippines
E-mail: ohmworx3@gmail.com, zarahloutabaranza@gmail.com, robert.roxas@up.edu.ph
http://upcebu.edu.ph

This paper describes the building of a tourism-related parallel corpus in English-Cebuano language pair. The source for building the corpus is the web because it is rich with probable translation pairs, specifically in bilingual websites. The resulting tourism corpus will be used as a training data for a statistical machine translation system. The corpus contained information on the Philippines in the context of destinations, food, festivals, and other related concepts. From the parallel corpus, a separate named entity list on these contexts is generated. The results show that the procedures used were able to build a tourism-related parallel English-Cebuano corpus from the web and the named entities were correctly identified.

Keywords: Tourism; Parallel corpus; English-Cebuano language pair, Named entity list.

1. Introduction

Development has become the watchword of the present time. This is supported by the fact that all disciplines are finding ways to put in a specific contribution so as to make development possible. Language is one of the many disciplines, which is continually explored to make the best out of it. The relationship between language and national development has always been directly proportional. Language is the key to unlock the door to affluence, thus bringing about the national development. Economically, tourism is a major contributor to the development of the Philippines, contributing 5.9% to the total gross domestic product (GDP) in 2011[1] and 11.13% in 2013[2]. Despite this improving tourism performance, the country still has to keep up with other ASEAN countries as it ranked lower than the other ASEAN countries in terms of its tourism industry's total contribution to GDP. Although the tag line *"It's more fun in the Philippines"* had become phenomenal, there still remains a wide room for development.

To make Philippines a friendly destination for tourists, communication should play a vital role. On one hand, Philippines is one of the few nations in Asia where English is understandable to the local folks, and communication may not be a major constraint in the first look. Moreover, the hospitable and English-speaking Filipinos make foreign people feel at home as easy as possible. On the other hand, there are 186 languages listed for Philippines. Of these, 182 are living and four are extinct. Of the living languages, 41 are institutional, 72 are developing, 46 are vigorous, 13 are in trouble, and 10 are dying[3]. With all of these languages spoken by Filipinos, a need for translation to an intermediary language spoken by many will aid in good communication between tourists and even with fellow Filipinos. Good communication always comes with increased productivity.

Nowadays, machine translation technologies are being developed in order to address language barrier issues. A machine translation system automatically translates text in one language into another language. One type of machine translation system learns from a training data containing parallel texts of two languages. These systems are needed for the development of the Philippine tourism industry. Filipinos will be able to express more hospitality and friendliness to tourists with the help of the translation system. Tourists will also be able to understand and appreciate more of Filipino culture, tourist spots, and even, the Philippine languages.

Language and language studies empower those who are engaged in them. With language helping out tourism, tourism is expected to become an even more important weapon in the Philippines' economic arsenal. Furthermore, through tourism, the country aspires to become a stronger player in the integrated travel and tourism industry of today.

2. Review of Related Works

Parallel corpus, also known as parallel text, bilingual corpus, bilingual text, or bitext, plays a central role of today's language studies and processes. It is a collection of texts paired with its translation into a second language[4]. It is used as training data for statistical machine translation systems. Aside from this, parallel corpus is also used in cross language information retrieval, word sense disambiguation, bilingual terminology extraction, and induction of tools across languages[5]. As of today, there are several studies and researches pertaining to parallel corpus and its related topics such as building the parallel corpus, its source of parallel texts, and its observable applications addressing language problems.

Resnik and Smith, in their paper entitled The Web as a Parallel Corpus, described a technique of locating and extracting English-Chinese parallel texts from the web[6]. The idea that web page authors tend to use the same document structures when presenting the same contents in two different languages is used in locating pages which may be mutual translations. They found three major problems in doing the research[6]. First, the parallel texts from the web are available only in a few language pairs. With this, it will be hard to search the web for parallel text in new language pairs. Second, very large web-based parallel texts collections are not available to the community. Third, the web-based collections are difficult to distribute because of some legal issues involved in distributing contents of the web pages.

Bharati and his colleagues described an algorithm for English to Hindu sentence alignment using lexical information of the corpus and available lexical resources of the source and target languages[7]. The algorithm applies the rule of one-to-one mapping of sentences, which means once a source sentence is already paired to a target sentence, it can no longer be paired to any other target sentences. The algorithm is language independent and also addresses the problem of omissions and insertions of texts, which is a major concern in using a statistical algorithm and is based on sentence lengths such as the one employed in Gale and Church algorithm[8].

Toth and his colleagues used Named Entity Recognition in their implementation of sentence alignment hybrid algorithm[9]. Their alignment algorithm works with the help of exact anchors. They considered named entities as good anchors for their alignment. The features used to identify named entities using a supervised learning algorithm include words in the sentence, their corresponding part of speech tags, and ratios of capitalized and in lowercase words. This named entity system was trained on a subcorpus of the Reuters Corpus which consists of news articles from 1996, thus containing texts from domains ranging from sports to politics and to economy.

From the different literature, three major points in building a parallel corpus were generalized. These points are locating of bilingual sites from the web, extracting of bilingual texts, and aligning these texts to retrieve sentence translation pairs. These related works were used in building parallel corpus in the English-Spanish and English-Hindu language pairs. The procedures in building these parallel corpora can also be used in building a parallel corpus in English-Cebuano language pair in the tourism domain. The implementation of Named Entity Recognizer for sentence alignment gives the idea of generating a named entity list from a parallel corpus.

3. Methodology

This paper presents our approach in locating tourism-related bilingual websites, crawling their bilingual texts, and aligning these texts to come up with a parallel English-Cebuano tourism corpus. Figure 1 illustrates the basic flow of the system. Included in this paper is the Named Entity Recognizer that is capable of extracting named entities from the parallel English-Cebuano tourism corpus.

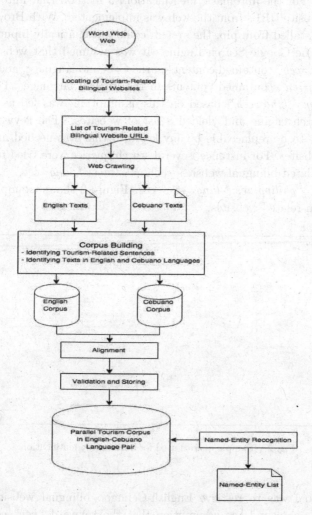

Fig. 1.   The system flow.

3.1. *The building of the English-Cebuano parallel tourism corpus*

Bilingual websites were identified and crawled from the web to yield English and Cebuano corpus. Then pre-processing was implemented to prepare the pair of sentences for text alignment. The aligned English and Cebuano sentences comprised the parallel English-Cebuano tourism corpus.

The list of bilingual websites was both automatically and manually identified. For the automatic identification, a method that automatically fetched website URLs from the web was implemented. With Browser from Splinter installed from pip, the system could automatically input a search query on the Google Search Engine. It was assumed that website URLs with *"lang=ceb"* contained contents in the Cebuano language, and the ones with *"lang=en"* contained contents in the English language. The search query *"key: *lang=ceb,"* based on this assumption, was fed as an input to the search engine and yielded a list of websites. The keyword *"key"* was meant to be replaceable by any keyword that was needed in order to specify websites. For instance, several search queries were tried to retrieve tourism-related bilingual websites such as *"travel:* lang=ceb,"* *"tourism:* lang=ceb,"* *"philippines:* lang=ceb,"* etc. Figure 2 shows example queries for tourism-related websites.

Fig. 2. Sample queries used for automatic identification.

The goal was to retrieve English-Cebuano bilingual websites in the tourism domain and the assumption that the keyword *"key"* covered all URLs. Thus such keyword was used as part of the input query. In order to retrieve the English counterpart of the collected websites, their URLs containing *"key:* lang=ceb"* were replaced with *"key:* lang=en."* The URLs with both Cebuano and English pages were retrieved and saved in a file. The web crawler was implemented to automatically extract the contents of the collected tourism-related bilingual websites, both their Cebuano and English texts.

Separate web crawlers were implemented for the manually identified tourism-related bilingual websites: *"http://www.visitmyphilippines.com/,"* which was under the domain of Department of Tourism; and *"http://justwandering.org/"* and *"http://www.pinoyboyjournals.com/,"* which were tourism blog websites. These websites contained tourism articles about the 16 regions of the Philippines in the context of food, destinations, festivals, etc. These separate web crawlers were also assisted by Python and the packages used by the automatic web crawler.

Before adding the texts to the corpora, these texts were split into sentences. These sentences would comprise the corpora. But in the alignment process, significant elements in each sentence should be identified. Significant elements are words, which are identified as nouns, verbs, adjectives, and adverbs[10]. The following pre-processing steps were performed to all English and Cebuano sentences in order to obtain the significant elements from each sentence. These steps were assisted by the Natural Language Toolkit:

(1) All sentence characters were brought to lower case using the function *sent.lower()*. This was done to eliminate case sensitivity.

(2) Punctuations were removed from the sentence. The resulting sentence was then split into words. These steps were done using the function *punc_tokenizer.tokenize()*, which yielded a list of the words used in the sentence.

(3) To identify the significant elements in a sentence, stop words should also be identified. Stop words are the frequently used short words such as prepositions and conjunctions, e.g., *"the," "in," "and,"* etc. For the English sentences, a list of stop words was obtained from the *nltk* corpus with the use of the function *stopwords.words('english')*. For the Cebuano sentences, a list of Cebuano stop words was manually generated by translating the English stop words to Cebuano. These English and Cebuano stop words were removed from the list of words used in the sentence, leaving behind the significant elements.

(4) The function *set()* removed the duplication of significant elements in

the list of words. The final list of words after the pre-processing steps were placed alongside with their corresponding sentences in building the parallel English and Cebuano tourism corpus.

The implemented alignment algorithm used both the statistical and lexical information of sentences in order to align sentences from the English corpus to their translations in the Cebuano corpus. A similarity function was used to calculate the score of each English-Cebuano sentence pair, which was used to determine if the pair was a probable translation pair.

As shown in Equation 1, the similarity function is defined as equal to the sum of their differences. This equation is a modified version of an existing aligment algorithm[10]. A lower similarity value of a pair of sentence meant that the sentences were having lesser differences, thus they were more likely similar or translations of each other. The following are the definitions of the components of the similarity function of each sentence pair (e, c) such that e is an element of the English corpus, and c is an element of the Cebuano corpus.

(1) $DictionaryDiff(e, c)$ is the number of significant elements in the sentence pair (e, c), which is not mutual translations of each other. This was the reason for placing significant elements alongside each sentence in both English and Cebuano corpora. To get the dictionary difference, each of the significant element in e was paired to each significant element in c, and using the online bilingual dictionary, "http://www.binisaya.com," the pair was checked if they were mutual translations of each other. Twice the number of mutual translations is subtracted from the total number of significant elements of the sentence pair (e, c). The number of mutual translations is multiplied by 2 to balance the equation because each mutual translation contains 2 significant elements. Equation 2 shows the dictionary difference component of the similarity function[10].

$$
\begin{aligned}
Similarity(e, c) &= DictonaryDiff(e, c) \\
&+ SignificantElementsDiff(e, c)
\end{aligned}
\tag{1}
$$

$$
\begin{aligned}
DictionaryDiff(e, c) &= SignificantElements(e) \\
&+ SignificantElements(c) - (2 * Translations(e, c))
\end{aligned}
\tag{2}
$$

(2) $SignificantElementsDiff(e, c)$ is the difference of the number of significant elements in the sentence pair (e, c). This was computed by getting the absolute value of subtracting the number of significant elements in e from the number of significant elements in c.

After solving the similarity scores of sentence pairs including e, a sentence pair (e, c) with the least score was chosen to be a probable translation pair. If (e, c) was already considered as probable translation pair, then both sentences e and c could no longer be paired to any other sentences to maintain an alignment type of one-to-one sentence. The result of the alignment process was a list of sentence pairs (e, c) with their corresponding similarity scores, which were considered probable translation pairs and were subject to validation. A sample computation of similarity scores of two sentence pairs is shown in Table 1, where the second sentence pair having lesser similarity score than the other sentence pair is considered as a probable translation pair and is subject for validation.

Table 1. Text alignment computation example of two sentence pairs.

Sentences	Significant Words	No. of Translations	Dictionary Difference	Significant Element Difference	Similarity Score
Many tourists love Cebu.	many, tourists, love, cebu	1	4+4-(2*1)=6	|4-4|=0	6+0=6
Nindot kaayo nga lugar ang Cebu.	nindot, kaayo, lugar, cebu				
Many tourists love Cebu.	many, tourists, love, cebu	4	4+4-(2*4)=0	|4-4 |=0	0+0=0
Daghang turista ang nakagusto sa Cebu.	daghang, turista, nakagusto, cebu				

3.2. *The Named Entity Recognizer*

The system also includes a named entity recognizer. Part of speech tagging was performed for each sentence which returned the word and its tag. This was needed in the implementation in order to ensure that part-of-speech tags of words were totally saved. Among all the tags saved, words with tag "*NNP*" were taken into consideration because this tag was for singular proper nouns, which was what the Recognizer was designed to look for. The list was iterated for words of this tag and was added to the list of named entities. This implementation retrieved single word named entities only. Consequently, an additional implementation for named entities composed of two or more words was also implemented. The following describes the detailed implementation for recognizing and extracting named entities composed of one or more words:

(1.1) For each word w in the returned list of the function *nltk.pos_tag()*, the tag component was checked. If the tag was not equal to "*NNP*", then w was disregarded. Iteration to the next words proceeded. Otherwise, further checking was performed.

(1.2) If the tag of the previous word was also "*NNP*," then w might be part of the previous named entity. With this, the previous word was concatenated with w. Then this new named entity would be added back to the list, replacing the last element of the list which was already part of the new named entity.

(1.3) Named entities that were composed of two or more words were also separated by words which were either prepositions or conjunctions. A maximum distance of two previous words of w was considered in checking a word in "*NNP*" tag. These word separators included "*of*," "*and*," "*in the*," "*of the*," etc. If a previous word within the set distance was a word in "*NNP*" tag, then this word and the word separators referred from the original returned list were concatenated with w. Then this new named entity was added back to the list, replacing the last element of the list which was already part of the new named entity.

(1.4) Otherwise, w was directly added to the list of named entities.

4. Results and Discussion

To get the language-pair English and Cebuano from the web, bilingual websites would be identified and crawled from the web to yield English and Cebuano corpus. The language pre-processing must be implemented to prepare the pairs of sentences subject for text alignment. The alignment result with English sentences and their corresponding Cebuano translations would comprise the parallel corpus.

A list of bilingual websites was generated from the method of locating websites using both automatic and manual approaches. For the automatic identification, several search queries were tried to retrieve tourism-related bilingual websites such as *"travel:* * *lang=ceb,"* *"tourism:* * *lang=ceb,"* *"philippines:* * *lang=ceb,"* etc. These queries located bilingual websites, but not all of them contained texts in the tourism domain. Although the tourism-related words used for the search queries appeared in some website URLs and contents, they only appeared a few times and were not the main topic or even related to the main topic of most of the websites. With the results of the automatic identification, the web was extensively explored to locate more bilingual websites of tourism domain. Three websites were identified using the manual identification: *"http://justwandering.org/,"* *"http://www.pinoyboyjournals.com/,"* and *"http://www.visitmyphilippines.com/."* These websites contained numerous articles about tourism in the Philippines, which included destinations, food, festivals, etc., with both English and Cebuano versions. Table 2 shows the collected text files for both approaches. The combined total number of sentences so far reached 33,339.

Table 2. Text files collected from both automatic and manual identification.

Quantity	Manual Collection	Automatic Collection
English Text Files	1,223	15
Cebuano Text Files	1,223	15
Average number of sentences per text file	28	73
Average number of words per sentence	19	10
Total number of sentence pairs	32,244	1,095

Websites with true Cebuano versions were only few in numbers given that Cebuano is not widely used as a language in the web. Most of the retrieved bilingual websites were powered by Google Translate, which is statistical machine translation solutions. Cebuano translations from websites powered by Google Translate were still very poor at the time of this writing, which could spoil the output of the machine translation system if they are used as training data.

The Named Entity Recognizer was tested using sentences. Out of the 120 named entities, 105 were identified by the Recognizer as named entities, where 92 of these identified were true named entities. The named entities incorrectly identified by the Recognizer included unfiltered titles of articles, which were written in upper case like common named entities. These titles were not in sentence structures and should not be considered in checking for named entities.

The results also included two or more named entities identified as one such as *"Cebu Transcentral Highway at Barangay Gaas in Balamban,"* thus reducing the number of identified named entities. The prepositions separating the three entities were considered as separators of a whole named entity where in fact these separators denoted location of one named entity to another named entity. The accuracy of the Recognizer was measured by getting the percentage of the correctly recognized named entities from the total number of entities, which was equal to 76.67%. Nevertheless, the Named Entity Recognizer returned a list of named entities from the tourism corpus and further restrictions were to be implemented to augment the accuracy of the Recognizer.

5. Conclusions and Future Works

Methods in building an English-Cebuano parallel tourism corpus and generating named entity list were presented. Tourism-related bilingual texts were extracted from the web and were pre-processed, which was necessary to align probable translation pairs. This work so far has built an English-Cebuano parallel tourism corpus with 33,339 sentence pairs. A named entity list, containing entities composed of one or more words, was also generated from the resulting tourism corpus with an accuracy rate of 76.67%. This was just an initial output and the task is on-going.

In the future, the web crawler for the automatic identification will be improved to retrieve more tourism-related bilingual texts. Bilingual websites, which are not powered by Google Translate, are to be explored further in order to retrieve more translation pairs from the web, which are of high quality. A more restricted implementation of the Named Entity Recognizer is to be worked on to improve its accuracy in identifying named entities. This parallel English-Cebuano tourism corpus, together with the named entity list, will eventually be fed as a training data for a statistical machine translation system.

6. Acknowledgment

This work is funded by the Commission on Higher Education (CHED) of the Republic of the Philippines for the ASEAN-MT project.

References

1. J. R. G. Albert, Contribution of tourism industry to the economy posts 5.9 percent in 2011. (November 2012).

2. T. P. Octaviano, Tourism contributing more to gdp. (March 2014), `http://research.bworldonline.com/economic-indicator/story.php?id=3521`.
3. P. M. Lewis, G. F. Simons and C. D. Fennig (eds.), *Éthnologue: Languages of the World*, 18th edn. (SIL International Publications, 2015), Date accessed: Dec. 15, 2015.
4. P. Koehn, Europarl: A parallel corpus for statistical machine translation, in *Proc. The Tenth Machine Translation Summit*, September 2005.
5. B. B. Megyesi, A. S. Hein and E. C. Johanson, Building a swedish-turkish parallel corpus, in *Proc. Language Resources and Evaluation Conference*, May 2006.
6. P. Resnik and N. A. Smith, The web as a parallel corpus, *Computational Linguistics* **29**, 349 (2003).
7. A. Bharati, V. Khrisna, R. Sangal and S. Bendre, An algorithm for aligning sentences in bilingual corpora using lexical information, in *Proc. ICON-2002: International Conference on Natural Language Processing*, Dec 2002.
8. W. A. Gale and K. W. Church, A program for aligning sentences in bilingual corpora, *Computational Linguistics* **19**, 75 (1993).
9. K. Tóth, R. Farkas and A. Kocsor, Sentence alignment of hungarian-english parallel corpora using a hybrid algorithm, *Acta Cybernetica* **18**, 463 (2008).
10. G. Sidorov, J.-P. Posadas-Durán, H. Jiménez-Salazar and L. Chanona-Hernandez, A new combined lexical and statistical based sentence level alignment algorithm for parallel texts, *International Journal of Computational Linguistics and Applications* **2**, 257 (Jan-Dec 2011).

Developing Course Content
for Micro-learning in Mobile Settings

Karen Pajarito and Rommel Feria

Department of Computer Science,
University of the Philippines, Diliman,
Quezon City 1101, Philippines
E-mail: {kbpajarito,rpferia}@up.edu.ph

The prevalence and continuous advancement of mobile technologies give way to the utilization of mobile devices for delivering learning content to learners. Education can take advantage of the benefits being provided by mobile learning, including self-directed learning and anytime-anywhere access of courses in mobile devices. Learners can use their waiting time (e.g. watching how to tie a knot while waiting for a ride home) to engage in learning experiences that can take place in seconds up to few minutes.

This paper presents the development of course content for mobile devices following the micro-learning approach using Micro-learning Course Authoring System or MicroCAS. The proposed platform consists of two main components: the web-based authoring tool used by the teachers for designing and creating learning content, and the mobile application, where the courses can be deployed and accessed by learners using their mobile devices.

Keywords: Micro-learning; Course content; Mobile learning; Web-based authoring; Learning objects.

1. Introduction

Micro-learning is not a new concept. Though it doesn't have a strict definition as multiple interpretations can be found in literature[1], this learning paradigm can be characterized by learning in a short amount of time (seconds up to a few minutes) and fine granular content. Only one point should be given per learning object; it should be narrow and focused. Since the lessons are short and will not take long to study, the learners can easily dedicate time for learning. There's no agreed accurate length of micro-learning experiences, but some literature[2–5] have suggested the maximum duration of 15 minutes.

In the discussion of micro-learning with respect to instructional design[2], splitting an e-Learning lesson in small units with 5-15 minutes of learning time distinguished the micro-level of instructional design to the meso and macro levels of learning content. The structure of these small units makes use of micro-content, which can be associated with a single Internet resource that could be referenced by a URL. Another literature on micro-level instructional design[3] relates these small units of instruction with small multimedia products such as short presentations, podcasts, or interactive simulations with a duration of approximately 1-15 minutes. The study has considered the file size of Web-based multimedia objects as download speed can be affected by the users' Internet connection. In the structured comparison made between micro-learning and macro-learning in terms of time and scope[4], the time spent in micro-learning activities should have a length of a few seconds up to about 15 minutes, which is a lot shorter compared to several hours of the larger e-Learning formats. In the case of micro instructional videos, the videos are always about 5-8 minutes long, and the longest is no more than 15 minutes[5].

Micro-learning is not meant to replace traditional learning materials. They can be treated as complementary learning resources that can help learners understand concepts, acquire new skills and solve problems. Instead of spending an hour studying a material telling and showing you how to tie a knot, micro-learning promotes the use of the direct approach in learning things. It focuses on what really matters, on what is really needed, and eliminates information that are not relevant to the objective of the learning content. With small bits of knowledge at hand, the learner can focus and easily go back to the lessons the learner wishes to repeat. The freedom to decide on which topics seem interesting and could be studied is on the learner. The use of mobile devices provides support to anytime-anywhere access to learning resources, which is one of the core properties of micro-learning environments[6]. Unlike the desktop computers, such devices and learning content could be easily moved or transferred from one device to another. Bigger amounts of content are harder to access instantly while on the move. Micro-learning deals with learning tasks that are broken into a series of distributed learning interactions[7]. Rather than learning everything at once, mobile applications supporting micro-learning would enable the learners to focus on specific narrow topics without consuming too much time and effort while they're on the move.

2. Related Work

Teachers use authoring tools to create and produce learning materials for their students. To produce educational slides and presentations, one of probably the most widely used authoring tool is the Microsoft PowerPoint application. The application comes with a library of various templates, layouts and other tools to give users an initial ground for their material. For those who prefer more interactive learning materials, there's the Adobe Flash application for creating videos and animations. All these materials can be accessed and delivered with the help of a computer and an application that will play the content.

In the case of authoring e-Learning content, e-Learning authoring tools allow the content creators and authors to develop learning materials without the requirement of programming knowledge and experience. These tools not only allow the creation of customized content, but also allow reuse and modification of existing contents. One e-Learning authoring tool that supports these features is called ViSH Editor[8], an open source web-based tool that allows creation of four novel interactive web learning objects (LO): *Flashcards*, *Virtual Tours*, *Enriched Videos* and *Interactive Presentations*. The authoring tool is one of the components of the ViSH e-Learning platform, an open-source e-Learning platform developed as part of the GLOBAL excursion European project. The site is available online and can be accessed through the Virtual Science Hub (`http://vishub.org`). Enhanced LOs produced and shared by users through the ViSH platform are called Virtual Excursions. The authoring tool is based on HTML5 and is based on the WYSIWYG (What You See Is What You Get) paradigm. It provides a user-friendly interface even to those who do not have a good IT background and support.

ViSH Editor follows an LO model defined by four levels of granularity[8]. The first level, is the atomic or most granular level, which includes various media files like images, audios, videos or flash objects, single elements such as paragraphs of text, documents or websites, and even more sophisticated elements like quizzes or web applications (e.g. SCORM packages). The second level corresponds to an LO called "slide", which consists of a collection of LOs from the first level. The third level corresponds to a combination of LOs from the second level, called "slidesets", which includes the Flashcards, Virtual Tours and Enriched Videos. The fourth and final level corresponds to one of the four new interactive web LOs, the Interactive Presentation, which can contain LOs from the third level.

ViSH Editor uses a slideshow format to present Virtual Excursion, where users can add, move or remove slides. A slide can be created based from the template selected by the user[9]. Users can also add different resources to the slide, which can either be uploaded to the system from the their personal computers or selected from the shared learning resource repository. Aside from the learning content in the slides, they can also create assessment items and add metadata to the Virtual Excursions. To be able to view and access the created learning content using the authoring tool, ViSH provides a fully client-side web application called ViSH Viewer[10]. Users need to be online to create and load Virtual Excursions using ViSH Editor and ViSH Viewer as both tools are accessible on any device with a web browser connected to the Internet.

Another learning platform similar to ViSH that allows users to create and edit learning objects through a web interface is called the J-GO System. It is developed for language learning based on lightweight learning objects and is designed for the Japanese language[11]. One of the main components of the system is the mobile application developed for the Android mobile platform. It is designed to work with the standard learning objects and display their content.

In J-GO System, a single learning object corresponds to a single lesson in the learning content, represented by a single XML file. Each object can contain a number of elements, which individually can also contain a number of smaller content elements, that are either word and character groups, fun facts and tests[11]. The content elements can be added in order to assemble a learning object. The objects and their metadata will be stored in the online learning object repository. The objects are reusable and can be referenced individually by their path or links to the original location. They can contain educational content consists of a number of elements, as well as multimedia elements such as images, audio and video. The repository was developed using PHP language while the learning objects are stored in a MySQL relational database.

To be able to transfer and store a copy of the learning objects in the mobile device, an XML file will be defined. The file will be then parsed by the mobile application. For this process, including the initial download of learning objects, an Internet connection is required. Once downloaded, the learning objects could be accessed and displayed in a web browser. The initial set of downloaded objects will be based on the learner's answers to the questionnaire presented upon first run of the application. The questions will determine the language the learner uses, the difficulty of the learning objects, as well as the length of the lessons.

Just like J-GO System, the Multimedia Presentation Authoring System (MPAS) produces e-Learning content for mobile environment. While the former is designed for language learning, the latter is proposed in order to create multimedia presentations integrating diverse media types including images, video, sound, and texts. MPAS provides an integrated authoring environment that utilizes media objects in creating synchronized multimedia presentation e-Learning content and allows authors to edit or reconstruct existing presentations based on Graphical User Interface (GUI)[12].

The proposed authoring tool uses Synchronized Multimedia Integration Language (SMIL). It is an XML based markup language based on the World Wide Web Consortium (W3C) recommendation for multimedia presentations. The authors don't need to know about the SMIL technology, nor need to have any programming background or knowledge in creating e-Learning content. Though MPAS system is composed of seven modules, the authoring part can be illustrated by two divisions dealing with slides and videos/audios separately, while the other two is taking care of the navigation and annotation of the slides. The authored multimedia presentation e-Learning content can be accessed by users on their mobile devices connected to the Internet. They can be stored locally on the author's device or make use of other e-Learning websites in a mobile environment[12].

3. The Development

In previous studies, some researchers used mobile devices to capture real-time and authentic learning-related scenarios[13,14] while others still preferred to work with larger computer machines (e.g. desktop computers) in creating learning content[8,11,12].

With the main goal of providing learners an alternative way to access and use learning content instantaneously with their personal mobile devices, and content creators a tool for producing learning content utilizing micro-content resources that can be used in different contexts, this paper presents the Micro-learning Course Authoring System or MicroCAS.

MicroCAS is a platform for the creation, delivery and presentation of micro-learning content for mobile devices. It is composed of two main subsystems: the web-based authoring system and mobile application. It is designed based on a client-server based architecture with the mobile devices representing the platform clients. Mobile devices such as smartphones and tablets can access the server through the mobile applications installed on them to be able to request and download preferred course content. The system architecture of the platform is shown in Figure 1.

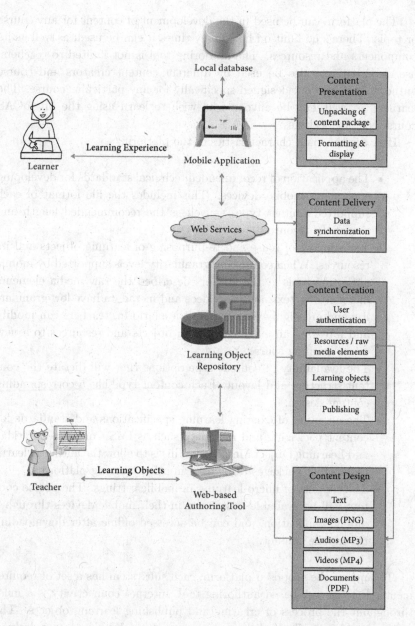

Local database

Content
Presentation

Unpacking of
content package

Formatting &
display

Learner

Learning Experience

Mobile Application

Content Delivery

Data
synchronization

Web Services

Content Creation

User
authentication

Resources / raw
media elements

Learning Object
Repository

Learning objects

Publishing

Teacher

Learning Objects

Web-based
Authoring Tool

Content Design

Text

Images (PNG)

Audios (MP3)

Videos (MP4)

Documents
(PDF)

Fig. 1.   MicroCAS system architecture.

The platform can be used in the development of content for any course or topic. There's no limit on how many times it can be used, as well as its components and resources. The authoring tool is not limited to teachers' use only, but can also be used by different content creators and course authors. It is also not designed specifically for any particular course. The learners, as well, can be anyone who wish to learn using the MicroCAS course content packages.

Here are the main characteristics of the platform:

- The application of recommended technical standards for developing content on mobile devices. This includes the file format of each supported content type, as well as the recommended length and size of the resources.
- The support of reuse and re-purposing of learning objects and its resources. When comparing granularity levels supported by mobile authoring tools[13], the authors described the raw media elements like pictures, text, audios, videos and metadata have low granularity, and are highly reusable. In the platform, teachers can modify and integrate all existing learning objects and resources to a new micro-learning course.
- The availability of content type options that will dictate the content structure and layout. Each content type has a corresponding content design.
- The adoption of existing learning specifications and standards for content packaging and metadata such as IMS Common Cartridge and Learning Object Metadata. This is to allow the authored learning content packages to be used in other learning platforms.
- The support of micro-learning in mobile settings. The course content will be available to learners in their mobile devices through a mobile application, and can be accessed offline after downloading the mobile content.

To support the proposed platform, each subsystem has a set of requirements. For the web-based authoring tool, Internet connectivity is a must throughout the process of creating and publishing learning objects. The teachers can access the tool through the use of a web browser on a desktop computer or laptop. For the mobile application, the learners have to be connected to the Internet as well to be able to install the application and download the preferred micro-learning courses to their devices.

3.1. *Content Design*

For the lifelong learners on the move, one of the design principles for content identified[15] is the micro principle. In this principle, learning content must fit into the fragmented time slots where content items are small, self-contained and granular, which are suitable for delivery on mobile devices. Just like in the proposed platform, content will be following the micro principle with respect to its subject, focus, length and size. A single learning object will represent a single lesson in the learning context. The resources used in the learning objects can be referenced by their URLs, thus can be downloaded separately.

To gain the attention of the learners, the micro-learning platform supports different resources and content types such as text, images, audios, videos and PDF documents. For each content type, a recommended file format will be supported. For the graphics and images, only PNG files will be accepted. The audio files are recommended to be in MP3 format while the video files should be in MP4 format. Both multimedia files should be 1 minute long only and cannot exceed the 3 MB size limit. The file formats chosen for the supported content types are recommended by various studies and learning organizations for use in designing mobile content. A web object can also be used in creating the learning objects, where the teacher can embed the URL of the web resource.

3.2. *Content Creation*

The main functionality of the web-based authoring tool component is to create and manage content. It is also used to assemble and create the course as a whole where course elements such as text and graphics will be used[16]. The responsibility of designing and creating the course is given to the teachers or any course authors. A teacher with basic computer literacy can use the authoring tool. Instead of providing a WYSIWYG editor, the content type chosen by the teacher will dictate the format of the course content. This approach will help the system to apply the micro-learning approach by structuring the content will limited amount of multimedia elements only. No two types of multimedia resources can exist in one learning object.

To protect the teachers' profiles and organize the course content authored by the teachers, the web-based authoring tool of the MicroCAS platform requires user authentication. A link to the log in page will be available in the home page upon entering the platform's URL in the web browser. Once the account details provided have been validated, the web application will forward to the dashboard page containing the most recent authored learning objects in the platform, as well as links to other modules such as user profile management and course content creation.

In the content creation module, the teacher can start with uploading resources that can be used in creating learning objects. The teacher can create the resources using external tools for capturing pictures, recording audios and videos and creating documents. Enhancement of the raw media elements using preferred editing tools depends on the teacher's preference before using them in the micro-learning platform. Once uploaded through the web-based application, a resource will be stored in a repository. It can be retrieved later through the authoring system and will be available to all the users of the web-based tool. Resources are not limited to a single use and can be re-used as part of the learning content being developed by other users.

3.3. *Content Delivery*

This module requires the combine effort of the web-based authoring tool and the mobile application. It contains the functions for executing methods for sending and receiving messages to and from the server. To access the course content developed by the teachers, the learners need to use their mobile devices. The communication between the server and mobile application will be through web services wherein messages will be in the form of XML-formatted packet of data. The XML format is widely supported by various mobile devices so the exchange of messages with the server will not be limited to a specific mobile platform client only.

When a client mobile application asks for course content, it will send messages to the server to request that required content package be delivered. The request message will contain the course information being requested. This information will come from the course listing displayed on the first screen of the application, which is also obtained from the server through web services. The requested course content package is created following an existing content formatting specification supporting established content packaging and metadata standards. The response message will have the packaged file containing the learning object, link to the path of the actual location of the resources, metadata information and an XML file containing essential packaging and content information about the micro-learning course.

The response message sent by the server to the mobile application contains the course content that will be downloaded to the mobile devices. All the files that will be received from the server will be saved locally. The mobile application has a local database designed to store the learning resources obtained from the content packages. Once it already has a copy of the course content, the mobile application will prepare and convert the content packages into learning content that will be formatted for display in mobile settings. Each course will be available in a single-page layout following essential mobile interface design principles. The design and format of the course will be according to the resources integrated with it. Almost similar to the content preview available to the authors developing course contents, the only difference will be on the position and size of the components of the learning material, as well reduced content information.

The course content developed using MicroCAS is not limited to the platform use alone. The web-based system will have an export feature for the authored content packages. This will let the other learning systems access and view the learning materials in their respective platforms.

3.4. *Content Presentation*

The mobile application is designed to access the course content authored by the MicroCAS micro-learning platform. To access the courses on an individual learner mobile device, the mobile application is required to be downloaded and installed. To cater a lot of users, it can be distributed via application store of the preferred mobile platform. If the target learners are a specific set of users, the mobile application can also be deployed through Ad Hoc distribution. In the latter type of deployment, the link of the application installer can be shared to selected people only.

Tools that allow the users to access the learning materials are web browsers and media players[16]. Both tools will be supported by the mobile application. Basically, the mobile application will serve as a course content player supporting various resource files such as images, audio and video files, PDF documents and web objects. The web objects will be opened in an embedded mobile web browser while media players will also be provided to allow playing of multimedia elements such as audio and video files.

The learner's access privilege is only limited to the viewing of the course listing and content of the downloaded courses. The initial display of the application will have the list of available courses published on the MicroCAS platform. No user account is needed to access the authored content; the courses are free and available to all the learners.

4. Summary

In this paper, we presented a platform for developing course content for micro-learning in mobile settings. The main objective of designing and developing this platform is the delivery of the micro-learning course content to mobile devices. We focused on the main modules of the platform concerning the content with respect to its design, creation, delivery and presentation. To summarize the process, the learning objects are created by the teachers using the web-based authoring tool, delivered to the mobile devices through synchronization of content packages, and downloaded content is then prepared and transformed for presentation to the learners through the mobile application.

Acknowledgment

This work is funded by the Engineering Research and Development for Technology (ERDT) Program of the Department of Science and Technology (DOST) and supported by the UP System Information Technology Foundation (UP SITF).

References

1. Z. Xinshun and W. Xiangling, A study on micro-learning in open and distance education under the fragmentation background, in *25th ICDE World Conference*, October 2013.
2. M. Kerres, *Microlearning as a challenge for instructional design*, in *Didactics of Microlearning*, eds. T. Hug and M. Lindner (Waxmann, 2006).
3. C. Snelson and P. Elison-Bowers, Micro-level design for multimedia-enhanced online courses, *MERLOT Journal of Online Learning and Teaching* **3**, 383 (December 2007).
4. I. Buchem and H. Hamelmann, Microlearning: a strategy for ongoing professional development, *eLearning Papers* **21** (September 2010).
5. H. Deng, Y. Shao, Y. Tang and Z. Qin, How micro lecture videos trigger the motivation of learners of coursera: A comparative study based on arcs mode, in *Educational Innovation through Technology (EITT), 2014 International Conference of*, October 2014.
6. S. Gabrielli, S. Kimani and T. Catarci, The design of microlearning experiences: A research agenda, in *Microlearning: Emerging Concepts, Practices and Technologies after e-Learning. Proceedings of Microlearning Conference 2005. Learning & Working in New Media*, eds. T. Hug,

M. Lindner and P. A. Bruck (Innsbruck University Press, Innsbruck, Austria, January 2006).

7. J. S. Beaudin, S. S. Intille and M. E. Morris, Microlearning on a mobile device, in *Proceedings of UbiComp 2006 Extended Abstracts (Demo Program)*, 2006.

8. A. Gordillo, E. Barra and J. Quemada, Facilitating the creation of interactive multi-device learning objects using an online authoring tool, in *IEEE Frontiers in Education Conference (FIE 2014)*, October 2014.

9. A. Gordillo, E. Barra, D. Gallego and J. Quemada, An online e-learning authoring tool to create interactive multi-device learning objects using e-infrastructure resources, in *Frontiers in Education Conference, 2013 IEEE*, October 2013.

10. A. Gordillo, E. Barra and J. Quemada, Enhancing k-12 science education through a multi-device web tool to facilitate content integration and e-infrastructure access, in *INTED2013 Proceedings*, 7th International Technology, Education and Development Conference (IATED, March 2013).

11. M. Milutinovic, A. Labus, V. Stojiljkovic, Z. Bogdanovic and M. Despotovic-Zrakic, Designing a mobile language learning system based on lightweight learning objects, *Multimedia Tools and Applications* **74**, 903 (2015).

12. M. Kim, C. Hong, D. Kwon and S. Hong, Multimedia presentation authoring system for e-learning contents in mobile environment, *Applied Mathematics & Information Sciences* **6**, 705 (2012).

13. B. Tabuenca, M. Kalz, S. Ternier and M. Specht, Mobile authoring of open educational resources for authentic learning scenarios, *Universal Access in the Information Society* , 1 (2014).

14. D. Kinshuk and R. Jesse, Mobile authoring of open educational resources as reusable learning objects, *The International Review of Research in Open and Distance Learning* **14**, 28 (June 2013).

15. X. Gu, F. Gu and J. Laffeyt, Designing a mobile system for lifelong learning on the move, *Journal of Computer Assisted Learning* **27**, 204 (2011).

16. O. Emeka, M. Charity, C. Philip and M. Onyesolu, E-learning system: Educational content delivery through mobile phones, *International Journal of Emerging Trends & Technology in Computer Science (IJETTCS)* **1**, 101 (2012).

Training to Pitch in Baseball Using Visual and Aural Effects

Yuki Tsukamoto and Kaoru Sumi

The Graduate School of Future University Hakodate,
Hakodate, Hokkaido, Japan
E-mail: kaoru.sumi@acm.org

This paper proposes a system that helps improve children's pitching form in baseball to improve throwing speed. The system uses Microsoft Kinect for motion sensing, onomatopoeia to teach users the timing of a pitch, and visual and aural effects to motivate them. The effectiveness of the system was tested through an experiment involving children as subjects. We also investigated how the impressions of visual and aural effects that effectively improve users' throwing speed by conducting an experiment using subjects.

Keywords: sports training, throwing, serious game, onomatopoeia, visual and sound effect.

1. Introduction

The average throwing distances recorded by children in baseball have recently declined to their lowest levels on record, according to a report released by the Japanese Ministry of Education, Culture, Sports, Science and Technology (2013). According to national children's physical fitness records, the average throwing distance in baseball for a male child in 1981 was 34.8 m; by contrast, this declined to 28.4 m in 2013. Likewise in 1981, the average throwing distance for a female child was 20.8 m, but had declined to 16.9 m by 2013.

Many children who are not skilled at sports feel self-conscious about being unable to perform as well as others. If they think themselves poor at sports, they are likely to seek out fewer opportunities to participate.

In past research, we developed a system to improve children's pitching form in baseball by encouraging them to think that sports are easy and enjoyable [1]. In related studies, sample movement and a first-person perspective for effective motion training [2] and anticipation in tennis were examined using realistic film simulations, movement-based response measures, and a portable eye movement recording system [3]. In sports, learning every part of the movement involved in a physical action is an effective training procedure [4].

Instruction by onomatopoeia has long been carried by out boys' baseball teams in Japan. We think that this is useful to teach children the rhythms involved in sports [5]. We proposed a pitching learning system that involved learning by example through onomatopoeia.

Serious games are defined as simulations of real-world events or processes designed to solve a problem. They are not intended solely for entertainment, but also to train or educate users [6]–[8]. Such games are applied over a wide range of uses because they have entertainment characteristics and hence the power to attract people. Game-based learning [9] and educational games are intended for educational purposes. Edutainment [10] means any entertainment content designed to educate as well as entertain. Gamification [11]–[13] is the use of game thinking and game mechanics in a non-game context to engage users and solve problems. Persuasive gaming [14] is a new initiative that deliberately uses games in rhetorical form to explore issues, or as a means of advocacy to encourage action and persuade people to see the world differently.

In this study, we develop a serious game for elementary school children to study pitching forms and rhythms in an enjoyable manner. The game format should increase children's desire to learn exercises. We use Microsoft Kinect for motion sensing, onomatopoeia to teach users the timing of the pitch, and visual and aural effects to motivate them. Our system is intended to motivate children, including those who are not particularly good at sports, to exercise by playing sports.

2. Sports Image Training System for Pitching Form

The purpose of this study is to improve the throwing speed of child pitchers in baseball by developing a system to improve their pitching form. An improvement in throwing speed leads to an increase in throwing distance. Our teaching methods made use of onomatopoeia and visual and sound effects. Figure 1 shows the onomatopoeic words "*Su*," "*Gu*," and "*Pa*" as well as hand gestures. In case of throwing, a player holds lightly "*Su*", then grasps his/her fist firmly "*Gu*", and opens the hand for throwing "*Pa*". There are two reasons for using onomatopoeia here. First, it helps teach children about throwing strengths and weaknesses as mechanics. Second, it helps children understand images of throwing models. We developed a training system using Unity 4.6 and Kinect v2. Unity is a three-dimensional (3D) game engine used to easily create 3D games. Kinect v2 comes from a line of motion-sensing input devices used to recognize gestures and sounds.

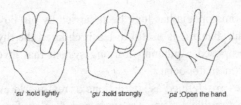

'su' :hold lightly   'gu' :hold strongly   'pa' :Open the hand

Fig. 1. Onomatopoeia *"Su"* *" Gu"* *" Pa"* and a fist image.

The teaching process begins with a child practicing throwing the ball in front of the Kinect v2. Then, a coach positioned near the system teaches the child rhythm and power (Fig. 2).

Fig. 2. The system and a coach.

The training system is described below (Fig. 3). We first describe the *Training stage*, which has two functions. The left side of Fig. 4 shows a real-time video of a user, and the right side shows sample movement based on motion data for a 23-year-old man with eight years of experience playing baseball. Unity's Mecanim function was used for the 3D motion data (bvh) in the sample. The system shows the onomatopoeic words used for guidance on the screen. A user practices by copying the sample movement. The coach then corrects the user's throwing rhythm. We chose two sets of onomatopoetic words to convey the rhythm of throwing:

"*ichi* (one), *ni-no* (two), *san* (three)" to teach rhythm ("*ichi*," "*ni*," and "*san*" are the numbers "one," "two," and "three" in Japanese), and "*su, gu, pa*" to accompany lessons on throwing strengths and weaknesses.

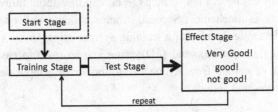

Fig. 3. Transition of screens.

Fig. 4. Training Stage of the system.

The system displays the user's skeleton data in the test window (Fig. 5). The user's motion in the test stage is shown in this window.

Fig. 5. Test stage of the system.

Video and sound effects are incorporated in the Effect stage. The results of throwing training are shown in the system with the aim of allowing the user to discern the sample throw by the experienced player. The sound effects help develop a sense of deep immersion in the experience. The system shown in the lower-right corner of the window is shown from 70 to 90 randomly when a "very good" effect is produced. The number conjures image of measured value of a speed gun (km/h). The system displays exaggerated visual and aural effects (Fig. 6). The number shown in the lower-right corner of the window is shown from 40 to 60 randomly when a "good" effect is produced. The system displays normal visual and aural effects (Fig. 7). When a "not good" effect is produced, the system displays depressed visual and aural effects and no number shown (Fig. 8).

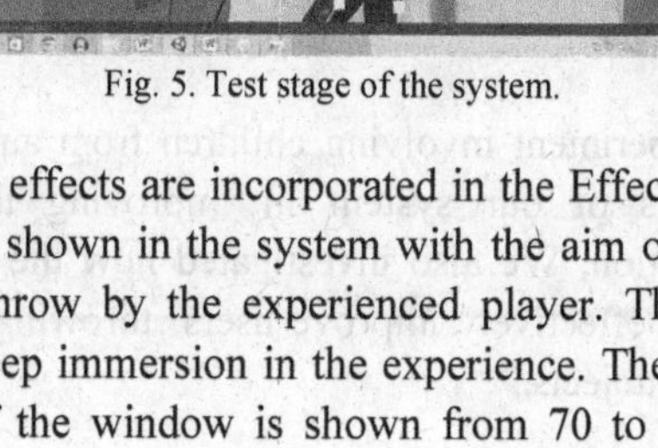

Fig. 6. Effect Stage *(very good)*.

Fig. 7. Effect Stage *(good)*.

Fig. 8. Effect Stage *(not good)*.

3. Experiment

We conducted an experiment involving children from an elementary school to test the effectiveness of our system in improving their throwing speed. Following the evaluation, We also investigated how the impressions of visual and aural effects that effectively improve users' throwing speed by conducting an experiment using subjects.

3.1. *Field Research at an Elementary School*

Our experiment involved two groups with a total of 24 male and female children. An effect group of 11 children (five male and six female) was subjected to significant changes in visual effects when they carried out throwing movements. The system first showed "not good" visual and aural effects. If they continued practicing, it subsequently yielded "good" effects. Finally, it showed "very good" effects. A non-effect group of 13 children (six male and seven female) was shown no change in visual and aural effects when they performed throwing movements, but instead were always shown "good" visual and aural effects. We conducted the experiment to determine whether pitching speed records improve the speed of throwing by comparing the results for the effect group and the non-effect group.

Our hypotheses were that (1) children's throwing would improve, (2) the throwing records of children in the effect group would improve to a greater extent than those of the children in the non-effect group, and (3) the children would be able to learn how to throw properly.

To compare exercise records before and after subjects' use of the system, we used a speed gun to measure throwing speeds. Subjects pitched the ball from within a circle 2 meters diameter and each subject's throwing speed was measured five times. We performed repeated measurements until the variation in measurements could reasonably be considered as error due to the speed gun. If after the fact records were significantly different from prior records ($\pm$ 20 km/h), the records were assumed to be in error.

We found that the average throwing speed of the subjects of our experiment was 0.85 km/h faster than that prior to using the system, and the fastest speed recorded for each subject was 1.12 km/h faster than before (Table 1). Table 2 shows the results for the effect group and the non-effect group. The average for the effect group was 1.29 km/h faster than prior to the use of the system. The fastest speed recorded for the effect group was 1.91 km/h faster than prior to using the system, whereas the average for the non-effect group was 0.56 km/h faster than before. The fastest speed recorded for the non-effect group was 0.57 km/h faster than before using the system.

Table 1. Throwing speed before and after using the system.

	Before	After	Difference
Average (km/h)	45.78	46.62	0.85
Fastest (km/h)	49.62	50.73	1.12

Table 2. Throwing speed of the effect group and non-effect group.

	Average (km/h)	Fastest (km/h)
Effect	1.29	1.91
Non-effect	0.56	0.57

Table 3 shows the results for the super-ordinate group, upper 5 children, and the subgroup, 5 children with the worst ranking in both prior and after the records. The average for the subgroup was 2.6 km/h faster than before the use of the system, whereas the average for the super-ordinate group was 0.5 km/h slower than before. These results show that the system has potential for effectively training children to improve their sporting abilities.

Table 3. Throwing speed of the super-ordinate group and subgroup.

	Before	After	Difference
Super-ordinate group	55.3	54.8	−0.5
Subgroup	33.2	35.8	2.6

Table 4 shows the results for the male and the female groups. The average throwing speed for the female group was 1.8 km/h higher than before the use of the system, whereas the average for the male group was 0.2 km/h slower. These results show that the system has potential to be particularly effective for female children.

Table 4. Throwing speed of the male and female group.

	Before	After	Difference
Female	39.2	41.1	1.8
Male	52.4	52.2	−0.2

3.2. *Visual and Aural Effect Function*

The results of our experiment at the elementary school suggested that users' throwing speed can be improved using visual and aural effects. We think the impression of the visual and aural effects changes users' mind motivated as it seemed to improve their pitches, thus improving the throwing speed.

We investigated the impressions created by several visual and aural effects to determine the kind of impression effective in improving children's throwing. The experimental material involve 12 types of visual and aural effects, including effects used in our experiment at the elementary school.

A total of 11 adult subjects participated in the experiment. Having thrown the ball, they were shown the visual and aural effects, and were asked their impression of each effect. We used 10 Japanese adjectives (Table 5) as evaluation indices based on [14] through questionnaires.

Table 5. Ten of adjective items.

Comfortable - Comfortless
Natural - Unnatural
Fast - Slow
Getting a compliment - Getting accused
Cool - Uncool
Heavy - Light
Stable - Unstable
Dynamic - Static
Showy - Sober
Faraway - Nearby

A five-point scale that we used ranged from −2 (minus as negative impression) to +2 (plus as positive impression), with 0 representing the center of the scale. Table 6 shows the average score of each impression. We found that speed line2 was associated with the impressions fast, cool, and faraway.

Handclap was strongly associated with comfortable and getting a compliment, phoenix with cool, showy, and faraway, and faraway with natural and faraway.

Table 6. The average score of each impression.

Comfortable	Natural	Fast	Getting a compliment	Cool
handclap(=1.45)	faraway(=1.36)	speed line2(=1.18)	handclap(=2.0)	phoenix(=1.09)
phoenix(=1.09)	happy(=0.63)	electricbeam(=1.09)	happy(=1.55)	speed-line2(=1.09)
happy(=0.82)	handclap(=0.45)	handclap(=0.82)	speed line1(=1.09)	frozen ball(0=.82)
Heavy	Stable	Dynamic	Showy	Faraway
blocks(=1.36)	happy(=1.18)	speed line1(=1.45)	phoenix(=1.45)	phoenix(=1.27)
rocket(=1.27)	faraway(=1.09)	phoenix(=1.45)	speed line2(=1.09)	faraway(=1.27)
fireball(=0.91)	handclap(=0.82)	speed line2(=0.82)	speed line1(=1.0)	speed line2(=1.27)

Fig. 9. *normal*;
The animation of a ball being thrown accompanied by a corresponding sound.

Fig. 10. *speed line1*;
The animation of a ball with speed lines accompanied by the sound of a ball being thrown, as well as cheering and applause.

Fig. 11. *break wall*;
The animation of a ball breaking a wall accompanied by the sound of a wall breaking.

Fig. 12. *electric ball*;
The animation of lightning accompanied by the sound of electricity.

190

Fig. 13. *faraway*;

The animation of a parabolic ball accompanied by the sound of a thrown ball.

Fig. 14. *fireball*;

The animation of a ball of fire accompanied by the sound of flaring up.

Fig. 15. *phoenix*;

The animation of a flying phoenix accompanied by the sound of flaring up.

Fig. 16. *cheer voice*;

The animation of a ball in a straight line accompanied by the sound of a thrown ball, as well as cheering and applause.

Fig. 17. *rocket*;

The animation of a rocket that bursts by flying into a wall accompanied by the sound of flaring up.

Fig. 18. *hand clap*;

The animation of a ball in a straight line along with people shouting and applauding, accompanied by the sound of a thrown ball, and cheering and applause.

Fig. 19. *frozen ball*;
The animation of a frozen ball thrown against a wall accompanied by the sound of breaking through the ice.

Fig. 20. *speed line2*;
The animation of a ball in a straight line accompanied by the sound of a thrown a ball, and cheering and applause.

4. Discussion

In this paper, we proposed a system to improve children's pitching form in baseball in order to improve throwing speed by using motion sensing, onomatopoeia, and visual and aural effects. We conducted an experiment involving children as subjects to test our system. We compared the average speeds of the effect group and non-effect group, the super-ordinate group and subgroup, and the male and female groups before and after the use of the system. The average and fastest speeds recorded for all groups were greater than prior to using the system. These results show that system can help users improve throwing speed.

We found that the average throwing speed of the subgroup was faster than before using the system, whereas the average speed of the super-ordinate group was slower than before. This suggests that the system can use onomatopoeia as well as visual and aural effects to improve the throwing speed among children with poor sports skills. We think that children who are poor at sports have more room for improvement.

The average speed for the female group was higher than before using the system, whereas that for the male group was lower than before. The system was thus more effective for female children. According to [15], female children are superior to male children in their ability to perform rhythmic ability test. We thus think that the recorded speeds for male and female children were different because we used onomatopoetic rhythmic training in the system. The results suggest that the system varies in its effectiveness for different subgroups of children.

We also conducted an experiment involving impressions of several visual and aural effects to determine the kinds of impressions that improve children's throwing. We tested the effects of 12 visual and aural impressions. The impression speed line1, which we used in our previous experiment, was "dynamic" in rankings by highest average score. A dynamic impression of visual and aural effects can contribute to improving throwing speed. However, other impressions may also contribute to this, and hence further research is needed to determine the precise causes of improved throwing speeds in our experiments. We think that the visual and aural effects change users' motivated mind such that they can throw better. Hence, the potential increase in their motivation to perform well also requires further research. We will continue to investigate the kinds of factors contributive to effective throwing among children in baseball.

5. Conclusion

This paper proposes a system that helps improve children's pitching form in baseball to improve throwing speed. The effectiveness of the system was tested through an experiment involving children as subjects.

References

1. Yuki Tsukamoto and Kaoru Sumi, Study of a System for Training in Pitching Form to Improve Throwing Distance using Kinect. JSAI2014, The Japanese Society for Artificial Intelligence 2014. pp. 178–182 (in Japanese) 2014.
2. Ungyeon Yang, Gerard Jounghyun Kim , Implementation and Evaluation of "Just Follow Me": An Immersive, VR-Based, Motion-Training System, Presense, Vol. 111 No. 3, pp. 304–323 (2006).
3. A. Mark Williams., Paul Ward, John M, Knowles and Nicholas J. Smeeton, 2003. Anticipation skill in a real-world task: Measurement, training, and transfer in tennis, Journal of Experimental Psychology Applied, 01/2003; 8(4):259-70.
4. Manfred Grosser and August Neumaier, Techniktraining. Theorie und Praxis aller Sportarten, BLV Buchverlag GmbH & Co. (1996).
5. Fujino, Y. and Yamada, T. (2006). Development of a "Japanese Sports Onomatopoeias" Computerized Dictionary for Understanding of Subtle Movement. In E. Pearson & P. Bohman (Eds.), Proceedings of EdMedia: World Conference on Educational Media and Technology 2006 (pp. 1034–

1041). Association for the Advancement of Computing in Education (AACE).

6. Abt, C., Serious Games, 1970. New York: The Viking Press.

7. Aldrich, Clark, The Complete Guide to Simulations and Serious Games, 2009. Pfeiffer. p. 576. ISBN 0-470-46273-6.

8. Reeves, Byron; Reed, J. Leighton: Total Engagement: Using Games and Virtual Worlds to Change the Way People Work and Businesses Compete, 2009. Boston: Harvard Business School Publishing.

9. Marc Prensky: Digital Game-Based Learning, 2007. Paragon House.

10. IE Hewitt: Edutainment - How to Teach English with Fun and Games, 2006. Language Direct.

11. Zichermann, Gabe, Cunningham, Christopher, 2011. "Introduction". Gamification by Design: Implementing Game Mechanics in Web and Mobile Apps (1st ed.). Sebastopol, California: O'Reilly Media. p. xiv. ISBN 1449315399. Retrieved.

12. Ab Huotari, Kai; Hamari, Juho, Defining Gamification - A Service Marketing Perspective, 2012. Proceedings of the 16th International Academic MindTrek Conference 2012, Tampere, Finland, October 3–5.

13. Sebastian Deterding, Dan Dixon, Rilla Khaled, and Lennart Nacke, 2011. "From game design elements to gamefulness: Defining "gamification"". Proceedings of the 15th International Academic MindTrek Conference. pp. 9–15.

14. Ian Bogost, Persuasive Games, 2010. The Expressive Power of Videogames, The MIT Press.

15. Tadahiko Fukuda, Ryouko Fukuda, 2009, "Ningen kougaku gaido: Kansei wo kagakusuru houhou", "Ergonomics guide: How to scientific sensibility", Tokyo Saiensu Sha (in Japanese).

16. Elisana Pollatou, Konstantina Karadimou & Vasilios Gerodimos, 2005. Gender differences in musical aptitude, rhythmic ability and motor performance in preschool children, Early Child Development and Care, Volume 175, Issue 4, pp. 361–369.

Profiling Moodle Servers for Usage and Activity

Dominique Gerald Cimafranca and Novie Joy Pelobello

Computer Studies Cluster, Ateneo de Davao University,
Davao City, Philippines
E-mail: dgmcimafranca@addu.edu.ph

Moodle is a web-based content management system used for distance learning. Ateneo de Davao (AdDU) introduced Moodle at the college level in 2011 and the service has been available to all units and departments since then. With over two years of activity logs and fully populated course modules, this study set out to answer the basic question of the extent of utilization of Moodle in the university.

What this study found was a wide variance in the adoption of Moodle across different units and departments. For two operational Moodle servers, at least 64% of courses were unused on the first server and at least 40% on the second server. This study presents more detailed usage profiles, such as the types of activities in course modules and the usage over time. This study also found that the most active courses on Moodle were those that made use of automated quiz assessment components.

Keywords: Moodle, Online Learning, Log Analysis.

1. Introduction

Ateneo de Davao University officially adopted Moodle as a learning management system to supplement classroom teaching during the summer of 2011. It started as a project of the university's MIS Office alongside other computerization efforts. Per the MIS Office, more than 500 instructors across college, high school and grade school units have already been trained how to use Moodle since its implementation.

This paper set out to determine how instructors and students at the college unit use Moodle in their classes.

The data that supports these inquiries is taken from the databases of Moodle. Every action taken by an instructor or student on Moodle is recorded in its database. Resources such as notes and links and activities such as quizzes and assignments are likewise supported by database entries. These records can be processed and analyzed by programs and queries.

The Moodle database is split into multiple related tables, each table holding the data for a particular aspect of Moodle. Depending on the version of Moodle being used and additional software loaded on the system, there may be anywhere from 200 to 300 tables. The usual database system used for Moodle is MySQL.

2. Methodology

For this paper, the researchers requested the database dump files for the Moodle servers from the University IT Office. The college unit of the university had two Moodle servers, with host names moodle.addu.edu.ph, henceforth called the M server in this study, and daigler.addu.edu.ph, henceforth called the D server. The M server was put into operation on April 4, 2011 and decommissioned in October 2013. The D server was put into operation on June 14, 2012 and continues to operate up till the time of the release of this report. The M server ran the older and now deprecated version 1.9 of Moodle and the D server continues to run version 2.9, with updates.

Owing to the differences in versions, the M server had 213 tables and D had 303. Nevertheless, the basic tables for the two are essentially the same so that the same queries can be used.

Because of the complexity of the relationship between the tables of the Moodle database, some pre-processing was required to transform the data into the appropriate form to be used by a data mining framework. Below is an example of an SQL query that denormalizes or flattens data from two tables:

```
SELECT COURSE.ID, COUNT(COURSE.ID) AS STUDENTS FROM
MDL_ROLE_ASSIGNMENTS AS ASG JOIN MDL_CONTEXT AS
CONTEXT ON ASG.CONTEXTID = CONTEXT.ID AND
CONTEXT.CONTEXTLEVEL = 50 JOIN MDL_USER AS USER ON
USER.ID = ASG.USERID JOIN MDL_COURSE AS COURSE ON
CONTEXT.INSTANCEID = COURSE.ID WHERE ASG.ROLEID = 5
GROUP BY COURSE.ID
```

The query returns a list of all current active enrollments in a Moodle system. In order to produce this list, the information has to be reconstructed from four different tables: mdl_role_assignments, mdl_context, mdl_user, and mdl_course. The output of the query will be a list of all course IDs and the number of students enrolled in each.

Some of the key Moodle tables the authors analyzed for this paper are:

mdl_log

This table logs every possible action taken on a Moodle server. Each action is an individual unit performed by a user. This table consists of the time the action was performed, the user ID of the user, the IP address of the computer the user used, the course the user acted on, the module the user used, etc. This table is of utmost importance for understanding what the users are doing on the system.

mdl_user
This table contains the information on all the users on a system. Important fields in this table are the user ID, the user name, the full name, the email address, the date of first access, the last login date, etc. The **mdl_user** table is referenced by other Moodle tables whenever user information is involved.

mdl_course
This is the central course table of a Moodle server. It holds key information about a course such as its name, the course format, the number of divisions of the course, its date of creation, the start date of the course, and other data about how the course behaves (for example, whether it is visible and whether students can enrol in it.) **mdl_course** links to and is used by other tables in the database, such as **mdl_course_categories**, which defines the category the course falls under, and **mdl_enrol**, which tracks user enrollments in a course.

A module is a subsystem of Moodle that corresponds to a capability that the server can perform. Some modules are essential for administration, like the users module, the login module, and the course module. Some modules correspond to activities and resources that users can access on the system. Among the latter are the assignment module (for submission of assignments), the quiz module (for taking quizzes), the resource module (lesson pages and files), and page modules (reference text, instructions, etc.) Each of these modules has a corresponding set of tables that link back directly or indirectly to the **mdl_course** table.

By running SQL queries against these tables, the authors capture a profile of the courses on the M server and the D server, the users enrolled in the courses, and the behavior of the users. This type of analysis can also reveal anomalies in the data held in the databases.

Selection of these tables and analysis of their data follows the work of Romero (2008) and Casey and Gibson (2010).

3. Results

The **mdl_log** table can show how busy the servers were. Counting the entries from this table returns the number of requests handled by the servers throughout their active period. As the logs had not been cleared since the time they were commissioned, it is also possible to fix the date in which the servers began operating.

M server, active for 928 days, served 4,305,814 requests. D server, active for 491 days, served 2,810,654 requests. From this we can see that, on the average, D was 19% more active than M, despite having fewer courses.

These simple queries reveal aggregate information about the servers, but not why the figures are the way they are. To dig deeper into the data, the authors made use of more creative SQL queries, discussed in the remaining sections.

3.1. *Finding Active Courses*

A basic question the authors set out to answer was this: of the 176 courses in D and 910 courses in M, how many of them were actually used in classes? The authors set forth two criteria:

1. that an instructor should have populated the course with resources and activities; and

2. that students should have been enrolled in the course.

Criteria 1 is simple to determine, though not straightforward. Information on resources and activities in Moodle are spread out across different tables. Fortunately, they all link back to an identifiable course. For the purpose of this paper, the authors counted resources, assignments, quizzes, forums, and wikis.

Resources in Moodle are instructor-generated content. They may be a page of text, an uploaded file, or a link to web site. Each resource item is stored as an entry in the **mdl_resource** table. Moodle 2.x introduces additional distinctions to pages and urls, which are stored in their own tables.

Resources provide a telling indicator of course activity. Courses with several resources point to instructors who took care to add their own content to the site. The number of resources attached to each course may be determined by the command

```
SELECT COURSE, COUNT(*) FROM MDL_RESOURCE
GROUP BY COURSE;
```

The summaries for the M server and the D server, based on the number of resources, are as follows:

Table 1. Determining activity by resources.

Resources	M server		D server	
	Course count	Percentage	Course count	Percentage
0	475	52.14%	61	34.46%
1-2	106	11.64%	12	6.78%
3-10	105	11.53%	41	23.16%
11-20	104	11.42%	39	22.03%
21-30	56	6.15%	19	10.73%
31-40	37	4.06%	2	1.13%
41-50	13	1.43%	1	0.56%
>50	15	1.65%	2	1.13%

Courses with zero resources may be considered inactive. It means that the assigned instructors never bothered to populate them with notes and lessons. As a further distinction, the researchers also distinguish courses with only 1-2 resources as possible inactive too, that is 11.64% for M server and 6.78% for D server. By the resource criteria, some 52.14% of courses on the M server and 34.46% on the D server can be considered inactive for not having any posted resources whatsoever. If courses which have less 3 resources are considered inactive, the count jumps up to 63.78% on the M server and to 41.24% on the D server. Further, only 1.65% of the courses have more than 50 resources for M server and 1.13% for D server.

Is resource count a sufficient marker for course activity? Unfortunately some courses eschew resources in favor of activities like assignments, quizzes, forums, and wikis. The count for each may be obtained in a manner similar to that for the resources.

By counting activities instead of resources, the following patterns emerge:

Table 2. Determining Activity by Assignments, Chats, Quizzes, etc.

Activities	M server		D server	
	Course count	Percentage	Course count	Percentage
0-1	673	73.87%	67	37.85%
2-5	110	12.07%	14	7.91%
6-10	21	2.31%	13	7.34%
11-20	62	6.81%	45	25.42%
21-30	26	2.85%	21	11.86%
31-40	15	1.65%	7	3.95%
>40	4	0.44%	10	5.65%

In order to generate the total count of activities in terms of assignment, chats, quizzes, wiki, and forum, the authors performed SQL instructions per activity. For assignment, the SQL statement used is

```
SELECT C.FULLNAME, COUNT(*) AS ASSIGNMENTS
FROM MDL_ASSIGNMENT AS A JOIN MDL_COURSE
AS  C  WHERE  A.COURSE=C.ID  GROUP  BY
C.FULLNAME ORDER BY ASSIGNMENTS DESC LIMIT
10;
```

For quizzes,

```
SELECT C.FULLNAME, COUNT(*) AS NUM FROM
MDL_QUIZ AS A JOIN MDL_COURSE AS C WHERE
A.COURSE=C.ID GROUP BY C.FULLNAME ORDER BY
NUM DESC LIMIT 10. For wiki, SELECT C.FULLNAME,
COUNT(*) AS NUM FROM MDL_WIKI AS A JOIN
MDL_COURSE  AS  C  WHERE  A.COURSE=C.ID
GROUP BY C.FULLNAME ORDER BY NUM DESC
LIMIT 10;
```

Courses with 0 to 1 activities may be considered inactive. It means that the assigned instructors never bothered to populate them with activities like assignments, quizzes, etc. 73.87% of courses on the M server and 37.85% on the D server can be considered inactive for not having any posted activities whatsoever.

Comparatively, the D server shows greater usage of activities in its courses than the M server. At most 26.13% of courses on M use activities; on the D server it is at most 62.15%. Furthermore, the D server shows 37.28% of courses incorporating 11-30 activities.

Criteria 2 evaluates a course based on the number of enrolled students per course. One way is to determine this is to run a query that will list current active enrollments. This is an SQL query that can do that:

```
SELECT   COURSE.ID,   COUNT(COURSE.ID)   AS
STUDENTS  FROM  MDL_ROLE_ASSIGNMENTS  AS
ASG  JOIN  MDL_CONTEXT  AS  CONTEXT  ON
ASG.CONTEXTID    =    CONTEXT.ID    AND
CONTEXT.CONTEXTLEVEL = 50 JOIN MDL_USER AS
USER   ON   USER.ID   =   ASG.USERID   JOIN
```

```
MDL_COURSE        AS        COURSE        ON
CONTEXT.INSTANCEID  =  COURSE.ID  WHERE
ASG.ROLEID = 5 GROUP BY COURSE.ID;
```

This query reveals that for the M server, 679 courses have no enrollments and 113 have only one. If we eliminate these as inactive courses, then that means only 13% or 119 of 911 courses on the M server are actually being used. But is this correct?

In examining the courses that have zero or one enrollments reveals that many of them actually do have resources and activities. Of these, the course with the most resources and activities, ChE121 General Chemistry for Chemical Engineers, has 126 resources and 6 quizzes and 4 forums activities but zero enrollments! Twenty-four (24) others have 50 or more resources and activities.

Why would courses active by the criteria of resources and activities have zero enrollments? One likely cause is that the instructor reset the course at the end of the term, removing past students from the roster. The database snapshot caught the server at a time when these enrollments had been removed.

Counting enrollments from the database, therefore, is not a reliable measure to determine whether a course is active or inactive. The query only returns current enrollments and not past enrollments. This would serve if this metric were monitored periodically, but not as a snapshot of the database.

A better approach would be to check the number of unique users of a course throughout its lifetime. This can be determined by looking at the **mdl_log** table. As **mdl_log** records all activities performed on the server, each user who accessed a course can be identified. We can then count the number of unique users who accessed the course. The query to perform this is:

```
SELECT L.COURSE, COUNT() AS COUNT FROM
(SELECT COURSE, USERID, COUNT() AS COUNT
FROM MDL_LOG GROUP BY COURSE, USERID) AS L
GROUP BY L.COURSE;
```

Breaking this down by the number of people who have access the course, the results for the M server and the D server are:

Table 3. Unique users accessing courses.

Unique users	M server		D server	
	Course count	Percentage	Course count	Percentage
0	5	0.55%	2	1.14%
1-10	512	56.26%	52	29.55%
11-20	102	11.21%	14	7.95%

Table 3. (*Continued*)

Unique users	M server		D server	
	Course count	Percentage	Course count	Percentage
21-30	89	9.78%	9	5.11%
31-40	45	4.95%	24	13.64%
41-50	43	4.73%	37	21.02%
51-60	27	2.97%	10	5.68%
61-70	18	1.98%	7	3.98%
71-80	12	1.32%	5	2.84%
81-90	10	1.10%	6	3.41%
>90	42	4.62%	1	0.57%

Assuming that courses which have been accessed by more than 10 users are automatically considered active, then it can be said that at least 43% of courses on the M server and 70% on the D server have been used by students. This matches more closely with the usage as based on the number of uploaded resources (48% and 66%, respectively.)

What if resources (including activities) and unique users were used together to filter for active courses? The dominant determinant of such a combination in both the M and D server is the number of resources.

This raises the question as to what level of each to use. The researchers decided to set baseline minimums so that courses with more than 10 users AND more than 10 resources are considered active. These baseline criteria are arbitrary but seem reasonable, considering that these are the boundaries at which the courses seem to cluster.

Using these criteria, then, the active courses on the M server are 213 (23.4%) and 96 (54.54%) on the D server. These figures match closely the resource count, as seen in the earlier section.

What of courses with atypical figures? For instance, what of courses with a high number of resources, but a low number of unique users? Or vice versa, minimal resources, but a high number of users? Being atypical, they will have to be subjected to individual inquiry. However, the researchers posit certain causes for this:

If the number of resources are high but the number of users are low, then (1) it may really be a small class and thus far, at the time of the snapshot, used only once; (2) the instructor populated the course with data but did not actually ask students to enroll; (3) the course may not have been used for teaching a class, i.e., the instructor used it as a repository; (4) the course may be a system backup of another course. Some 50 courses on the M server and 12 courses on the D server have this characteristic.

If the number of resources are low but the number of users are high, then it is likely the instructor may have used the course for only a small portion of the class, e.g., a few activities or to distribute a few files. Some 112 courses on the M server and 14 courses on the D server fall under this criteria.

If the known active courses and the atypical cases are combined, then these comprise 375 courses on the M server (41%) and 122 on the D server (69.3%).

3.2. Activities on Moodle

Below are the breakdowns of the top performed actions on the Moodle servers:

Table 4. Breakdown of Activities per server.

M Server			D Server		
Action	Count	Percentage	Action	Count	Percentage
view	2,198,735	51.06%	continue attempt	933,381	33.21%
continue attemp	912,309	21.19%	view	894,683	31.83%
login	301,777	7.01%	login	203,805	7.25%
logout	134,938	3.13%	review	198,853	7.07%
error	130,406	3.03%	logout	103,730	3.69%
view all	125,403	2.91%	error	56,256	2.00%
upload	115,892	2.69%	save submission	40,259	1.43%
review	75,135	1.74%	upload	38,491	1.37%
view forum	28,537	0.66%	run	38,316	1.36%
view discussion	26,309	0.61%	view summary	35,107	1.25%

These figures were retrieved using the query:

```
SELECT ACTION, COUNT(*) AS S FROM MDL_LOG
GROUP BY ACTION ORDER BY S DESC;
```

The "view" action happens whenever a user loads a resource for reading. The "continue attempt" action is associated with a quiz, when a user moves on the next question.

What can be concluded from these figures? Quizzes form a significant part of the usage of Moodle in Ateneo. Quizzes were slightly more prevalent in on the D server than on the M server.

3.3. Usage of Moodle Over Time

By analyzing the log files of the Moodle servers, the researchers were able to get a profile of the usage over time. A first pass analysis can start with the monthly activity on the Moodle servers, which can be retrieved using the following query:

```
SELECT COUNT(*),
DATE_FORMAT(FROM_UNIXTIME(TIME),"%y-%m")
AS MONTH FROM MDL_LOG GROUP BY MONTH;
```

For the M server, the monthly usage breakdown, by number of actions taken on the Moodle server, is as follows:

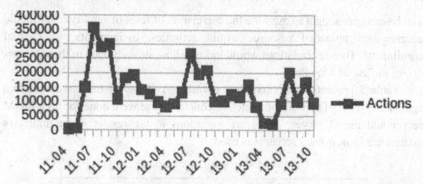

Figure 1. Monthly activity graph for M Server.

For the D server:

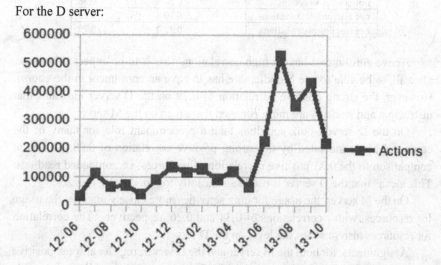

Figure 2. Monthly activity graph for D server.

As can be seen from the charts, Moodle activity typically peaks in July, followed by a small dip in August, another smaller peak in September, before dropping off in October. July and August correspond to the months for prelim and midterm examinations in Ateneo.

Activity in the second semester, on the other hand, doesn't fit any predetermined pattern. Looking at the M server charts, there was a tapering from October to March in 2011, and in 2012, a sharp peak into February before dropping in March.

3.4. *Relationship of Level of Activity to Moodle Resources*

The researchers sought to examine the correlation of level of activity of a Moodle course with uploaded resources, quiz activities, assignments, and actual enrollments. These correlations would indicate how strongly each of these factors drives the use of Moodle.

Table 5 presents the Pearson's r correlation values of the various factors against the level of activity of an active course. These were done for both the M server and the D server. There are variations in the results which indicates differences in how each server was used.

Table 5. Correlating against actions.

Variables	M server r-value	D server r-value
r of resources vs actions	0.34	0.23
r of quizzes vs actions	0.26	0.58
r of assignments vs actions	0.10	0.15
r of enrollments vs actions	0.40	0.79

Active enrollments have a high correlation. This is to be expected because, after all, to be able to use Moodle, one has to have an enrollment in the course. However, the strong positive correlation of 0.79 on the D server indicates that instructors and students are more engaged there than on the M server.

On the D server, quiz activities take a predominant role for many of the courses. This is indicated by the strong positive correlation of 0.58. This is in comparison to the 0.23 positive correlation of resources, i.e., uploaded readings. This means that the D server is used significantly for conducting quizzes.

On the M server, the usage for quiz activities more closely matches the usage for resources, with r correlations of 0.34 and 0.26, respectively. The correlation for resources also matches the level on the D server.

Assignments, for both the M server and the D server, register at weak positive correlations of 0.10 and 0.15, respectively. This suggests that, while assignments are being used in Moodle courses, these constitute a relatively lower proportion compared to quizzes.

4. Conclusion

This research started out with the basic question of the extent of the utilization of Moodle in the college unit of Ateneo de Davao University. After the deployment of the system, after the training conducted to faculty, was Moodle in fact being used? A snapshot of the database collected at the start of the research shows that the Moodle systems served over 8,000 users in 1,086 different courses. These courses and users generated almost 7 million requests. Whether this is meaningful and relevant to the original intent of a learning management system – this required some depth of exploration.

Enrollments and courses by themselves do not necessarily translate to active use of Moodle. Courses may be created but not used. Likewise, students may be enrolled in these courses, but still not engage in any meaningful activity. In the case of the older M server, up to 64% of the courses, or 581 in total, are simply dummy courses. This number is less on the newer D server, but still significant at 40%, or 73 courses in total.

The first step then is to establish some baselines as to what constitutes an active course. After looking at the patterns of data from the Moodle servers, this baseline for the school seems to be set at the presence of at least 10 activities and at least 10 enrollments. This is based on the distribution of the count of activities and users for courses, these being the boundaries at which the figures seem to cluster.

Delving deeper into the actual activity on Moodle, what is Moodle being used for? Breaking down the actions shows similar usage for both Moodle servers with slightly different percentages. Automated quiz activities are clearly a major driver for Moodle usage, but that seems more true for the newer D server than for the older M server.

The other major use of Moodle is for accessing course content. In this regard, then, Moodle is performing its intended function in the university. However, other features of Moodle, such as assignments and discussion forums, don't see as much use. Again, these choices are driven by the faculty who design the courses.

The figures for activity type on Moodle are further borne out by the correlation between the level of activity to Moodle resources. The Pearson's r correlation of resources, quizzes, and assignments vs. the level of activity on a Moodle server is an indicator of what the server is being used for. As it turns out, the correlation of resources vs. actions on the M server and the D server are relatively equal at 0.34 and 0.23, respectively. However, the D server shows a much higher correlation of quizzes (0.58) than the M server (0.26). Assignments, for both servers, show relatively low correlation.

The difference in the correlation between enrollments vs level of activity between the M server and the D server, 0.40 vs. 0.79 respectively, shows that the users have been more engaged on the D server than on the M server.

The time usage profiles confirm the level of Moodle activity. The monthly usage graphs taken over a 32-month period for the M server and a 17-month period for the D server show similar patterns. Moodle usage is higher in the first semester than in the second semester. There are also spikes in Moodle usage near the time of prelim and midterm exams.

The most striking takeaway from this study is the variance by which Moodle was adopted by different professors and instructors. The university initiative introduced Moodle to the community at large through training and enablement, but adoption of the technology was left to departments and individuals. While the effort bore fruit with some, a greater many tried it but sparingly or abandoned it altogether, hence the pattern revealed by this study. This highlights the critical role of teachers and course creators in the success of learning management systems. Thes are factors borne out in teacher-centric studies such Wong *et al.* (2014) and Stoyanov *et al.* (2014).

5. Acknowledgments

The researchers would like to acknowledge the University Research Council of Ateneo de Davao for their funding support for this paper, and the University IT Office for access to the data.

References

1. Romero C., Ventura, S. and Garcia, E., Data mining in course management systems: Moodle case study and tutorial. Computer Education (2008).
2. Casey K. and Gibson P., (m)Oodles of Data: mining Moodle to understand student behavior (2010).
3. Wong K. T., Hamzah M. S. G. and Hamzah M. B, Factors driving the use of Moodle: An empirical study on Malaysian practising teachers' perspective (2014).
4. Stoyanov S., Sloep P., de Bie M. and Hermans V., Teacher-Training ICT, creativity, MOOC, Moodle – what pedagogy? (2014).

A Template Matching Method for Explosive Gas Identification

Ralph Jason G. Caballes

Department of Computer Science, University of the Philippines Cebu
†E-mail: ralphjason.caballes@yahoo.com

Sandra Mae W. Famador

Department of Computer Science, University of the Philippines Cebu
E-mail: swfamador@up.edu.ph

This paper addresses the problem of gas identification from an output of a gas sensor. Gas detectors are capable of detecting presence of certain types of gases but sensors that accept multiple analytes like MQ2 do not identify them. Identification of the analyte is very important to properly handle explosive gas. Template for each analyte is generated and used for template matching. A Gaussian type noise embedded in the input is also considered. Sample templates and percentage of accuracy in using template matching are shown. Gases used in the experiment include LPG, butane, propane, methane, alcohol, hydrogen and smoke. Smoke, which is not explosive, is also considered and classified as part of other gas detected.

Keywords: Analyte, MQ2, Template Matching, Gas sensor, Gaussian noise, LPG, i-butane, propane, methane, alcohol, hydrogen and smoke.

1. Introduction

The goal of a Gas Detection System or GDS is to provide reliable and fast detection of flammable and toxic leaks before a gas cloud reaches a concentration and size, which could cause risk to personnel and installation. [1] A GDS makes use of a chemical sensor to detect presence of gas. A gas sensor from a GDS is a device that indicates presence of certain chemical composition and converts it to an electrical signal.

A chemical sensor is a device that provides information about the chemical composition into a useful electronic signal that can be used for further study. Chemical information may originate from a chemical reaction of the analyte of the system investigated. These sensors can be used in different areas such as medicine, home safety, environmental pollution and many others. Current application of these sensors are the Carbon Monoxide Detector, which detects the presence of carbon monoxide gas. The Glucose Detector used to measure the concentration of glucose in person's blood. A Pregnancy test, which is used to detect the presence of hormone known as chorionic gonadotropin or hcG which is produced by women's system placenta when pregnant, and many more. One typical chemical sensor that detects gas is the MicroQuest2 (MQ2) sensor. This sensor is used for gas leakage detection. It can detect gas such as LPG, i-butane, propane, methane, alcohol, hydrogen and smoke. There are other gas sensors available as well, such as TGS2620, TGS2620, TGS2442, and TGS832. These sensors are sensitive to Methanol n-Propanol, Hexane and Dicholoromethane. [2]

This study shows how to identify gas that is detected by a gas sensor using template matching. Its importance is to help identify some explosive gases.

The number of terrorist attacks employing improvised explosive devices (IEDs) has increased dramatically in the last 10 years. [3] These devices can be designed to use explosive gases to destroy humanity or the environment. Proper detection of explosive can lead to proper handling of the situation and can prevent enormous damages. This study is part of a bigger study on the detection of Improvised Explosive Devices.

The rest of this paper looks at related research, the method used in this study, the result of the method used and its conclusion.

I. RELATED WORK

In recent literatures, many papers talk about chemical detection, an example of this is "Detecting gases wirelessly and cheaply." This study was conducted by an MIT chemists, Timothy Swager. Swager finds a new way to detect hazardous gases and environmental pollutants wirelessly using a simple sensor that is readable by a smartphone with near-field communication capabilities. This new sensor is capable of detecting gaseous ammonia, hydrogen peroxide, and cyclohexanone, among other gases. The sensor developed in Swager's lab requires almost no energy and can function at current temperatures. The sensor used in detecting gas are made from a modified near-field communication (NFC) tags which is later on modified to what they called as chemically actuated resonant devices (CARDs). This research was funded by the U.S. Army Research Laboratory and the U.S. Army Research Office through the MIT Institute for Soldier Nanotechnologies; the MIT Deshpande Center for Technological Innovation; and the National Cancer Institute. [4]

Gas sensors are widely used by some researchers in conducting experiments in gas detection. One good example is the microcontroller based project that detects dangerous gas in the kitchen, leak in cars or in a service station and storage tank in the environment. The project is based on the detection of gas concentration from 200 to 1000ppm. It is highly sensitive in sensing gasses and is consist of heater coil which is added with resistance. The flow of the study starts from Gas detection then gas detected was send to an Analog to Digital Converter (ADC). Converted data is passed to a microcontroller ports for further proceedings. A driver communicates to a subsystem to which the hardware is connected. The driver commands an issue to a device like a buzzer to alarm if there is a gas detected. [5]

A paper on Haze Monitoring System in the City of Kuala Lumpur using Zigbee Wireless Technology Implementation used MQ2 sensor and PIC16F887 for data collection and Zigbee technology. The gases/haze detected by the sensors are being converted to a digital signal which is transmitted to Zigbee wireless technology to a personal computer. The Zigbee technology has an operating frequency of 2.4GHZ and suitable for indoor and outdoor communication applications. The data received by the Zigbee is processed to classify the level of air pollutant in accordance to air pollutant index. [6] A review on using gas sensor is being presented in Gas Sensors Based on Conducting Polymers. The paper focused on the sensing mechanism and configurations of the fabricated sensors by using conducting polymers such as polyaniline (PAni), polypyrrole (PPy) and poly (3,4-ethylenedioxythiophene) (PEDOT). These polymers are being used as the active layers of gas sensors. The sensors made from these polymers have many improved characteristics compared to some sensors that are made of metal oxides. This papers also tackles the different factors that affects the performances and disadvantages of these sensors. [7]

A review on Label-free biological and chemical sensors conducted by Heather Hunt and Andrea Armani, provides a brief overview of the different types of biosensors and their performance. They also talk about optical devices, surface functionalization methods to increase device specificity, and fluidic techniques. The paper gives overview on various optical transducers (Mechanical, optical or electrical) and its functions. The main goal of the paper is to provide the researchers best sensing unit that comprises an array of numerous devices with varying transduction methods and specificities that is capable of capturing the behaviour or signal of interest. [8]

Another review was made on Chemical Sensors for In-Situ Monitoring of Volatile Contaminants. This paper presents a study of different sensors and some technologies that are competent enough in detecting and monitoring volatile organic compounds. It focuses on sensors that can be used in geologic environments for long-term monitoring applications. The different sensors evaluated are the following: chromatography and spectrometry, electrochemical sensors, mass sensors, and optical sensors. This paper concluded that electrochemical sensors are the most viable sensor for in-situ chemical sensing. [9]

Another application in using chemical sensors is electronic nose or ENose. It is a device that can recognize chemical compound or elements. According to Dr. Amy Ryan, ENose can detect an electronic change of 1 part per million. [10] Many application of ENose are available worldwide, one of which is the Electronic Nose Based on Metal Oxide Semiconductor Sensors as an Alternative Technique for the Spoilage Classification of Red Meat. The goal of this study is to develop an ENose to control the quality of red meat. It uses Electronic nose and bacteriological measurements to analyse samples of beef and sheep meat. Principal component analysis (PCA) and support vector machine (SVM) based classification techniques are used in investigating the performance of the ENose. The system is capable of distinguishing unspoiled from a spoiled beef or sheep meat. The study used partial least squares (PLS) collaboration model to validate if the ENose findings correlates to the result of the bacteriologist. [11]

2. Methodology

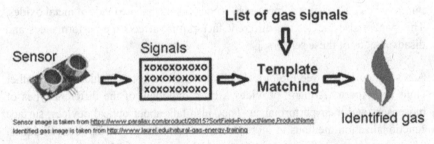

Sensor image is taken from https://www.parallax.com/product/28015?SortField=ProductName,ProductName
Identified gas image is taken from http://www.laurel.edu/natural-gas-energy-training

Figure 1. Flow diagram of gas identification using template matching.

Gas sensor, like MQ2 as produced by Hanwei electronics Co., Ltd., is a transducer that transforms chemical composition to a useful analytical signal as shown in Fig. 2.

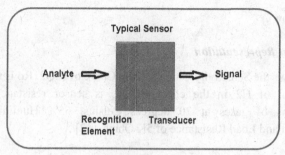

Figure 2. Gas sensor.

Different kinds of sensors are available in the market ranging from metal oxide to infrared. A gas sensor is a transducer that produces a decimal output. Most wide range gas sensors can only detect several types of gases but will not identify what particular gas is detected. This study used the decimal output of a gas sensor to produce a template.

Figure 3 below shows the flow diagram of the process:

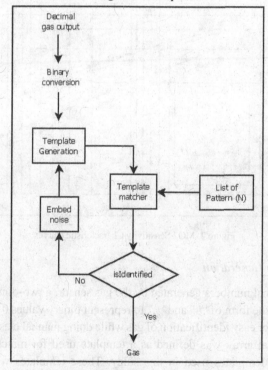

Figure 3. Flow Chart for Template Matching.

3. Discussion

3.1. *Element Representation*

Figure 4 shows the Sensitivity Characteristic Curve of MQ2. Ro is the resistance at 1000 ppm of H2 in the clean air, Rs is sensor resistance at various concentrations of gases at 20 degrees Celsius, 65% Humidity 21% O2 concentration and Load Resistance of 5K Ohms. [12]

In another study conducted by one of the authors [13], patterns were generated from the decimal output of the gas sensor. A pattern defined the characteristic of a certain gas. Figure 4 was one of the basis for pattern formation. Other patterns were derived from actual experiment of [13]. These patterns were used in this study to identify presence of specific gas.

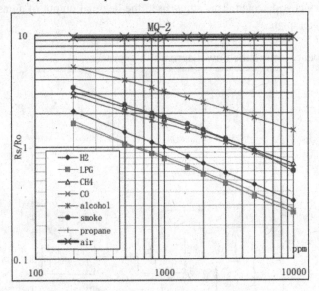

Figure 4. MQ2 Sensitivity Characteristic Curve.

3.2. *Template Generation*

From the decimal numbers generated by the gas sensor, a two-dimensional array was created in the form of "#" and '_', to represent binary values 0 and 1. "#" and '_' were used for easy identification of gas while doing manual classification. The two-dimensional array was defined as a template used for matching. Figure 5 shows sample templates used in this study. These templates were fed to the template matcher to identify the gas present in the environment.

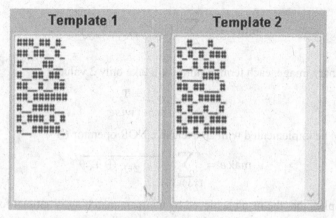

Figure 5. Sample templates.

3.3. *Template Matching*

Template matching, a method of parameter estimation is used in this study to identify the presence of gas such as LPG, i-butane, propane, methane, alcohol, hydrogen and smoke.

We define a template in a window as a discrete function, $T_{x,y}$, where x,y are coordinates of the points. Here, $(x, y) \in W$, where W contains coordinates of the points.

The use of template matching in an image requires rotation, translation and scaling. Given an image, $I_{x,y}$ a template $T_{x,y}$ will traverse through $I_{x,y}$ to get an exact match. In this study, rotation, translation and scaling requirements are not applicable. A two-dimensional matrix was created from a decimal output signal of gas sensor and was treated as image to consider additive noise.

In cases where the input is corrupted by an additive Gaussian noise, the noise has a mean value of zero and the standard deviation of σ.

For $I_{x,y}$ corrupted by a Gaussian noise, the maximum likelihood solution was chosen. In logarithmic form

$$\ln\left(L_{i,j}\right) = n \ln\left(\frac{1}{\sqrt{2\pi\sigma}}\right) - \frac{1}{2} \sum_{(x,y)\in W} \left(\frac{I_{x+i,y+j} - T_{x,y}}{\sigma}\right)^2$$

The input image is transformed to binary image to minimize computation. The minimization problem solution is given by

$$\min e = \sum_{(x,y)\in W} \left(I_{x+i,y+j} - T_{x,y}\right)^2$$

For a binary image, each term in min e will take only 2 values.

$$\begin{array}{ll} 1 & I_{x+i,y+j} = T_{x,y} \\ 0 & otherwise \end{array}$$

This can be implemented with an exclusive NOR operator $\oplus$

$$\max e = \sum_{(x,y)\in W} \overline{I_{x+i,y+j} \oplus T_{x,y}}$$

This implies that the result achieved by template matching is optimal for images corrupted by Gaussian noise [12].

3.4. *Identification*

From Figure 3, matching was made for each line and each array. Whenever a match was found, identification of gas was made but if there was no match found, another template was generated and traversed the same path as the previous template. If no match was achieved another pattern was considered.

4. Result

The result of this study is tabulated to see the efficiency of template matching. Template matching was tested to see if it can identify a particular gas. Table 1 shows sample patterns and sample templates to illustrate the method. From the table, Patterns represent the ideal and actual patterns of each gas type. Templates are those generated by the gas sensor and converted to array to be used for matching and identification.

We assume that Patterns (m,n) represent the gas signal values, where m is the pattern number and n is the gas type such as LPG, i-butane, propane, methane, alcohol, hydrogen and smoke. Template x is the template formed by the digital output of the gas sensor, where x is the number of template. The minimum size of template used in this study is 5x5. Matrix produced less than this size may lead to an error in gas identification. A template can have a bigger size but should not exceed the size of a pattern.

Figures in Table 1 are snippets of the actual pattern matching. Column 3 or percentage matched is the result of the experiment.

Table 1. Simulation results.

Pattern (m,n)	Template x	Percentage matched
| ```
####_#
#_####
###_##
######
####_
_#####
``` | ```
_##_#
_#_##
##_###
###_##
##_##
##_#_#
``` | 61.11% |
| ```
####_
#_###
_#_##
#_#_#
#_#_#
``` | ```
####_
#_###
_#_##
#_#_#
#_#_#
``` | 100% |
| ```
#####
#####
_####
#_###
_##_#
``` | ```
_##_#
#####
_###
###_#
####_
``` | 68% |
| ```
##_##
###_#
#_###
####_
_#_##
###_
_###
##_##
##_##
``` | ```
###_
_####
#_###
#####
_####
#_###
##_#
_##_
_##_
``` | 55.56% |
| ```
#_#####_#
#######_#
##########
######_##
###_#####
###__###
####_##_#
``` | ```
#__#####_
_####_#_#
_#_#_####
#####_
_#_##_#_#
_#__#_###
######_##
``` | 63.49% |

5. Conclusion and Future Work

This paper presents a possible way to correctly identify a gas as detected by a gas sensor. The use of template matching can identify the type of gas present in an environment. As seen in the Percentage matched column, there is a way to identify the gas from the output of a gas sensor. In one pattern, a 100% accuracy is obtained while in another pattern it has a 55.56% accuracy. 100% accuracy means a template matched one of the patterns that describe a certain gas. 55% accuracy requires another template to be matched. Since templates are extracted from the decimal output of the sensor, more templates generated means higher template matching.

Future work considers the use of more Artificial Intelligence algorithms to identify or classify gas present in an environment. Right identification of gas is necessary to prevent explosion and damage to human or to the environment. Output of this study is integrated in another study to attain the bigger objective, that is, to create an autonomous Improvised Explosive Devise Detector.

References

[1] NORSOK Standard S-001 Technical Safety – 4th edition. 2008.

[2] J. Srinonchat, "Development Of Electronic Nose And Program For Monitoring Air Pollutions And Alarm In Industrial Area" [February 2013]. International Journal of Computer and Electrical Engineering, Vol. 5, No. 1.

[3] Chu Yun, "Solid State Gas Sensors For Detection Of Explosives And Explosive Precursors" [2013]. Open Access Dissertations. Paper 119.

[4] http://newsoffice.mit.edu/2014/wireless-chemical-sensor-for-smartphone-1208. Accessed on August 03, 2015.

[5] K. P. Dewagan, J. Rajpurohit, "Multiple Gas Analyzer And Indicator" [July-August 2012]. S. R. Manihar, International Journal of Modern Engineering Research (IJMER); Vol. 2, Issue 4, pp. 2753–2755; ISSN: 2249-6645.

[6] K. A. Othman, N. Li, E. H. Abdullah, N. Hamzah; "Haze Monitoring System In City Of Kuala Lumpur Using Zigbee Wireless Technology Implementation" [July 3–5, 2013]. Proceedings of the World Congress on Engineering 2013 Vol. II, WCE 2013, London, UK.

[7] H. Bai and G. Shi, "Gas Sensors Based On Conducting Polymers" [2007]. ISSN 1424-8220.

[8] H. K. Hunt and A. M. Armani, "Label-Freee Biological And Chemical Sensors" [2010]. Nanoscale, 2, 1544–1559.

[9] C. K. Ho, M. T. Itamura, M. Kelley and R. Hughes, "Review Of Chemical Sensors For In-situ Monitoring Of Volatile Contaminants" [March 2001]. SANDIA REPORT; SAND2001-0643.

[10]   http://science.nasa.gov/science-news/science-at-nasa/2004/06oct_enose/. Accessed on August 03, 2015.

[11] N. E. Barbri, E. Llobet, N. E. Bari, X. Correig and B. Bouchikhi, "Electronic Nose Based On Metal Oxide Semiconductor Sensors As An Alternative Technique For The Spoilage Classification Of Red Meat" [2008], MDPI, ISSN 1424-8220.

[12]   http://www.seeedstudio.com/wiki/Grove_-_Gas_Sensor%28MQ2%29. Accessed on August 03, 2015.

[13] Famador, S. M. W. "MQ2 Gas Pattern Generation for IED Detection." [2015]. University Of The Philippines Cebu. Unpublished Manuscript.

[14] Mark S. Nixon and Alberto S. Aquado, "Feature Extraction and Image Processing" [First Edition 2002].

Crime Modelling and Prediction Using Neural Networks

Jonathan Albert U. Tumulak and Kurt Junshean P. Espinosa

Department of Computer Science,
University of the Philippines Cebu,
Cebu City, Philippines
E-mail: {jutumulak, kpespinosa}@up.edu.ph

With the increase of urbanization in cities, there is also the rise of crime incidence. It is important for the police force to stay ahead in proactive policing. In this paper, the researcher presents a simple approach to predict crime in a geographic space using grid thematic mapping and neural networks. The study particularly focuses on the possibility of using historical crime data in predicting future crime incidents. The dataset is divided into monthly, weekly, and daily data called as a snapshot for training the model. The study area, Cebu City, is divided into a square grid of various sizes and crime incidents, from each cell in the grid of each snapshot, will then be recorded. This data is then fed into the neural network to predict possible areas where crime would happen for the next time interval. Initial results have shown that the model is accurate enough to predict crime areas when the data snapshot is divided monthly and weekly and grid size is set to a large size of about 1000 by 1000 meters and 750 by 750 meters. The best model was able to yield an F1 score of 0.95. Although the created model is simple, this can be a stepping stone to further crime modelling and prediction studies. This tool can be used to aid decisions and policy-making in the deployment of police resources throughout the city.

Keywords: crime; hotspot; neural networks.

1. Introduction

1.1. *Background*

Throughout human civilization, crimes have been present ever since. This has been a challenging dilemma in society that must be dealt with accordingly with solutions and methodologies which would enable law enforcement to function with utmost efficiency. According to Bogomolov *et al.* (2014), crimes have affected the "quality of life" and the "economic development of a society". Clearly, something needs to be done in order to prevent, and eventually, eradicate all forms of crimes in a society.

A crucial factor in solving crimes is recognizing that a crime "takes place at some location" (Chainey, Tompson and Uhlig, 2008). This principle presupposes that felonies are not random in nature, and that they are likely to "concentrate at particular places" in which subject places have a higher rate of criminality. These concentrations are commonly called as hotspots, areas that have high numbers of crime. This technique is popularly used by law enforcement, especially in Cebu City, to identify areas with high crime volumes. Using this data, it can help in deciding where to deploy police resources.

The study will investigate whether or not it would be possible to predict where the next crime hotspots would be given data on previous hotspots. It will also answer if it would be possible to specifically predict where the next crime would happen. With this information, the police would be able to effectively deploy and prevent any crime that may happen in an area. More so, the police would be more productive based on their ability to respond in a timely manner, and more importantly, as a deterrence in discouraging would be criminals.

2. Literature Review

The study called "Artificial Neural Networks and Crime Mapping" (Olligschlaeger, 1997) aims to develop a system by using Geographic Information System (GIS) together with artificial neural networks to pinpoint new upcoming drug hotspot areas. 911 calls were used as indicators to predict emerging street-level drug markets. The calls include: weapon-related calls, robbery calls, and assault-related calls. A map of the city of Pittsburgh with all the call data was then divided into a grid with a size of 2150 square feet for each cell. In each cell, the number of calls per month was obtained. Their data spanned for 3 years from 1990 to 1992. The proportion of residential to commercial property was also included as an indicator variable. Also, drug dealing was a seasonal affair, so a seasonal index was added depending on the month. Three methods were used to estimate the "one-step-ahead" forecasting model. One was an ordinary least squares regression with six independent variables for each cell in the neighborhood. Another was a neural network similar to the "Game of Life" neural network with constant weights, and a similar neural network was also used as a model, but with spatially varying input-to-hidden unit weights. Data from 1990 to 1991 was used to estimate regression parameters and as the training set. The 1992 data were used as the test set. C programming language was used in implementing the model and run on SPARC 20 workstation. Learning rate was set to 0.0001 with maximum of 15000 iterations. The researcher found that the regression model and constant weight network performed similarly, but the varying weight model did significantly better at modelling the hotspot areas compared to real actual hotspot areas.

Chainey *et al.* (2008) remarked that Hotspot mapping is a "popular analytical technique" that is useful in identifying areas to deploy police and crime reduction resources. In their study called "The Utility of Hotspot Mapping for Predicting Spatial Patterns of Crime", they tested popular crime hotspot mapping techniques like point mapping, thematic mapping of geographic areas, spatial ellipses, grid thematic mapping, and kernel density estimation (KDE) can accurately predict where crimes would happen in the future. In grid thematic mapping, they suggested that as a starting point for the grid cell size is approximately the distance in the longest extent of the study area, divided by 50. They introduced a measure called prediction accuracy index (PAI) to quantify the accuracy of each mapping technique. The results show that prediction accuracy depends upon the different techniques with KDE outperforming the others, as well as upon the type of crime to be predicted.

A recently published study called "Once Upon a Crime: Towards Crime Prediction from Demographics and Mobile Data" by Bogomolov *et al.* (2014), used human behavioral data derived from mobile phone network activity may be used in predicting crime. Given a feature of an area, defined as a "Smartstep cell", they would predict if that cell will become a crime hotspot or not. Basically, they transformed it into a binary classification task given set of features from their dataset. The model used in the study is a decision tree classifier based on the Breiman's Random Forest. This study is a huge change from the conventional historical knowledge or criminal profiling to predict crimes. The results show that the developed model has an accuracy of almost 70% of predicting crime hotspots.

The literature shows us that there are various ways of tackling the problem of crime prediction and mapping, each with its own strengths and weaknesses. Research in this field is still young and there has not been a globally accepted technique that is in use today. The challenge here is to apply some of these existing techniques to create a crime prediction model for Cebu City and determine if its performance is sufficient. The Cebu City Police Office is currently not using any crime prediction techniques to proactively make decisions in police patrolling and deployment. By making use of these techniques, the Cebu City police will be more effective in suppressing criminal activity.

3. Methodology

The following section will discuss the methodology that will be used by the researcher to predict where possible crimes would happen.

3.1. *Creating the Map Grid*

In order to create the map grid, the researcher used the Google Maps JavaScript API v3. The area of Cebu City had to be defined to act as the study area. The researcher manually defined the city's bounds by using map bounds available on Google Maps since the existing city bounds was not available. To create the city bounds polygon, the researcher used a tool (http://www.birdtheme.org/useful/v3tool.html) to generate the coordinates that would be used to create the city polygon.

With the city polygon in place, the API object called "Rectangle" was used to create the square grid overlay. The researcher used a start coordinate north east of the city and set a limit coordinates on the northwest and southeast of the city. From the start coordinate, coordinates to the east and south given a distance is calculated. This distance can be changed as desired, but for this experiment, the distance is set to 1000 meters, 750 meters, 500 meters, and 250 meters while taking note of the performance of each cell size. With the two new coordinates, a square can be formed. The vertices of each square are checked if it resides in the city polygon. If it resides, the square is placed on the map. The process repeats until the city polygon is completely covered in a grid. Figure 3 is an image of Cebu City with square grid overlay. With the configuration of 1000 meters by 1000 meters, there is a total of 344 square cells covering the city. This number of cells would change depending on the size of each cell grid.

Fig. 3. Cebu City map with 344 square cells.

Cell merging will also be incorporated into this experiment. Merging cells with the least number of reported crimes would lessen the number of cells in the grid. In these experiments, cells will be merged if the number of crimes occurred in a group of cells will be less than 15. This will now have two cell sizes in the grid. Figure 4 shows a sample merged square grid overlay with a total of 197 cells.

Fig. 4. Cebu City map with 197 square cells.

3.2. *Data Collection and Preprocessing*

Crime report data was collected from the Cebu City Police office. The dataset was from the Crime Reporting System Form 1 (NCRS Form 1) which contains various information of crime incidents. The fields that will be useful in this experiment are the date the crime was committed, type of crime, address of the committed crime including the latitude and longitude. The dataset spans for 2 years from the months of January 2013 to December 2014.

Red for occurrence of crime, Green for absence

Fig. 5. Grid snapshot of January 2013.

With the collected dataset, it is fed to the map grid where it translates the individual crime data into a monthly, weekly, or daily crime grid snapshot. Crimes of each month, week, or day are grouped together and placed on the map. The application then counts the occurrence of crimes of each cell in the grid. Figure 5 shows an example grid snapshot. Green shows where there is no occurrence of crime while red shows there is an occurrence of crimes.

Data from each month is then written into a text file that contains the number of occurrences of crimes in each cell. This data would contain the month number and the counts of each cell in the grid. Another experiment would be done if there is any difference in the performance of the model if the data used is the presence or absence of a crime (1 or -1) instead of the crime counts for each cell in the grid.

3.3. *Model*

The new generated file will now be used for the training of the model. In this experiment, a simple feed forward neural network with back propagation will be used. This will be implemented with Python and a library called "Neurolab" will be used to create the neural network. Inputs of the neural network are the month number and the counts of crime incidents of each of the 344 cells in the grid, a total of 345 input neurons, but this would change depending on the size of the cell grids. The number of neurons in the hidden layer is set as the same as the number of the input neurons. The number of output neurons would be equal to the number of cells in the grid (In the initial experiments, the number would be 344). The grid snapshot of the current month will be used as inputs and the model will predict the state of the grid snapshot for the next month. It is assumed this way because crime incidents for Cebu City seems to be reoccurring at the same places based on the sample data collected. For now, the learning rate is set to its default value of 0.07 and back propagation algorithm used will be resilient back propagation. Learning rate is set to its default value so that it would be uniform throughout the experiments and see which model would perform better. Resilient back propagation is used because it performed the best and reaches its local minima faster than other algorithms provided by "Neurolab". In training the neural network, the dataset will be divided 70% as training set and 30% as test set. This means that data from January 2013 to April 2014 will be used as training data and from May 2014 to December 2014 will be used for testing. Training epochs was set to 1000 to speed up the computation. Figure 6 shows an example of a neural network.

The results of the neural network model would then be inputted back to the JavaScript map application in order to visualize the results. The application will show the predicted areas where there is a presence or absence of crime in that cell area.

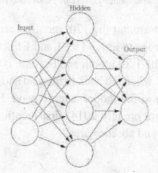

Fig. 6. Neural Network.

3.4. *Statistical Analysis*

The results generated by the neural network will be analyzed using the Sum of Squares Error (SSE) of the output values and the target values. In visualization of the map grids, Accuracy and F1 Score will be used to check if the model accurately predicted a similar pattern to the actual data.

4. Results and Discussions

The proponent of the study performed a simple experiment to test if the neural network was working as intended. Learning rate was set to its default value of 0.07 and resilient back propagation was used in training. Input neurons were set to 345 neurons, 345 hidden neurons, and 344 output neurons. Maximum number of epochs was set to 1000. Data consisted of the crime counts for each monthly cell grid involving all crime types in the city. Figure 7 shows the graph of the accuracy and F1 Score of the experiment.

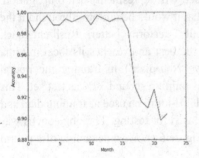 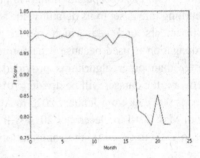

Final SSE: 56.0
Average Accuracy: 0.974721941355
Average F1 Score: 0.940022560443

Fig. 7. Accuracy and F1 Score of 1000x1000 meter grid.

It can be noticed that around the 17th month, accuracy and F1 score drops significantly. Accuracy drops to around 0.91 and F1 score drops to around 0.80. This is so because, from the 17th month and beyond, is the testing data.

Looking at the results when fed back to the grid and comparing it to the actual patterns, the performance of the model is quite good. Figure 8 shows the actual data and the predicted data on July 2014, first month of the test data, where it predicted crime presence and absence areas.

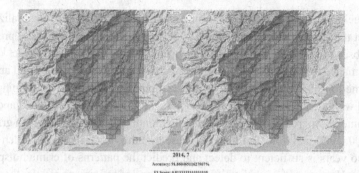

2014, 7
Accuracy: 91.86046511627907%
F1 Score: 0.813333333333335

Actual data on the left, Predicted data on the right

Fig. 8. Actual and Prediction of 1st Experiment.

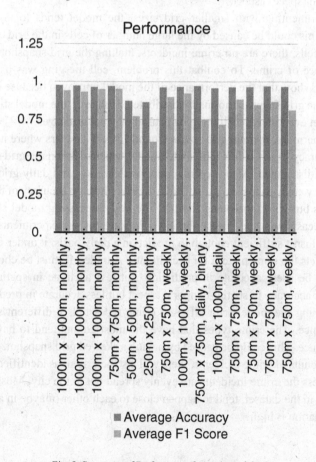

Fig. 9. Summary of Performance for each model.

Seeing the results of the experiments, the model is able to generalize and predict the crime incidents of Cebu City. Using the crime counts or the presence and absence of crime for the grid snapshot did not have much effect on the performance of the model. The proponent chose to use the presence and absence of crime for the grid snapshots to lessen computation and speed-up training. The model with the best performance, as shown in Figure 9, was the second and third experiments wherein the data was split into monthly grid snapshots and a grid size of 1000x1000 and 750x750 meters. These monthly grid snapshots which spans for two years is sufficient to detect and predict the patterns of crime hotspots in the city. However, it would be difficult for the police officials to efficiently deploy resources when predictions are not accurate enough in terms of temporal (time) and spatial (space) aspect.

Experimenting with smaller grid sizes, the model tends to under fit the dataset. This could be caused by the large number of cells in the grid and in most of those cells, there are no crime incidents, making the grid snapshot skewed to the absence of crime. To combat this problem, cell merging was used and the results did show that the performance of the model improved because it helped in making the grid snapshot normally distributed. However, the model still underfits the dataset even though cell merging is used in small grid sizes.

Furthermore, optimal grid size is around 750x750 meters where it retains the high accuracy of the 1000x1000 meter model, where data on the grid snapshot is normally distributed. Also, experimenting with weekly and daily grid snapshots show that weekly snapshots are still able to retain the high accuracy of the monthly snapshots but with time being shorter. The best forecasting model should have daily forecasts with the lowest possible grid size, but the experiments show that the model isn't sufficient enough to predict on a daily basis, it under fits the data and predicts the same pattern for each month. A trade-off must be chosen for the model to be used: accurate in prediction, but less accurate in spatial-temporal aspect, or accuracy in spatial-temporal aspect but less accurate in predicting.

Training the model with different crime types tells a different story about performance. The crime types that have the most counts tend to have a higher performance. This could be caused by having a skewed grid snapshot. Since there are less counts of crime incidents, there will also be less areas identified as a crime area, unless the crime incidents are evenly spread out in the city. Most crimes, as observed in the dataset, tend to happen close to each other (maybe in areas where the population is high).

5. Conclusion

The results showed in the previous chapter are very promising. Grid thematic mapping with artificial neural network is able to predict future crime areas from the previous historical data, with a few trade-offs. The model can perform well when data are split into weeks or months, and the cell size is large enough to prevent skewness of the grid snapshot. The average F1 score of the best performing model with a grid size of 750x750 meters and monthly grid snapshots is 0.95. This may help the police officials in the deployment of resources in the predicted areas. However, the prediction area is still large at 750x750 meters and a time aspect of a week or a month will deter any police officer in covering such area and time span.

The dataset also plays a substantial factor in the performance of the model. The dataset collected only contain data spanning two years. As a result, the model wasn't able to have a training set with two full years, where half of the second year is used as a test set. This could have an effect in detecting the patterns because the model hasn't seen concrete patterns from the two full years. Moreover, the system is limited to predicting only areas where crime would happen, not the predicted crime counts of each crime area.

6. Acknowledgments

We thank the Cebu City Police Office and all its constituents, especially, Ms. Aileen Recla, for accommodating us, providing the data for this study and giving useful insights. We would also like to thank Mr. Ryan Ciriaco Dulaca for his unconditional support in collecting the data set from the Cebu City Police Office.

References

1. Bogomolov, A., Lepri, B., Staiano, J., Oliver, N., Pianesi, F. and Pentland, A. (2014). Once Upon a Crime: Towards Crime Prediction from Demographics and Mobile Data. arXiv:1409.2983 [physics]. Retrieved from http://arxiv.org/abs/1409.2983
2. Carrington, P. J. and Schulenberg, J. L. (2003). Police Discretion with Young Offenders (p. 168). Departnt of Justice Canada. Retrieved from http://www.justice.gc.ca/eng/rp-pr/cj-jp/yj-jj/discre/org/styles.html
3. Chainey, S., Tompson, L. and Uhlig, S. (2008). The Utility of Hotspot Mapping for Predicting Spatial Patterns of Crime. Security Journal, 21(1), 4–28. doi:10.1057/palgrave.sj.8350066
4. Crime Statistics at a Glance. (2013). (No. AG-13-03).

5. Diaz, B. (2014, June 1). Report: Cebu City's crime rate up 22%. The Freeman. Cebu City. Retrieved from http://www.philstar.com/cebu-news/2014/06/01/1329740/report-cebu-citys-crime-rate-22

6. Etimade, F. (2012). People Participation in Urban Governance in Cebu: A Reader. Cebu City: Ramon Aboitiz Foundation Inc.

7. Hagenauer, J., Helbich, M., Leitner, M., Ratcliffe, J., Chainey, S. and Edwards, R. (2012). Data mining of collaboratively collected geographic crime information using an unsupervised neural network approach. Presented at the AutoCarto 2012, Columbus, OH. Retrieved from http://www.cartogis.org/docs/proceedings/2012/Hagenauer_etal_AutoCarto 2012.pdf

8. Helbich, M. and Leitner, M. (2012). Evaluation of Spatial Cluster Detection Algorithms for Crime Locations. In W. A. Gaul, A. Geyer-Schulz, L. Schmidt-Thieme and J. Kunze (Eds.), Challenges at the Interface of Data Analysis, Computer Science, and Optimization (pp. 193–201). Berlin, Heidelberg: Springer Berlin Heidelberg. Retrieved from http://link.springer.com/10.1007/978-3-642-24466-7_20

9. Kişi, Ö. and Uncuoğlu, E. (2005). Comparison of three back-propagation training algorithms for two case studies. In Indian Journal of Engineering and Materials Sciences (IJEMS) (Vol. 12, pp. 434–442). CSIR. Retrieved from http://nopr.niscair.res.in/handle/123456789/8460

10. Moore, M. H., Trojanowicz, R. C. and Kelling, G. L. (1988). Crime and Policing. National Institute of Justice Perspectives on Policing, 2, 15.

11. Nath, S. (2006). Crime Pattern Detection Using Data Mining (pp. 41–44). IEEE. doi:10.1109/WI-IATW.2006.55

12. Olligschlaeger, A. M. (1997). Artificial Neural Networks and Crime Mapping (From Crime Mapping and Crime Prevention, P 313-347, 1997, David Weisburd and Tom McEwen, eds. - See NCJ-170277) (pp. 313–347). Retrieved from http://citeseerx.ist.psu.edu/viewdoc/summary?doi=10.1.1.131.8483

A System that Converts Music Score Sheets with Round Notes into One with Shape Notes

Michael Alan V. Ygnacio and Robert R. Roxas

Department of Computer Science, University of the Philippines Cebu,
Gorordo Ave., Lahug, Cebu City, 6000, Philippines
E-mail: mvygnacio3@up.edu.ph and robert.roxas@up.edu.ph
http://upcebu.edu.ph/

This study presents a music notation software, which facilitates note reading, sightsinging, and encoding for music amateurs and enthusiasts. The system can accept scanned images of music score sheets as input and renders them into a software playable music score sheets. The software renders automatically the music score sheet containing round notes into shape notes. This greatly eliminates the problem of incorrectly encoding the correct properties of individual musical notes like proper positions, duration, shapes, etc. At the same time, the time consuming tasks of encoding the musical notes is also greatly shortened.

Keywords: Music score sheets; Round notes; Shape notes; Music notation software.

1. Introduction

Making music score sheets from a songbook by encoding the notes using a music notation software is a long and tedious process and prone to error. The common input process of music notation software is to encode manually the notes one-by-one. Some programs use MusicXML file as input. A MusicXML contains the data found in a music score sheet. MusicXML was designed for sharing music files between applications, and for archiving sheet music files for use in the future[1]. To utilize the use of MusicXML, some notation programs have the ability to scan music sheets and store the data into MusicXML files, which would then be used. Audiveris[2], an open-source image processing software, can read images of music sheets and store the data in a MusicXML file.

Most existing music notation software renders music score sheets into round notes only. Reading round notes, on one hand, can be difficult and confusing sometimes. Shape note reading, on the other hand, is known to facilitate the reading of the notes. It allows the reader to sing the notes quickly without having to waste time in memorizing and deciphering the notes in the different keys[3]. A software that automatically assigns the shape of the notes based on the given key signature and the position of the cursor on the music staff was developed[4]. This is computationally possible because the position of the different key signatures in any music staff is clearly defined.

The objective of this study is to utilize the functions of Audiveris[2] and add an important feature to the above-mentioned software[4]. That important feature is the ability of the system to automatically encode the scanned music score sheets into it. This is done by extracting the MusicXML data from a scanned music score sheet image and automatically rendering the corresponding music score sheet in the notation that uses shape notes. With this, it is possible to simply scan a music score sheet from a songbook, have it read by the system, and render it automatically in shape notes. The study, however, focuses on vocal music score sheets only, and thus it cannot read music score sheets, which are intended for some specific musical instruments. This study will be a significant endeavor in learning and reading vocal score sheets. The system will also be beneficial for choir singers and music teachers in learning an unfamiliar song from a songbook because the system can render that particular song into a playable one.

2. Review of Related Works

With the advancements in technology, there are several kinds of music notation software that are capable of composing music score sheets, but most of them do not implement the use of shape notes. Some of them also have the capability to import MusicXML files and render the data into their application interface. Finale[5] and Noteworthy[6] are both music notation software that can create, edit, print, and publish music score sheets. Both software can also import MusicXML files and render the musical data found within the file. Both software are capable of encoding shape notes. Finale can now automatically render the shape of a particular note based on its position in the staff and the given key signature. In Noteworthy, the user has to manually specify the shape of each note in order to render it in shape note format thus making the process tedious and prone to error.

An open-source image processing software called Audiveris[2] can read scanned music score sheets. It can identify the properties of the whole music score sheet, from the staff to the notes found in it. It can store the music score sheet properties into a MusicXML file. This MusicXML file is used in some music notation software, that have a feature to accept MusicXML file, as an input for playback and visualization. Ms. Cortes' software[4] has the capability to automatically render shape notes, but is unable to import neither scanned music score sheets nor MusicXML files. It uses an open-source project called jMusic[7]. It provides composers and software developers with a library of compositional and audio processing tools. It provides support to musicians with its familiar data structure based on note or sound events, and methods for organizing, manipulating, and analyzing musical data[7].

This study provides a system that can accept scanned music score sheet images, most likely from songbooks in round notes format, and renders them in shaped notes format. The existing software like Finale and Noteworthy do not convert music score sheets in round notes format to shape notes format.

3. Preliminaries

To make it more understandable, we discuss some few background information in this section. Figure 1[a] shows a staff containing shape notes together with their corresponding note names. This is the target format that our systems aims to create. In most cases, we encounter the so-called round notes. Figure 2[b] shows an example staff containing round notes, which is the round notes version of the one shown in Figure 1. Because this format is very common in most songbooks, this becomes the intended input to our system.

Fig. 1.   Example staff containing shape notes and their corresponding note names.

[a]Taken from: http://www.wikiwand.com/en/Shape_note
[b]Taken from: http://www.easyeartraining.com/learn/the-space-between-hearing-and-singing-intervals/

232

Fig. 2. Example staff containing round notes.

As we know, the spaces and the lines in any music staff have predefined areas for the different key signatures in which the note *"do"* starts. Figures 3[c] and 4[d] show these different key signatures. So any software that automatically assigns the shape of the notes based on the given key signature and the position of the cursor on the music staff is computationally possible[4].

Fig. 3. The predefined positions of different key signatures in a staff with Treble Clef.

Fig. 4. The predefined positions of different key signatures in a staff with Bass Clef.

[c]Taken from http://www.musicnotes.com/blog/2014/04/11/how-to-read-sheet-music/
[d]Taken from http://www.musicnotes.com/blog/2014/04/11/how-to-read-sheet-music/

4. Basic Flow of the System

Figure 5 shows the basic flow of the system. It starts by accepting scanned music sheets, converting it into MusicXML file using Audiveris, and automatically rendering it in shape note format.

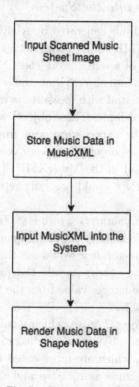

Fig. 5. Basic system flow.

4.1. *Input Scanned Music Score Sheet Image*

In this stage, the user would use the system to input a scanned image (*.jpg, .png, .PDF*) of a music score sheet. The image would then be read by Audiveris, and its output will be a MusicXML file, which will be used later by the system to render the music score sheet in shape notes format.

4.2. *Store Music Data in MusicXML*

The Audiveris software would read the input image file of a scanned music score sheet and generate a MusicXML file, which would contain the necessary music data generated. This generated MusicXML file must be true to the original music score sheet so that the system can render correctly the music score sheet in round notes format into one in shape notes format.

4.3. *Input MusicXML into the System*

At this stage, a MusicXML file generated by Audiveris would be input into the system. The MusicXML would contain tags that would include the attributes and properties of a music score sheet. The system would parse these tags and assign them into objects that would be represented according to their attribute such as a staff with measures, a measure with notes, and a note with its type as an example. These objects would be the *Score, Part, Phrase,* and *Note*. All the music score data from the MusicXML input would be stored in the *Score* object. For every voice or part represented by tags *<part id= "P1">*found in the MusicXML, it would be classified into its own *Part* object. A *Part* would basically represent a staff or a single voice in the music score.

The function *setKeySignature(key)* and *setTimeSignature(numerator, denominator)* are called to identify the *Key Signature* and *Time Signature* of each *Part*. The parameter *key* would be the integer value from the tag *<fifths>*under the tag *<key>*, while the parameter numerator and denominator would be the integer value from the tags *<beats>*and *<beats-type>*under the tag *<time>*.

Every *Part* has an object *Phrase*, which would store the *Note* objects within a staff. The *Note* objects would become instances of the notes found in the music score, which are represented by tags *<note>*. A note would contain properties such as its *Step* and *Octave* found in the tags *<step>*and *<octave>*tag, respectively under the *<pitch>*tag. These note objects would be classified and stored within a *Phrase*. The objects would then be classified and used in the latter part of the system's main functions for rendering and playback.

4.4. *Render Music Data in Shape Notes*

At this stage, the system implements the function of Ms. Cortes' software[4] that automatically renders the notes into shape notes. The data parsed from the MusicXML file would then be read by the system and render the notes accordingly. The *Note* objects would be gathered from the *Phrase* objects where they were stored. The notes would then be rendered into their staff or *Phrase* accordingly.

There are a few ways to automatically render the MusicXML data into shape notes. One is by using the key signature. This is because the lines and spaces in a staff have defined "do" note depending on the key signature as shown in Figures 3 and 4. Another approach is to use the data on staff number and the octave number because these are also defined in the staffs.

Still another approach is using the *PitchValue*. In order to identify the shape of the note, the *PitchValue* of the note is computed using the equation shown in Eq. 1.

$$PitchValue = (Octave * 12) + Step + 12 \tag{1}$$

Knowing the *PitchValue* of the note can determine the shape of the note and the position it will take within the staff. This systems uses the *PitchValue* data in rendering automatically the shape notes.

5. Results and Discussion

The prototype system was run and fed with a scanned music score sheet image. That scanned music score sheet image is shown in Figure 6. Audiveris read and stored the data into a MusicXML file. This file was then input into the system, and the notes, together with the other music score data in the file, were rendered on the application interface. Its output is shown in Figure 7.

Figure 8 shows code snippets of the generated MusicXML data produced by Audiveris from the sample music score sheet image shown in Figure 6. The <*note*>tags in the figure represent the first four notes in the first measure of the *Soprano* part.

The MusicXML generated was read by the system, which then rendered the data into its application interface. The notes that were displayed were automatically rendered as shape notes as shown in Figure 7. The scanned music sheet image in Figure 6 was compared to the rendered music score sheet shown in Figure 7. It was shown that the notes were translated correctly into their proper positions and shapes.

Although the system successfully rendered a music score from a MusicXML, the result relied on how Audiveris accurately stored the data from the scanned image into the MusicXML. If Audiveris, for example, mistakenly read a quarter note as a whole note, it would store a whole note in the MusicXML file. Then the system would render a whole note on the staff rather than a quarter note. This problem was outside of the scope of the study and, therefore, would fall under future works for improvement.

Fig. 6.   Sample scanned music sheet.

Fig. 7.   Output music score sheet rendered from the MusicXML data generated by the sample music score sheet shown in Figure 6.

There was one note, however, with the accidental "*natural*" in the 2nd part or second staff, particularly the second note in the second measure as can be seen in Figure 7. There was no accidental "*natural*" in the source music score sheet as can be seen in Figure 6. This can be rectified by updating the system to correct this error. But this initial result shows that it

```
<note default-x="91">                          <note default-x="182">
    <pitch>                                       <pitch>
        <step>E</step>                                <step>B</step>
        <octave>4</octave>                           <octave>4</octave>
    </pitch>                                      </pitch>
    <duration>1</duration>                       <duration>1</duration>
    <voice>1</voice>                             <voice>1</voice>
    <type>quarter</type>                         <type>quarter</type>
    <stem default-y="-6">up</stem>               <stem default-y="-55">down</stem>
    <staff>1</staff>                             <staff>1</staff>
</note>                                        </note>
<note default-x="130">                         <note default-x="232">
    <pitch>                                       <pitch>
        <step>B</step>                                <step>A</step>
        <octave>4</octave>                           <octave>4</octave>
    </pitch>                                      </pitch>
    <duration>1</duration>                       <duration>1</duration>
    <voice>1</voice>                             <voice>1</voice>
    <type>quarter</type>                         <type>quarter</type>
    <stem default-y="-55">down</stem>            <stem default-y="10">up</stem>
    <staff>1</staff>                             <staff>1</staff>
</note>                                        </note>
```

Fig. 8. Snippet Codes of the MusicXML data generated from source shown in Figure 6.

greatly eliminates the problem of incorrectly encoding the correct properties of individual musical notes like proper positions, duration, shapes, etc. At the same time, the time consuming tasks of encoding the musical notes is also greatly shortened.

6. Conclusion

A system that converts music score sheets with round notes into one with shape notes was presented. The results showed that the software, given that the MusicXML had the correct data and format, could convert round notes automatically into shape notes. The output rendered by the software was a readable and a playable graphical music score sheet. This greatly eliminates the problem of incorrectly encoding the correct properties of individual musical notes like proper positions, duration, shapes, etc. At the same time, the time consuming tasks of encoding the musical notes is also greatly shortened.

7. Future Works

The software still has limitations that should be improved. Some musical symbols like the *slur* and *beam* were not yet implemented in this study and would need to be done. Audiveris also needs further development to enhance its capability to properly and accurately read the music data from a scanned music score sheet image. The accuracy of the rendered music score sheet in shape notes format is heavily dependent on the accuracy of the generated MusicXML file.

References

1. I. MAKEMUSIC, Music xml: What is musicxml? (2016), http://www.musicxml.com/.
2. H. Bitteur, Audiveris open music scanner. (2013), https://audiveris.kenai.com/.
3. M. Beadle, Shape note singing. http://mountaingrownmusic.org/shape-notes.html.
4. A. R. N. Cortes, A notation software for a cappella music with automatic rendering of shape notes and capable of converting an open score to a closed score. (2013), Special Problem, University of the Philippines Cebu.
5. I. MAKEMUSIC, Finale. (2016), http://www.finalemusic.com/.
6. I. NoteWorthy Software, Noteworthy composer. (2016), https://noteworthycomposer.com/.
7. A. Sorensen and A. Brown, An introduction to jmusic. http://explodingart.com/jmusic/jmtutorial/t2.html.

Author Index

Printed in the United States
By Bookmasters